A Legionnaire's Journey

Leslie Aparvary

To Luc and Alex with sincere good wishes from your brother in law

Calgary 1989 Dec. 27

Detselig Enterprises Ltd.
Calgary, Alberta

© 1989 by **Leslie Aparvary**   *Eagle Bay, British Columbia*

Canadian Cataloguing in Publication Data
Aparvary, Leslie, 1921 –
   A Legionnaire's journey

   ISBN 0-920490-93-X

   1. Aparvary, Leslie, 1921 –   2. France.
Armée. Légion étrangère – Biography.   I. Title.
U55.A63A3 1989   355.3'5'0924   C89-091206-8

Back Cover Photo: Courtesy of Grizzly Photography

Detselig Enterprises Limited
P.O. Box G 399
Calgary, Alberta T3A 2G3

Printed in Canada   SAN 115-0324   ISBN 0-920490-93-X

Foreword

The French Foreign Legion has captured the imagination of many an author. It has given inspiration to, among others, Eugene Rejto, the celebrated and highly acclaimed literary giant of Hungary. But of the relevant literature available to date, few authors have committed their personal experiences to paper. Leslie Aparvary is one who counts among the few.

The anarchy and the political chaos of the post-World War II years compelled the author to take to the road. It was not a thirst for adventure, but chance, that led him to Indochina as a soldier fighting for the French Foreign Legion.

The author's experiences were written in his journal and form the basis for this autobiographical work. The work, however, does not carry with it the standard characteristics and usual implications so often ascribed to memoirs of this nature. Leslie Aparvary sets forth scenes laced with witty dialogue, and with his captivating and picturesque descriptions of landscape, the author rises above the mundane status of a mere diary recorder. He conjures a convincing and gripping story that has not one hero but many. Leslie Aparvary has no desire to place himself in the limelight. Rather, he places himself in the role of narrator of, and commentator on, the events that inspired the work.

The journal has found its way out of the author's desk drawer after a forty year lapse. He has refused to depart from the original or change facts established at the time. He presents everything as he saw it; through the eyes of a Hungarian youth driven away by persecution and deprived of home and country.

The author infuses life into the struggles and strifes of the lives and miseries of the soldiers who fought in a part of the world where the value of life, be it that of one man or one hundred, was considered tantamount to zero. These soldiers served in an army that has been called, "the world's toughest and hardest."

The years following WW II nourished this army with adequate manpower. The economic and political climate of the time forced men by the hundreds of thousands to escape from Soviet and occupied countries. Fate propelled a portion of these refugees into the hands of the French Foreign Legion, where they fought for, and often lost, the very lives they had tried to save in the first place.

I have heard the author relate many of the events he describes herein, am convinced of the authenticity of what he has written and recommend the work highly.

Joseph Fulopp
Past President
Canadian Hungarian Veteran's Association

Contents

Translation from original Hungarian manuscript by *Kathy Angyalfi*

Detselig Enterprises Ltd. appreciates the financial
assistance for its 1989 publishing program from

Alberta Foundation for the Literary Arts
Canada Council
Department of Communications
Alberta Culture

The names of people in this biography have been changed.

Preface

May, 1945

The genesis of hope. The war had died but the spring survived, as had I. I remembered the injury all too well. It happened during the last days of World War II. I revived, to find myself lying in the recovery room of a hospital in a small Austrian city. I was a convalescent strengthened by the warmth of the sun and the scent of the flowers streaming through the open windows. I saw the white and gentle clouds beckoning me on their voyage, they were eastward bound, bound for my beautiful fatherland, to my home.

I was transferred to an American prisoner-of-war camp near the end of May, and after almost two months of hospitalization, my eyes beheld those same clouds. There was hope after all, a slender chance that soon I might sail along with them to Hungary.

During our detainment in the prisoner-of-war camp, the Hungarians labored endlessly over the pros and cons of returning home. I found it incredulous that the subject was even considered a topic for discussion. Despite the outcome of the War and the grave consequences of the Yalta Conference, was the security of our native country not a thousand times better than life in some foreign state?

Not only I, but hundreds of thousands of other Hungarians, were painfully disappointed to later learn that our fantasy of a stable and peaceful life was exactly that. The realities of existence were in stark contrast to the expectations of a people who paid a most painful price to discover the cost of peace.

I was as optimistic as the rest when I left Linz to return home that sunny day in June. Not even in my wildest dreams did I imagine that exactly three years later I would be standing on the very same platform heading west instead of east.

The War may have ended, but man's thirst for revenge was just beginning to kindle, and Moscow did everything in its power to encourage the revolt.

The conspirators were Hungarians, most of whom could barely read or write. To ensure themselves a higher standard of living they became willing pawns of the Russians through promotions as house wardens, party functionaries and police officers. Protected by their uniforms, the state and the security of positions that were considered exalted at the time, these Hungarians committed what were no less than hideous atrocities against the people. In the wake of state crimes, the people understood what was entailed when such a mob was raised to supremacy. There is no need to itemize the resulting trials of daily existence. The predicament we found ourselves in is perhaps best summed up by the late Cardinal Mindszenty: "Before, we were victims of the ravages of war, and now, we are patients who bear the heavy burden of peace."

There was literally nothing to do but take it or leave it, and I, like so many others who were not willing to fight fire with fire, stood by and endured. Compromise meant toleration, but the cross became too heavy a burden, and what had been a fleeting thought, sparked into a persistent and burning desire to escape to the West.

A series of personal incidents augmented my urgent need to leave. In the fall of 1947 my brother-in-law was falsely denounced by the authorities, detained and locked away in the Markó Street Prison. That my father, though retired in 1938, was a member of the Royal Hungarian Mounted Police was not in my family's favor either. Clouds of doom hovered over our heads as the evidence to suggest that my family was on a blacklist mounted.

Within the bearings of an uncertain future, miracles have been known to happen even in the most hopeless instances. My brother-in-law was released from the Markó Street Prison around March, 1948. At my sister's urging, he immediately applied for an exit visa and passport for both himself and my eighteen-year-old sister. Since the chances that his request would be granted were extremely slim, especially because of my sister's youth, they were more surprised than anyone when, a few weeks later, word arrived that the documents were ready to be picked up.

Following their departure from the country in early June, 1948, I began having thoughts of escaping too. I was finally persuaded after a chance encounter with a police officer who was well-acquainted with my family. We bumped into each other one evening as I was starting home from work. He was walking towards me, and when we were abreast he stopped just long enough to whisper these words of warning: "You'd better look out for yourself. You're near the top of the list." That was it, then he hurried past. The whole thing happened so suddenly that I had no time to even stop. I made it home, explained what had happened and told my family that I had no choice but to leave immediately. The alternative was certain imprisonment, and as for thousands of other Hungarians, the chances for eventual release were slim. My brother-in-law was one of the fortunate few and I did not trust fate to deal me the same hand.

In the early hours of June 22, 1948, I departed for the first destination of my journey, Sopron – a city near the Austrian border. It was essential that what I carried fit into a slim briefcase, and thus, my wordly possessions included personal documents, underwear and a slab of bacon. I was especially grateful for the bacon because in giving it to me, I knew that my mother was depriving herself of the last bit of food in the house. Once my fortune was rounded out with a few hundred forints (Hungarian currency), I was ready to tackle the world. I stayed in Sopron for a few days, just long enough to nose about and investigate the possibilities for escaping over the nearby border. I succeeded with the help of two acquaintances, one of whom was generous enough to provide me with a letter of introduction. It was addressed to the owner of a tavern in a village in southern Burgenland and virtually guaranteed that I would receive further assistance.

Escape from Hungary was of such pressing importance that I did not question my dubious fate. I saw only the face of the policeman and heard his foreboding voice telling me that I was doomed. With this one image in my mind, I set out.

Chapter One
Burgenland

June 26 - 27, 1948

The small village I was referred to was located in the southeastern part of the Austrian province of Burgenland. I reached the outskirts of the village in the early afternoon and made a beeline for the tavern in question. Much to my horror, I saw that Soviet officers were patrolling the streets and demanding identification from everyone who crossed their path. I twisted and turned down streets every time I saw the patrol, and within minutes I was completely disoriented and hopelessly lost.

I groped my way down the dusty avenues. My energy was drained and I was ready to drop from exhaustion when suddenly the tavern appeared. Just in the nick of time too. My tongue was so swollen from thirst that I was ready to risk stopping at a house to ask for water. The terror of possibly finding Soviets inside restrained this rash impulse.

Instead of a simple glass of water, the good Lord had blessed me with and entire tavern. The stench of liquor and oily floors battered my nose as I stepped through the door. The tavern was strangely deserted in this heat. The doorbell summoned the boss who looked me over from head to toe, then in German asked:

"What do you want?"

"Do you speak Hungarian, sir? I'm sorry, but my understanding of German is pretty poor."

He nodded, though he didn't trust me entirely, then repeated the question in Hungarian. I handed him the letter and explained the reasons that brought me here.

He was so enraged after he heard my story that he let loose a lengthy stream of obscenities. When he finished, he turned back on me, sent me to the recesses of hell and again condemned me for bringing nothing but trouble over his head. He paused to catch his breath, and I grabbed the chance to get a word in:

"I'm dying of thirst. Could you please get me something to drink?"

He was so taken aback by my interruption, he was at a loss for words. His wife, "Golden Flower," used this moment of hesitation to barge in. Having heard Hungarian through the open door leading to their residence, she pitched into me at once.

"What the hell are you doing here? Can't you see that the village is full of Russians? You're crazy! No one in their right mind walks the streets at a time like this!"

So that's why this tavern is so empty, I thought.

"If the patrol comes around and finds you here, all three of us will be kaput!"

Her husband gave her my letter, then told her where I was from and why I was here. Golden Flower tamed down a bit after that, but only because the letter writer was her relative. As to what happened to her husband later, I have no idea. However, after seeing her two hundred and fifty pound figure and hearing the outrageous insults her husband threw at her relatives I sensed that his prospects for a fine future were none too bright.

I was swept through their house and into the stable on the opposite side of the yard. By this time the tension in the air eased a little, so eeking up a bit of courage, I made reference to my aching thirst once more. They complied, and produced a rejuvenating wine spritzer. I gulped this down instantly. The bartender then pointed through the open door to a haystack:

"See that haystack? Go hide in it, and don't even *think* of moving until I call. The Soviet patrol comes around at least five times a day and if they find you here, it could mean the end for all of us."

I settled in and noticed indents indicating that I was not the first tenant. Affected by sheer fatigue, and the wine spritzer, I was dead to the world in minutes.

June 28, 1948

For two days I have been inhaling the fragrance of this hay. How much longer? There's no way I can stand another two days without water. Time moves too slowly and the heat gets worse every minute. Hunger doesn't bother me as much as my thirst. I wondered if the Soviets will come. I heard them nosing around here five times yesterday! There it is again, the sound of those boots. The Russians are coming!

Someone pulled the haystack away from the entrance.

"You can come out now. The coast is clear."

The bartender's words sounded more beautiful than the song of angels. I ran to the well and dipped my head into a large barrel of water. The bartender drew fresh water and I drank until I nearly burst. I was led into the house, reunited with my briefcase and introduced to Fritz. Fritz would accompany me to Vienna, serve as a guide and act as my right hand man until I found assistance elsewhere.

We took a train that backtracked to Sopron before going on to Vienna. The Hungarian Secret Police (AVO) took up positions on both sides of the train while at the Sopron Station. They also came on board, and walked up and down the aisles. I was paralyzed with fear during every moment of their presence. I imagined that they would discover that I was travelling illegally and arrest me. I aged five years during their five minutes on board. I breathed such a sigh of relief when they finally left that I attracted the attention of my fellow passengers.

The train left the station almost immediately after the Police were gone. I took one last look at Sopron, uttered one last "God be with you" to my home, said a short prayer for those I left behind in the slave camps and the train was on Austrian soil.

Chapter Two
Vienna

June 28, 1948

It was almost evening by the time the train pulled into Vienna's West Banhof Station. All the consulates were closed, and Fritz and I spent the night with a friend of his.

When we stepped inside the house I sensed that it was the wrong time to intrude. At least the bartender had been open in expressing his displeasure. He had simply told me where to go. Here eyes flashed with the same anger and loathing, but instead of a verbal reprimand, a tense and unsettling silence filled the air. I nodded to Fritz when I could no longer cope with the awkward stillness and told him that I was really tired and needed some sleep. The host led me into a small pantry that was used as a storage space. Among the pile of collectibles was a bed without a pillow or blanket. I would do for one night. I satisfied the demands of my stomach with my homemade bacon, said a prayer for those at home, and with great difficulty shoved aside the sad reality and settled into the restless world of nightmares.

June 29, 1948

I wrestled with Soviet and Hungarian border guards who were in constant pursuit as I fought my way across minefields to the border. I dragged my weight, advancing a few inches at a time. One final surge before victory was complete. I gathered all my strength to plough across the border, only to trip on the edge and tumble headlong into a deep ditch that had heaved into sight a moment too late. I smashed my head against a rock and woke up to find myself on the floor.

Everything was quiet. I crawled back into bed and used the time to ponder my future. What did it hold for me? Would I reach Ankara according to my original plans? Could I rely on the Americans for help? What might I do with my life in Turkey? How does my sister manage to exist there? Would she be able to help me if I showed up on her doorstep?

If Ankara didn't pan out, I could always join my sister in Brussels. Still, I would rather end up in Turkey, in a land that was far more stimulating to the imagination.

"Aufstehn!"

It was the harsh voice of the housemaster ordering me out of bed.

"I've been 'auf' for a long time now," I replied in Hungarian.

At this, he smiled and sent me to the kitchen for coffee.

Well I'll be darned. How come things are so much better all of a sudden? Here's this guy offering me coffee, after all that hostility last night?

Fritz urged me on: "Eat fast. Have to run to the American consulate. Time is pressing, can't waste much of it. Every hand is needed in the fields back home."

It was almost nine by the time we finished breakfast. Fritz suggested that I leave my briefcase behind: "Not much point in lugging it around, you know. Anyway, we'll be back by this afternoon, and if need be, the landlord will take you to the embassy tomorrow."

Without giving the matter a second thought, I did as I was told and left it there.

Off we went to the American Embassy. My heart raced when I spotted the star spangled banner and a heap of new questions flooded my mind.

Standing by the front gate was an armed sentinel who pointed toward a hallway where we found several people already waiting. We were summoned into an office where people were airing their annoyances at one of the numerous desks. A sympathetic-looking American ushered us over to his table. I gathered what little German I had and tried to make him understand that I was a Hungarian refugee seeking sanctuary with relatives abroad. To enhance my request for aid, I showed him a letter from my sister in Ankara. That bit of evidence, however, failed to produce the desired response because my sister had copied my name in a Turkish style that the American was unable to decipher.

We were not getting very far with my broken German, so the American asked Fritz to interpret. From thereon in Fritz acted as my spokesperson. He jabbered, gesticulated and a few minutes later, we were on the street.

According to Fritz, the American was reluctant to believe my claim that the letter was from my sister because my name, as presented to him, did not correspond with that on the envelope. Having made the claim, they would, however, carry out an investigation to see if I was telling the truth. And if it so happened that I was, then they could not understand the discrepancy in the names.

"What do you mean they don't understand? Didn't I ask you, sir, to please explain the reason behind the inconsistency?"

"I did," he answered. "But the American insisted on setting up an inquiry, and added that the policy will likely take several weeks to complete."

"Several weeks? You know I can't wait that long! Where will I stay? What will I live on?"

"Relax," he said. "The possibilities are far from exhausted. There is always the British Embassy."

We tried that source, only to discover that we could not get past the front gate. Fritz suggested the French Embassy, and seemed utterly convinced that there, I would not be rejected. I kissed Ankara and Turkey good-bye to concentrate on the possibility of joining my older sister in Brussels.

The polite reception at the French Embassy was a pleasant surprise after the last two bitter encounters. Some polite conversation, and a note with directions and an address was slipped into our hands. By now I was feeling much obliged to Fritz for all this running around, what with all that farm work waiting for him at home.

It struck me as somewhat peculiar, however, that as we made our way to the address Fritz was pounding the pavement like one who had made this journey many times before. No big deal. It means nothing. The guy happens to know the city well, that's all. I mean, I know Budapest well-enough too. If someone asked for directions to the Basilica I could guide him there on the straight and narrow.

Rain had started to pour during all this wandering from one consulate to the next and by the time we reached our destination I was soaked to the skin. I cared, but Fritz, who had a raincoat, did not.

Fritz handed the slip of paper to the sentinel who glanced at it, smiled and directed us to the appropriate building. Fritz, again, seemed totally familiar in the surroundings and maneuvered around with ease. We turned up and down corridors until we reached a door that Fritz opened without the slightest hesitation.

A gentleman dressed in military attire stood up from his chair as we entered. He was most cordial as he came forward in welcome, but that he shook hands only with me was a tad conspicuous. I was led to his desk, asked to sit down, then politely questioned.

He called Fritz over to interpret when he realized that the German language posed a problem for me. With Fritz's help I completed the identity papers that were necessary, I was told, to keep accurate records. After all, the French Embassy would provide free lodgings and food during my stay and accounts had to be rendered. This was a military garrison and I, as a civilian, could not stay long. However, assistance in crossing the Russian zone was virtually guaranteed.

This was a reasonable explanation that tallied with the facts, though not quite as I had expected.

It took half an hour of translating before the form was completed. Fritz pushed the paper to me with instructions to sign. Without my signature, the embassy's hands were tied and they could do nothing for me.

What choice do I have? If I refuse to sign then they will put me back out on the street, and then what? Where will I go? Spend the rest of my life roaming the streets? Cross the Soviet zone by mistake and be thrown into Markó Street Prison, or worse, transported to Siberia? I wish there was some place where I could hide out for a few weeks. Fritz's friends would never consider taking me in for that long, not if they were upset over even a ten minute stay. There's no other solution but to sign.

I did. And unwittingly, I committed myself to five years of service with the French Foreign Legion.

The junior officer, or rather the Master Sergeant as I later found out, pulled six hundred shillings from his desk drawer and handed it to Fritz, who stuffed the money into his pocket and turned to leave.

I had been sold to the French Foreign Legion for six hundred shillings.

The betrayal, needless to say, could not be proven had I tried. According to the signed and sealed official documents, I had volunteered without coercion.

I remembered my briefcase and tried to follow Fritz, but he protested with unusual vengeance. He wasn't going back to his friend's, he was going straight home to his village. I was a stranger, I could get easily lost, and the Soviets would pick me off the streets in no time if I was found loafing about alone. I had to admit, he was right. It would be ludicrous to risk capture now when I was so close to freedom.

"But what about my briefcase?" I asked. "All my identification, all my underwear is in it, and of course, that juicy slab of bacon from home."

"Relax," said Fritz. "You'll get it back, don't worry. My friend will bring it to you tomorrow."

With that, he tore out of the room so fast that he was gone before I could say another word. The Sergeant told me to follow him, using a voice that was not quite as friendly as before. He led me into a large room where I counted approximately twenty people. As I stood in the doorway the curious faces stared at me, and I heard Hungarian from one the corners. Naturally, I gravitated toward that area.

Introductions were exchanged, then I asked if they had heard anything in connection with our journey from here. I was eager to join my sister in Brussels and told them that the person who had brought me here had also promised that the French would help me cross into the American zone.

When I finished, a short, dark-eyed fellow with curly black hair explained how and why the French would assist me through the Russian sector.

My immediate inclination was to laugh. This guy had to be putting me on.

"Are you actually trying to tell me that I dropped into the French Foreign Legion, just like that? I think you've read a few too many tales about the Legion, buddy."

"You think I'm kidding? Just try and go through the gate. My friend, we are prisoners here! Go and see for yourself. You could try climbing over the brick wall, but even that is hopeless. It's much too high and the guards are pretty alert."

I could not believe what I was hearing. No, none if this is true. This guy was just pulling my leg. And to prove that I was right, I got up and started for the street. At that moment, the Non-Commissioned Officer (NCO) stepped out of his office. All signs of politeness had vanished as he rudely ordered me back into the room with instructions that no one was to leave it without permission and an escort.

So it's true after all, I thought. Dear God! What kind of a trap did I fall into? Books that I had read about the Legion and their vivid portrayal of Saharan expeditions in scorching heat, blood thirsty Arabs and desert outposts came alive once more.

I was powerless, desperate and close to tears. I would tear my escort to pieces if I could lay my hands on him now. But then, why did I want to tear him to pieces? Why not myself? What a fool I was, to blindly trust a complete stranger. I was 27-years-old, old enough to know better. If I was sold to the Legion, I had no one but myself to blame.

It took some time before I was able to calm down and realize that for the time being, this might be the surest way of reaching the American sector. Once there, I could say 'God be with you Legion' as I walked away. So, I said to myself, you have turned into a legionnaire! Remember when you were a student secretly reading those tales of the Legion under your desk during algebra class? Did you ever stop to consider that one day you might become one of those brave soldiers or that one day, you may even be the hero, like Pete Checker, in a Percival Wren novel? But if heroism is the topic, why did fate choose this tale instead of, say "The Princess and the Beggar"? I would have preferred the role of the beggar to that of Pete Checker any day! No longer was I a passive reader, I was a true to life character playing out the very roles I had devoured with such passion. Fate, however, could take an unexpected turn and just as it had sucked me into this mess, so it might draw me out!

What upset me more thàn anything was not that my price had been a mere six hundred shillings, but that I had lost a good briefcase and everything in it – especially that juicy slab of bacon.

My speculations were broken by the creak of the door. Supper was brought in. During the meal, I took stock of the five Hungarians with whom fate had brought me.

The chap who explained that I had entered the Legion was Leo Fürstin. Leo was a third year medical student studying in Vienna. He was approximately 25-years-old, with slightly protruding cheekbones and unusually white teeth that sparkled when he laughed. It was no accident that brought him here, but the happy go lucky and carefree existence of the American soldiers and their young ladies.

American soldiers stationed in Vienna were often lonely and desired companionship on their evening excursions. The young girls and bored wives were gladly at their service, not only for the sake of a good time but to acquire gifts like silk nylons, American cigarettes, lighters, chocolates and other valuables that were in short supply due to the privations of the War. Scarce goods such as these were guaranteed after every jaunt. In addition to the aforementioned gifts, another which was not noticed until two or three months down the road was frequently bestowed.

Enter Leo. He set-up a small clinic in his home and was more than willing to assist the ladies in need for a fee of several hundred shillings. His surgical skills, however, were not quite honed, and so, his efforts at assistance were not always one hundred percent successful. The patient had to be rushed to the hospital in these instances. One patient, in her desperation, spilled the beans and gave Leo away.

This was more than enough evidence for the Police, who in no time at all were on Leo's doorstep. Leo was in the middle of one of his "good samaritan" acts when the Police arrived. The unexpected intrusion gave him only enough time to strip off his gloves and gown, grab his raincoat, and leap through the open window.

The Police set-off in hot pursuit. They were on his trail and Leo was running out of wind and time. He had no choice but to run through the barracks gate and straight into the arms of the Legion. So there it was, and here he was, grieving the loss of a most lucrative business.

The second chap, Walter Szoros, was 28-years-old and a scant bit taller than me. Walter claimed to have escaped from Bratislava, or Pozsony, as the territory was known when still part or Hungary prior to 1920. Walter's lot was one of hardship and misery, and like many others accustomed to a higher standard of living, he too became fed-up with the ravages of the mob and bid his homeland farewell. He joined the Legion of his own accord; thinking it to be the easiest and surest way of crossing over Soviet occupied territory. Time would dictate the path of his future, but one thing was for certain, Walter had no intention of remaining in the Legion any longer than dictated by necessity. In addition, he was a excellent pianist and when we were able to sneak down to the barrack canteen, he made it a priority to play.

Then there was Angel, an enigma who made it difficult for me to draw conclusions concerning his personality. Rarely did he speak, and when spoken to, he merely nodded in silence or mumbled a few words in response. He did, after some persuasion, offer a chilling account of his life history. He began by saying that he was wanted by the Police in almost every European city.

He had been dodging the authorities between Vac, a city north of Budapest, and Vienna. The Hungarian police were on his tail until the border and from there, both the Russian and Austrian police were in pursuit. For months he was in one end of a country and out the other until the Legion, as a last resort, seemed the only feasible place to hide.

Try as he might, Angel could not come to terms with the privations, poverty and forced labor of the post-war years. Instead, he used his ability to speak Russian, and would persuade a few cooperative Russians to be his accomplices in robbing a store or two, loading the pickings on a truck and selling the loot in remote villages where chances of encountering the Russian patrol were slim. The profit would then be equally divided.

A store was robbed, a village was selected and they were on their way. Angel always rode on the back of the truck along with one or two Russians. He would kill these men as soon as they reached a place that posed little threat of interference, the driver would hear the shots, stop to investigate and be shot too. Angel would throw the corpses in a ditch which he then neatly covered with hay, branches or whatever else was at hand. He rid himself of the goods and returned to Budapest as the sole profiteer, only to lure other Russians into his trap and do it all over again.

The Police were aware of the crimes and were hot on his heels by the summer of 1947. Angel was forced to leave, without his loot, and after a long stretch of weary hiding and steady harassment, he opted to enlist with the Legion.

The fourth was Johnny Bacsa, barely 24 and the youngest of the group, came from a farm in Transdanubia. He dispelled our downcast spirits and concerns over a none too bright future many times over with his sunny disposition and down-to-earth sense of humor.

The last member of this group was a laborer, approximately 30-years-old who was a self-indulgent boor and generally unappealing person. His anger was visibly expressed when the food arrived. He cursed the cooks for being late with the chow and starving a ravenous man half to death. He had little to say except describe his exploits as a safecracker and gloat over the good old days when there was nothing to do but "neck with the chicks."

It was a relief supper came to a close and cut him off. He may have gone on forever. The laborer guzzled down his wine, grumbled over the quantity of it, accused the cooks with vile abuses of hoarding the booze for themselves, and stretched out on his bed. Within seconds, the walls trembled from the infernal snoring he created.

Sleep escaped me; I was kept awake by the infernal snoring of that darn laborer as well as by my anxieties over the black future. I could not accept the irrevocable fact that I was committed to the French Foreign Legion. Not for a second was there any dispute in my mind that somehow, no matter what the cost, I had to try and escape. It was ludicrous to think that I would stay here and lose five years of my life. Even if I did honor the commitment, there was no guarantee that I would live to see the end.

How was I to tell my family about this? Good God! What will they think when I write to tell them where I landed?

Falling asleep with all this on my mind was a valiant effort, but when I did, the Arab relief arrived to cover for the Hungarian board guards and I battled with them all night.

June 30, 1948

I awoke with a start to find that someone was trying to shake the living daylights out of me. Johnny was doing the dirty deed.

"Hey Scout!" he screamed. "Who the hell were you fighting with all night? You were kicking the wall so hard that the entire building almost collapsed on me."

"I was kicking the wall? You must be out of your mind. My head was facing the wall."

"Like hell! Maybe that's where it was to start with, but believe me, that's not how you ended up."

The name 'Scout' came into being when Johnny decided to bestow nicknames on us all. I altered my uniform to fit the bill. Trousers became shorts, the tunic became a jacket to match, while kneehigh socks and oxfords completed a look which was very similar to that of a boy scout.

In honor of his shining career as an illegal abortionist, Leo was blessed with the title 'Fetus.' Walter was baptized 'Chesko' out of respect for the home he escaped from. Angel ended up with the title, 'Little Angel.' In Johnny's estimation 'Lucifer' was more apt because if everything we knew of him were true then Lucifer was an archangel by comparison. The laborer, a man who was held in disdain by all, and not worthy of a nickname, or so thought Johnny, continued to be referred to simply as 'Safecracker.' As the man responsible for our baptisms, Johnny was given the title 'Godfather.'

Fetus and Chesko were woken by the racket Johnny and I created, neither was terribly impressed. Chesko flung a pillow at him, told him where to go and promised him a fair beating.

"But I had no other choice," Johnny said in defense. "This idiot was about to kick a hole right through the wall. Not that I care much about that, but his next kick was aimed right at my head. Sorry, but even my nerves of steel will not tolerate that kind of insult. I'd much rather shake the wind out of him."

Walter and Leo would have continued to rake Johnny over the coals had the Safecracker not woken up. He worked himself out of bed and quite likely out of some dream world that focused on women because he immediately broke into a heartfelt rendition of a classic epic with raunchy lyrics.

His howling woke up everyone in the room and in a matter of seconds three boots were flung at his head. They unfortunately missed their mark. The Safecracker gathered the boots and claimed ownership saying that since they were thrown at him it was only fair that the boots not be returned. The rightful owners, however, were reluctant to acknowledge their loss and converged on the Safecraker with clear intentions.

The situation was becoming enticing when the door opened and breakfast was wheeled in. The Safecracker didn't even have a chance to return a blow, for those who had brought the meal assessed the situation and very quickly put an end to a fight that hadn't even begun. The boots were returned to their rightful owners, while the Safecracker got off with a couple of slaps and no breakfast. Eat or fight he was told, and since he chose the latter he could quit the habit of eating for this morning.

At some point in the afternoon we sneaked down to the canteen where Walter, or rather Chesko, sat at the piano. He transformed the moment his fingers touched the keys. The pleasures he brought to us were, however, mixed, and I'd rather he hadn't started. For what he played evoked painful memories that merely emphasized our separation from the world we left behind.

I was fit to be tied and almost killed Chesko. He, as if sensing my rage and wanting to rub it in even more, started to play another song. This was the last straw. I bought a half-litre of wine and guzzled it down. This was not a good idea. In a matter of minutes my legs gave out, and like a felled tree, I sprawled to my stomach. Had Fetus and Chesko not carried me off to bed I might have spent the night on the floor. As it was, I woke up in my bed shortly after supper with one hell of a headache.

"Is that squash about ready to burst?" asked Godfather, with a malicious smirk.

"See what you get for trying to imitate grown-ups? Wine is meant for real men, not for some greenhorn office worm like yourself. And to drink wine on top of coffee! Man, you're real raw. About as inexperienced as Bessy my cow when it comes to ploughing."

"Listen you Transdanubian, if you don't shut your face you'll be on the floor in a minute with a head the same size as mine."

"No, you listen. More than once I've been threatened like that, but they never get around to it 'cause they find themselves lying in the dust first. I don't give anyone half a chance to make a move on me, you understand."

"Come off your high horse old chap. Hell, you could run circles under my armpits!"

"Christ Almighty! You should know better than to judge a man by his size."

"Yeah, but all I can do is hear your voice. I can't see a man behind it."

"Just remember this, Scout. You're talking to someone who used to throw men your size two at a time from the bar on Saturday nights."

I sensed serious overtones intruding on this joking manner and quickly changed the subject. Supper arrived and helped dissolve the growing tension.

It was during supper that the NCOs told us that tomorrow our group was to start out for Marseille.

The main topic of conversation among the five of us was how to effect our plans for escape.

Little Angel sighed, "Fine for you guys to talk about that! You can do it, because you've got nothing to worry about. But me? No matter where I escaped to, no matter where I went, the cops would be on my neck in no time at all."

Down to four hopeful escapees. For the time being we had no idea how to execute the plan, or how to continue once freedom was in hand. The foremost objective was to cross the Soviet zone. Concrete plans were impossible to work out until that was done. Once Russian territory was behind, we hoped that everything would take care of itself.

We were discussing our plans long after midnight. God only knows what time it was when we finally fell asleep.

July 1, 1948

We were at it again, well-before the eight a.m. breakfast hour. All of us that is, except the Safecracker who was in his usual immobile state and still snoring up a storm.

Breakfast arrived, word of our departure did not.

Lunch was served and still nothing.

Supper came and we were still in the dark.

A few hours after supper, a NCO showed up and explained in German that everyone was to remain in place next morning because a captain was coming to brief us on the details of the journey ahead. After this, sleep eluded us even more than the night before.

July 2, 1948

The Captain came as promised. Behind him trailed the NCO with a box in his hand. The Captain explained that the next morning, we were to board the Parisian Express and travel to a camp in an unidentified city where we would join forces with a like group of men. The following day we would proceed to another camp and remain there for an undisclosed length of time.

The Captain pointed to the box in the NCO's hand,

"This box contains passports. Every man will be given one before we reach the Soviet zone. Once you have your passport in hand, you are to leave our coach and spread yourselves throughout the train. Go wherever you want, but you must return to our reserved coach immediately after the Russians have finished inspecting your documents."

So much for French strategy, but the question remained: Why did the Captain want the group to separate? Even more important, why put a distance between the group and its escorts?

I later learned that this tactic was necessary to protect the French government from the possibility of political conflict. Should the Soviets board the train, detect a fraud, and happen to arrest any of us on that basis, the man in custody would be left defenseless. He would be unable to accuse the French government of involvement, or say that he was a member of the French Foreign Legion. He would get nowhere by saying that he was in the Legion, for the two escorts who remained behind in our compartment would refuse to support the claim. No one, but the man in custody, would be hauled off the train by the Soviets and he alone would suffer the consequences.

Precautions such as these would not be necessary in neutral territory. Complications would not arise because the Americans were not inclined to seek involvement when it came to the doings of the French government. For this reason, and to avoid the risk of capture, the French were virtually guaranteed that none of the legionnaires would risk escape. Especially not in the Soviet zone, for they knew that we were not foolish enough to throw ourselves into the clutches of those we were trying to flee from in the first place.

The Captain finished explaining the plan and once he was convinced that his orders were understood he calmly turned and exited.

Not to be dismayed by the tactics of the French which seemingly afforded no way out, the five of us sat around a table to try and formulate a plan of escape. It was clear that to break loose by jumping off the train while still in Soviet territory was an asinine idea. Better to wait for a safer time and place. To leave the train in Austria had no rhyme or reason, especially since I wanted to go to Belgium. Why risk an already hazardous journey from so far away? Why not take advantage of the free food and ride instead, remain with the Legion as far as France and be that much closer to our final destination? I no longer remember why, but I found myself changed out of my Scout's attire, and into a French uniform adorned with gold-colored buttons. The others followed suit but none looked as charming.

The thought of departure the next day livened our spirits and at Chesko's suggestion, we made a go of sneaking down to the canteen.

Chesko first struck up and old Hungarian folk song, "I Will Leave Your Village Soon." A most appropriate selection, and we could not help but break into song. The French soliders on the premises, who were quietly sipping their wine and were not particularly fond of shoddy would-be legionnaires, did not take kindly to our serenade and showed us to the door.

"It's all your fault, Little Angel," accused Godfather. "They booted us out only 'cause of you and that rusty voice of yours."

"I wouldn't say anything if I were you," retorted Angel. "What about your voice? The sound of Bessy your cow mooing is sweeter to the ear than your singing, which sounds exactly like the whining of a cat when its tail is being pulled. Maybe somebody was pulling your tail!"

"That kind of talk will get you into trouble real quick. Where's your respect towards a Transdanubian? Let me assure you, if you want to talk about tail pulling, there's ample to pull on me. But you? Can't seem to see more than a couple inches worth."

They continued their bickering while Fetus, Chesko and I went back to the canteen. We kept our conversation subdued so not to again disturb the sons of the French tricolor. After all, we too would become kindred servants of that flag, and as such, would have every right to breathe our last in the swamps and jungles of Indochina or in the cursed Sahara.

July 3, 1948

The order came during breakfast: everyone was to stay put and get ready to leave right after the meal. However, it wasn't until four in the afternoon that the truck rolled in to take us to the West Banhof Station. We were ordered to, and herded on, the last coach of the Parisian Express with the greatest of haste.

The haste was to avoid the questioning faces of, and possible interference from, the bystanders. The French went to great lengths to shroud the fact that they were gathering recruits by the hundreds from every corner of Europe.

The train compartments were tailor-made for the group of Hungarians in that they afforded room for six people. The six of us crammed into one, and thus spared us from having to mix with the other nationalities. Wandering about was clearly prohibited, and to enforce it, the escorting NCOs circled the corridor with a watchful eye. The reason for this precautionary measure was a mystery to me as we would all be issued passports and ordered to scatter.

It was time to leave, and the long row of train cars started for the unknown, transporting me further and further from home. As the engine pulled, its steel heart was unable to feel for the two dozen men in the rear who had lost everything. The rhythm of the train wheels seemed to say; There is no return . . . only forward . . . only forward, forward! I asked, but to where? Where would we stop? Would we have any hope for a better future, or would the final destination be some Indochinese swamp, or jungle, or the hellish Sahara desert? The wheels did not answer.

We sat in silence, caught up in the moment of loss, even the Safecracker had nothing to say. I wondered: Would there ever be a road leading back? Would there be time again to feel the warm embrace of my mother, hear my father's voice or see my faithful dog, Aigo, run out to greet me?

One of the escorts entered, haphazardly distributed the passports, told us to disperse in about twenty minutes, and then turned on his heels and left.

While everyone examined their passports, I saw no point in looking. I knew it to be a forgery. The six of us decided to separate from each other for the sake of protection should any one of us be apprehended. With that, we scattered.

I made a beeline for the dining car. In no time at all one of the waiters took my order. I watched the countryside glide past while the supper was being prepared, and contemplated the serious and sometimes cruel ways of fate. I wondered if those at the Yalta Conference, those in a position to do something, had washed their hands of the fate of millions of eastern Europeans.

My thoughts were interrupted by the waiter bringing the soup. No sooner had I started to eat when I felt the train slow, a sure indication that the Russian zone border was ahead. As the train slowed, my heart beat increased in direct proportion.

I was so tense that I could hardly swallow. The sickening sense of dread was like that which I had experienced in the Burgenland village when I first spotted the Soviet patrol circling the streets. The difference was that there I had been able to escape attention, but here a face-to-face encounter was imminent.

No sooner had the train jerked to a complete stop, a Soviet soldier was inside the dining car, and as I was closest to the door, standing beside me. He was polite, yet firm:

"Document!"

He took my passport, looked in it, flipped through it, tried to read it, and glanced at me then back at the passport. I sat through it breathless and very close to a heart attack.

After what seemed like an eternity, he returned the passport with a smile that was intended to convey friendliness.

"Haraso."

Everything was in order, and with a salute, on he went.

What a load off my mind!

I glanced inside the passport. Any imbecile could surely see that the picture inside did not correspond with my own face. The fellow in the picture had curly hair, light eyes and a round face. I was exactly the opposite. Perhaps it was dictated by fate that I not look inside sooner, for had I been aware of this gross discrepancy, I might have been anxious enough to give myself away.

The train started moving again, and I, under all that pressure, had completely forgotten about the explicit orders to return to our reserved coach. What is more, I had not finished eating since service in the dining car ceased during the passport inspection. Once the train was on its way, the waiter brought out the rest of my meal.

No sooner had I started to eat when one of our escorts discovered me. With his eyes blazing with anger, he quietly demanded to know why I had not returned as ordered. True, I hardly understood a word of his French, but from his gesticulations, all that he was trying to convey was perfectly clear.

I mimicked his mannerisms to lend some comedy to the scene, then in Hungarian explained that I had not returned first of all because I was still eating, and second, because we weren't even close to the American zone yet. I assured him though, that I would do as told, but only after supper. I had no idea how much of my recital he understood, but he was not inclined to leave me alone.

The other escort flew into a violent rage when we finally showed up, and screamed at me for not having returned sooner. Leo and the others looked at me with astonishment when I stepped in. They were certain that I was roaming the highway and enjoying my freedom by now. Not only had I not escaped, but of the twenty-four men, no one went missing.

It was night by the time we reached the city of Bregenz, the first designated stopover of the journey. The trucks we had boarded stopped in front of a small building where we joined the waiting group. Roll call, back on the trucks and we headed back for the train which would take us, so we were told, to Kehl.

Where exactly is this city? As per instructions in Vienna, it was there that we would be stationed for some time.

Haste and darkness had separated me from my Hungarian friends and among a group of people who were babbling in an assortment of languages. Rather than socialize, I occupied myself with thoughts of Brussels. I imagined my sister fainting from surprise when I appeared on her doorstep. Now it was only a question of picking the right moment and place to make my move. If intuition served me right, that place would be Kehl.

It would only be a matter of familiarizing myself with the locale. I had to know precisely what direction to go in. If only I had a map to show me where Kehl was, how far it was from Belgium and what cities I would have to cross to get there.

During the course of all this planning I fell asleep. I woke to the sound of bodies shuffling around me. It could only mean that Kehl was just around the corner.

Chapter Three
Kehl

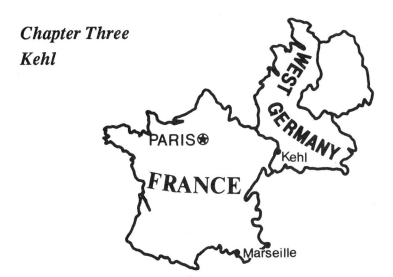

July 4, 1948

The camp in Kehl was typical of the military concentration camps that most emigrants have crossed through. It differed from the camp in Vienna only in that the atmosphere was decidedly more military. Highrise style barracks were replaced with single storey wooden barracks set out in neat rows. We could no longer be lazy and sleep in until 8:00 a.m. Reveille was at 6:00, followed by an hour and a half of preliminaries laced with a touch of exercise before breakfast. We fell in line to the strident commands of the officers and NCOs and marched to the tables for the morning meal. Lineups again after breakfast for group work assignment. One group cleaned the streets, another scrubbed the barracks and the third was sent on work duty outside of camp. The authorities made certain we were not bored during our residence here.

My five Hungarian friends and I were together in the corner of the same barrack. At the very first opportunity we four promising escapees congregated to discuss the details of our imminent getaway for the umpteenth time. Until now, the talks had been unproductive and it was time to seriously address the issue.

By now we knew that Kehl was situated along the Rhine, and at the same elevation as Strasbourg, which meant that it lay in a direct line with Paris. To launch an escape from any place more ideal than this was impossible to imagine. What we failed to realize was that the French were also very much aware of this.

We detailed a plan and set the attempted escape date for three or four days later, depending on how quickly we could get a map. Little Angel assumed responsibility for this, saying that stealing one lousy map was child's play when compared to the vast amount of robbing he had done.

I admired the lad's sense of honor. Fully aware that he could not come with us, he was willing to take the gamble and steal for us. I should say obtain, because a duty-bound legionnaire never steals. Little Angel was a man held in high esteem.

July 6, 1948

Reveille at 6:00, lineup, breakfast, lineup, and group work assignment. Fetus, Little Angel, Johnny and I lucked out and were not only in the same group, but one assigned to work detail outside of the camp.

"I'll get a map for you by noon!" boasted Little Angel. "Provided, of course, that there is one in the house we're going to."

"Just be careful, Little Angel," I warned. "I don't want to see you get caught and beaten up like that shoemaker was."

"You should never worry about me, Scout!" came the arrogant reply. "It's a lot harder to nab me than you think. I've given too many police the slip to fail now."

We were dispatched to do some gardening for a private home – working under the constant supervision of an armed guard. The lady of the house came out, told the escort that there were things inside to be done and asked him to send someone in to help. Little Angel jumped at the chance.

"The map is on its way, if there is one!" he said between his teeth.

That the lady strolled in and out of the house many times made Little Angel's task that much easier. He emerged around eleven, his face boasting a sardonic smile.

"I've got it!" he whispered, carefully slipping the map into my hand. "I got it, now you guard it."

We drew into a corner after supper to study the map and established that the only possible route was to head for Paris.

The odor in the barrack, caused by the work detail's leaving foul smelling water puddles on the floor, was a nuisance so we decided to continue our discussion in the canteen where a few rounds of cognac could be enjoyed as an added bonus.

On the way to the door I slipped on one of these puddles, fell on my left arm and dislocated my elbow. The pain was excruciating. The others helped me down to the infirmary.

The doctor instructed my friends to hold me as tight as they could, then grabbed my arm and with one violent jerk set my elbow back in place. Needless to say, no anesthetics were used and the procedure was sheer agony. The doctor saw what pain I was in and gave me a comforting pat on the back.

"Come now, a legionnaire can surely stand such a trifle without anesthesia. You'll be fit as a fiddle by the morning."

He offered me a cigarette. He might have offered more than one, perhaps the whole pack, first because he tortured me so and second because as new recruits, we did not get any. The first installment of our pay or "premium" was not due for many months. Fist fights commonly broke out over a discarded butt.

The doctor secured my arm with a splint, tied the ends of the sling around my neck, gave me a few pills and told me to come back in the morning.

To kill the terrible pain which still lingered, I suggested that we go to the canteen. A few glasses of cognac had to be a far more effective pain killer than any pill.

We returned to the barracks early to further study the map. Chesko went to fetch the map, but returned with a panic stricken look on his face – it was gone. Someone had stolen it during our absence. Whoever it was must have seen Chesko hide it under his pillow before we left for the infirmary. Livid with rage, our first inclination was to string Chesko up on the nearest lamppost.

"No point to stringing him up," said Little Angel. "We'd have to take the blame, and besides, it's not gonna bring the map back. But don't worry. I'll get another one soon as we go on outside work assignment again."

It was Little Angel again, a wanted criminal around the continent, who offered to help us get out of this fix.

July 7, 1948

Sleep eluded me all night. I wanted to scream from the pain. By 7:00 a.m. I was standing in front of the infirmary waiting for what seemed like an eternity until it opened at 8:00. This morning, of all times, the doctor arrived half an hour late. He removed the binding and revealed an arm that was swollen to the size of a small watermelon.

The game is up for me, I thought. So much for Paris and Brussels! And how easy it would have been to reach Paris via Strasbourg, even with the Rhine as a minor obstacle. I sincerely hoped that the others would go through with the plan. I had no other choice but to wait until we reached Marseille.

The doctor finished rebinding my arm and gave me another handful of pills with instructions to take three every hour.

On my way back to the barracks I saw my friends sweeping the streets. So much for a map today. Feeling terrible, I spent the rest of the day swallowing pills.

July 8, 1948

The pain had subsided and I felt a whole lot better. After the doctor removed the bandage I saw that the swelling had reduced considerably. Those pills must have been some kind of a miracle drug. I should be good as new by tomorrow, and just maybe, I can still join the gang.

It was around ten when he finished with me. On my way back to the barracks, I noticed that Chesko and company were cleaning the streets again. What a pain. No map again today.

"What's going on? Didn't you guys luck into work outside?"

"That's not all," said Godfather. "Word is, that we're off to Marseille tomorrow."

"Well, what did you decide? Are you going to try and leave tonight? " I was disappointed over my stroke of bad luck and sorry that my quick recovery was all for nothing.

"If the rumor is true, then we haven't got much choice but to go along," replied an indifferent Chesko. "I for one don't want to run the risk without a map."

"You could leave tonight, map or no map. Why wait for tomorrow?" I said, secretly hoping that they might change their minds.

"If we had a compass, I wouldn't hesitate for a second," sighed Fetus.

We waited all day for further announcements regarding the trip and began to hope that nothing would come of it. There was no way I would be left out if my arm continued to heal like this.

"Hey Scout! Bet you anything that your arm will save you from the Legion," philosophized Little Angel.

This hadn't even occurred to me. Maybe he was right. Maybe my stroke of misfortune would work itself out for the best. I put great store in fate now, as in Vienna, as always, and if fate got me into this mess then just maybe fate would get me out of it. If only Little Angel's words were indeed prophetic.

July 9, 1948

We were anxious to hear some word about the departure before the breakfast lineup, but nothing.

"Johnny, are you absolutely sure that you heard we were leaving? They would have said something a long time ago if it's really true."

"I'm quite serious. Ask Leo or Chesko. We overheard two legionnaires talking about it when we were sweeping the streets yesterday."

"How the hell could you understand what they were saying when you don't speak a word of French?"

"That may be true, but they were speaking in German and Leo understands German. Right, Leo?"

"Yep. But the question is, where did they get the information? Anyway, it doesn't matter. If we can get some work outside of camp today and somehow find a map, then we can still get away tonight. But map or no map, I think we should still go. I have no desire to rot in Indochina."

After breakfast they trotted off to work while I went back to the infirmary.

I was seeing stars and howling after the doctor removed the bandage and began twisting my arm. He bound it one last time, gave me some more pills and pronounced the arm healed. It would not be necessary to come back and see him again.

I did not see Fetus and the company of sanitary authorities on my way back. Great, I thought, Little Angel is stealing a map.

Stepping into the barrack I saw the street sweepers sitting on their beds.

"What the hell is this? Weren't you sent outside?"

"We've lost our last chance," said Fetus. "Orders have been given that no one is to leave the barracks. We will be loaded into freight cars starting this afternoon."

A population census revealed that two people had gone missing. The two Germans who slept beside Chesko had escaped. They had stolen our map and escaped with it!

I had to admire their efficiency. Instead of speculating and planning for days on end, they simply picked themselves up and left. We, on the other hand, would soon find ourselves not in Paris but in Marseille.

Dinner, then supper, passed and bedtime came without a word about departure. It suddenly occurred to me that the two Germans who had escaped with *our* map were responsible for the delay, and until they were caught, no one was going anywhere. Fate was not being kind at all, and trying to escape from Marseille will be much more hazardous.

July 10, 1948

As we marched to the dining barracks for breakfast we were met by a most unpleasant sight: the two recaptured Germans. My God! It would be many weeks before they regained any semblance of human form.

I'm sure our thoughts were the same when the four Hungarians exchanged glances. Not one of us had any desire to be on display like that. The public display of the Germans had made its desired impact.

We were told to prepare for an 11:00 a.m. departure.

Loading began at precisely 11:00. I was disappointed to see that we would be continuing our journey aboard cattle cars instead of an express train complete with dining facilities. The one luxury was the thick layer of straw which was covered with blankets strewn on the floor.

The six of us again found ourselves in the same car along with Germans, Poles and Italians. There were seventeen men in the car, including the veteran legionnaire who was assigned to each car to maintain order. Our superior gave us no trouble whatsoever. In fact, not even an hour had passed before he was drunk and asleep. We kept a watchful eye on him rather than he on us.

The train pulled into Lyon around midnight. With the exception of our watchdog, who lay in the corner reeking of wine, the guards on duty jumped off the moment the train stopped to prevent us from leaving.

The train next to ours ignited someone's curiousity, and having outwitted the attentive guards and forced open a door he discovered several jars of honey. Little Angel ran over and brought back several jars of it.

The Safecracker turned on Little Angel after he had stuffed himself: "You're such a fool. Instead of honey, it might of occurred to you to check out the next car. You might have turned up something that can come in handy for a legionnaire to attract dames with, like bras and panties. Honey's no good at all."

Little Angel snarled at him, "To hell with you! All you ever do is shoot off your mouth and stuff yourself. Why didn't you go? You're a good for nothing lazy bum waiting to be served hand and foot. You're nothing but a bloody parasite, a disgrace to society. You have no honor."

Little Angel was certainly one to speak of honor.

The train soon rolled on and we were lulled to sleep by its rhythmic swaying.

July 11, 1948

We woke to find the sun high in the sky, the train still rushing ahead at full speed. The guard finally revived, saw the jars of honey and championed one for his breakfast. It didn't occur to him to ask where it had come from.

Curious to know how much further it was to Marseille, Leo asked the guard but he merely hemmed and hawed, shrugged his shoulders, curled up and went back to sleep. He was certainly not one to be counted on as a source of information.

The train dashed along, and we spotted a road sign to Marseille. We were one short step away from the next concentration camp.

Chapter Four
Marseille

July 11, 1948 – August 3, 1948

It was late in the afternoon when our train pulled into the Marseille train station. As in Vienna, we were scurried away from the station, and out of public scrutiny, with great haste. We were herded into trucks and after a short ride, rambled through the gates of the St. Nicholas Fortress.

The faded structures in paltry tones of yellow and grey within a huge gravelled enclosure were anything but enticing. The flat roofs of the buildings next to the wall formed a walkway that ran in a half circle around the fortress. The courtyard was dusty and bleak, and armed sentries guarded the gate. However, from atop of the back wall of the fortress, the scene opened onto a tiny gulf whose outlet led to the island on which the "If Castle," where Count Monte Cristo had been imprisoned, was built. Beyond, the Mediterranean Sea appeared in full view.

Rarely were we permitted to leave the boundaries of the fortress, and even then, only with an armed escort. Conditions here were significantly worse than in Kehl. Abusive treatment was rampant and often beyond the point of tolerance. This behavior on the part of the authorities was understandable considering that every nation of Europe was represented amongst the almost 200 men present. With such cultural diversity, many of these men did not understand the word discipline. Those of us who had had military training were better able to adjust to the situation. That we could not understand a single word the NCO screamed did not matter much because he flung his arms while talking, and from that we could surmise what he was trying to communicate. It is hardly surprising that under these conditions, and after screaming his lungs out with no apparent result, the poor NCO resorted to physical abuse. Wonder of wonders, those who were altogether dense and incapable of following the slightest of orders, knew right away what was expected of them after one kick. I trust that not just an officer of the Legion, but the Archangel Gabriel would have lost his temper with such a shoddy group.

We legionnaires in training learned what it meant to serve an army where men perished like flies. Some chose suicide over suffering in the Sahara or Indochina. Others still, the fortunate few, were discharged due to physical inadequacy. These men were permitted to travel, at the expense of the French government, to any place in the world of their choosing. Of those that remained, some had the good fortune to be assigned a comfortable desk job, but the majority were delegated to combat units and more than a few sacrificed their lives in the name of their adopted homeland. On the grounds of serious illness a man could regain his freedom before the five year contract expired. These were perhaps the most fortunate of the lot, provided that the illness in question was not terminal. And then there were those who, after surviving the initial five year ordeal, turned around to re-enlist for another five years.

Where visits to Marseille were permitted, there was little reason to complain about, except the brutality. Life was carefree and the food was tasty despite its lacking in quantity.

A cushy position fell into my lap one day. I was awarded the high distinction of office dispatcher. The numerous perks that went along with the position included enough extra food to feed Leo and the gang many times over, cigarettes and respect. I was no longer abused, even by the toughest of the tough, with their usual coarse language or rude behavior. I also began to notice that contrary to popular opinion and my experiences until then, the NCOs were essentially pretty good guys. Around the office they were always very polite, even with me, and stopped using the same vulgar language they did with the men outside. I, in turn, did my best to please and put enormous effort into learning French. I was not ridiculed for this effort. On the contrary, they assisted my mastery of the language by correcting my pronunciation and expanding my vocabulary so that by departure time, I was babbling well-enough to be understood.

A NCO told me one day that I was to be included in a group departing for Sidi-Bel-Abbes. The ship, *Sidi-Brahim,* would take us to Oran, from where the journey would continue by train.

I hurried to tell the good news to my friends.

"Are we on the list too?" asked Johnny.

"How the hell am I supposed to know? Besides, I didn't see any list. You'll find out soon enough one way or the other."

Little Angel turned on me, "I'd think you'd have enough brains to check it out. You're a good for nothing stupid office messenger."

"What do you mean, good for nothing? Who's responsible for the extra food and all those cigarettes? I've gone out of my way to provide for you."

"Come off your high horse and quit your bragging. Anyone of us would have done the same, given the advantages of your position. You just lucked into it, that's all. You've got to show some tact. But they don't teach you that, do they. All they do is teach you how to lick stamps and stuff like that. What you need is a gentleman like myself to teach you the art of finesse, to show you how to be slick and cagey. Sign up for lessons. I'll show you!"

"Look you guys, you'll know in a few days. But if you're so tense about it, I'll do a little snooping and find out tomorrow."

The next morning, I grabbed a rag and went from one office to another, dusting the rooms. I piled and repiled stacks of books and papers, hoping to find the list. No luck. What with all the commotion I caused, it was surprising that I was not booted out.

One room left to go, the office of the Commander. It was empty so I was free to snoop around undisturbed. At last I came across a typed sheet, the heading of Sidi-Bel-Abbes on top, a long list of names below. The first name was mine, followed by all my friends. That is all but the Safecracker. This omission thrilled me to bits.

I dropped everything and ran to tell the guys. It was not met with much enthusiasm. Each had hoped to be disqualified for medical reasons.

August 4, 1948

The four days flew by, and the trucks came to take us to the *Sidi-Brahim.*

When I saw the ship I wasn't sure whether to laugh or to cry, it was in such a deplorable state of disrepair. The "ship" was the type used to transport livestock.

"We're going to go to Oran on this?" I asked.

We embarked and were immediately escorted to the large storage area which, resembling a swimming pool, was accessed by steps down the side wall. These were our living-quarters. We slept on the bare steel floor without blankets or straw, but if the four-legged creatures were able to adapt, so could we.

The guards gave us permission to come up on deck after the ship reached open sea. We passed the Balearic Isles late in the afternoon, it occurred to one of the Italians that basking in their shade was much preferable to tanning in the Sahara. He made a splendid dive into the water and swam directly for one of the islands. He was a fool who should have known that to reach the island was impossible.

In less than half an hour he was drenched and standing on deck once more. His escapade resulted in a delay for which he would be duly reprimanded once in Oran.

Thirty-six hours of rowing later, we docked in Oran's harbor, where we were greeted by officers and NCOs alike. The hosts waited patiently until we fell in line. Having done so, one of the officers delivered a short speech, and though we couldn't understand a single word, I assumed it to be a message of welcome. His manner was calm, polite and in direct contrast to the endless screaming that was the norm in Marseille.

"Scout," whispered Johnny, "I think we took a wrong turn somewhere. This can't possibly be the Legion. This guy's gotta be a theologian from some seminary."

The trucks came and took us to the barracks, where a second pleasant surprise awaited. The barracks were surrounded by tall walls of stone, but in all other respects, the building looked like anything but a barracks. I would gladly stay here for the five years. Everything was painted in warm hues of green, red and white, creeping vines along the walls, flowers and palms in the courtyard and the cooing of doves filled the air. It was like stepping into Eden after the dismal environment in Kehl and Marseille.

To dispel any false optimism, supper reminded us that yes, this was the Legion. Some inedible concoction made of camel steak was supposed to pass as food. After bending my knife out of shape trying to cut it, I aborted any ideas of chewing it. Also included was something that pretended to be creamed vegetables. It turned my stomach just to look at it, and I retired for the evening on an empty stomach.

We spent the night on rush mats in the courtyard. The temperature was mild, palms swayed gently in the evening breeze, millions of stars shone and sleep eluded me. I was not accustom to sleeping on cement and the once beautiful dove calls were now an irritating nuisance. I tossed and turned but gave up the battle and sat inside one of the gazebos until morning.

August 6, 1948

We left for Sidi-Bel-Abbes, approximately eighty kilometres to the south of Oran. The blistering heat was so distracting that I was not interested in the view of fields rich with fig trees, vineyards and orange groves, which contrasted with miserable hovels and arid desert wilderness. Nothing helped to alleviate my discomfort from the intense heat, not even stripping off almost every last stich of clothing. I was, however, willing to sacrifice half of everything I owned for a cold bottle of beer. I wasn't sure what I had to offer, but at the time, I was desperate enough to promise anything.

Doors and windows were flung open in an effort to combat the midday sun, but it didn't make any difference. If anything, it made things worse because the resulting rush of air blew hot sand in our faces and made us even more miserable.

We arrived in Sidi-Bel-Abbes around one in the afternoon, and none too soon.

Chapter Five
Sidi-Bel-Abbes

Oran
Sidi-Bel-Abbes

ALGERIA

August 6, 1948

Excluding the palm tree lined streets and the intense heat, Sidi-Bel-Abbes was little different from a small European city. Carefree strollers sauntered in the squares beside apartment buildings and stores on clean avenues. Europeans and Africans intermingled on the terraces of sidewalk cafes.

It was a pretty city, or at least that is the conclusion I drew from what I was able to see as we were driven to the barracks. I was overcome with a feeling of well-being. It was a joy to see that we had ended up in such a nice place rather than some forsaken fortress. We could mingle in the city and despite the uniform feel like civilized beings again. At least that's what I thought. Reality, proved to be completely different.

Sidi-Bel-Abbes was the headquarters of the French Foreign Legion. The base consisted of two separate groups of buildings. One side of the boulevard housed the offices and living quarters of those personnel who were permanently assigned here while the other side, included the garages, storage areas and living quarters of those legionnaires who were just passing through. On this side, the separate residences, were intended to accommodate different groups of people. CP-1 (Company Passenger 1 Building) housed those legionnaires who were waiting to be discharged and those who were waiting to be transferred from one city to another, while CP-3 building accommodated new recruits like ourselves.

When we entered the courtyard I was pleased to notice the presence of trees, bushes and flowers. Though not quite as aesthetically satisfying as in Oran, the setting was, nevertheless, far superior to the bleak landscape I remembered in Marseille.

This is one section of the military station located in Sidi-Bel-Abbes. The buildings that surround the square courtyard, the Quartier Vienot, housed the offices and apartments of those in permanent residence. The buildings with chimneys in the lower left hand corner, the CP-3, were the temporary quarters for the candidates of the Legion.

I had some time to look around while waiting in line for further orders. From my vantage point all was agreeable. All but the three-storey building in a distant corner of the vast courtyard. This structure was isolated from its surroundings by a tall iron gate. Armed guards stood in front of the gate, and we could not gaze into the yard because iron plates covered the gate's slates and blocked the view. There was no questioning that this was the camp prison.

After a short interval, we were led past this very gate, and my world crumbled.

Were we to be housed in this building? Was this the infamous CP-3, the quarters for new recruits?

With the gate barely closed behind us, we stood within the revolting grey cemented yard and face-to-face with the officers and NCOs in charge. The authorities in Marseille had been gentlemen by comparison. Only officers completely hardened and devoid of any and all human compassion were assigned to serve here. To so much as idly saunter toward the gate was interpreted as a serious misdemeanor worthy of brutal physical punishment.

Every room had iron bars covering the windows. These bars were built so close together that our heads could not fit between them. A thin piece of matting was supplied as a bed. Each room also contained a table with two benches. The ethnic majority of the room claimed the table for their own. Leo and I being the only two Hungarians in a room with eighteen Italians, five Germans and five Spaniards, didn't have a hope in hell of sitting down to eat even once in a while, so we ate all our meals squatting on the floor.

And to think that I had daydreamed of strolling under palm trees past buildings embraced by flowers, and sitting on terraced cafes. This dream did not come true. In Marseille, we had been permitted to move freely about on the walkway which surrounded the fortress, to gaze out on the gulf and at the sun bathers beyond. Here, we were prisoners in the strictest sense of the word.

In rare instances we went on excursions outside the prison, but only in small groups, and never without two armed guards. Rather than issue a word of warning should somebody step out of line, the guards chastised with a kick so powerful that the offender keeled over in pain.

There was one NCO whose brutality exceeded all imaginable limits. We despised him to no end, but there was nothing we could do about it. Little Angel, however, thought otherwise.

One evening, he sneaked out and concealed himself beside the wall that led to the toilets. Little Angel had had enough of the NCO's sadistic behavior and decided that no matter what the consequences, the man was going to get what was coming to him. Little Angel waited hours for the officer to show up. When the NCO was within reach, Little Angel jumped on him with such a force that the NCO was knocked against the wall. Little Angel took advantage of his opponent's vulnerable position and soundly worked him over. The attack came so suddenly that the officer had no chance to identify his assailant or to defend himself. Little Angel was incredibly lucky in that the officer did not put up a fight and attract attention, and that nobody happened by while the fight was going on.

A thorough investigation ensued, but Little Angel escaped suspicion because the NCO could not identify the culprit. Angel's revenge did not change anything. It didn't tame the officer's spirit, if anything, he treated us worse than before.

The doctor in Sidi-Bel-Abbes subjected us to the most thorough and rigorous medical examination yet. I went in hoping that the doctor would diagnose me inept because of my arm injury. He focused a lot of attention on my arm, but pronounced me apt and fit for military service. Once the final personnel decision was made, we received the first installment of our salary – 5700 francs or $14 US.

August 22, 1948

It was announced that volunteers were being sought for a paratrooper battalion to be established in the near future. The volunteer aspect of the matter was strongly emphasized. The advantages of being a paratrooper were elaborated and included, an increase in salary and a better chance of promotion. The greatest inducement was a promise to those who volunteered that they could leave CP-3 within a few days. Now that, if nothing else, made a substantial impact. The sooner we were allowed out, the better.

I'm going to be the first soldier to volunteer from this battalion. It can't possibly be any worse than life with these animals. And if I had to die, to do so while teetering through the air seemed more fitting an end than to rot in the stinking Sahara. Besides, I was already in a lurch just by being here, and what the hell, I may as well be in it all the way. It was just a matter of time before the Vietmins used me for target practice. As a paratrooper, at least I could fraternize with St. Peter before I returned to dust.

I called my Hungarian friends together after the speech to seek their opinion. Did they have any desire to volunteer as a paratrooper?

Johnny declined at once. Godfather declared that he preferred to play it safe. He had escaped serious injury so far and had no interest in volunteering for a chance to break his neck. One down, three to go.

"Well, all right," I said to him, "if that's how you feel. Go ahead and suffocate in the Sahara while we enjoy the fresh cool air a thousand metres above you."

"What do you mean 'we'?" cried Little Angel. "You expect us to voluntarily get into more danger than we already are? You're nuts! Go ahead if you want, but I'm staying."

"Do you know what? I have a feeling they wouldn't take you even if you did volunteer. Don't forget that paratroopers are the cream of the crop in armed forces the world over, only truly promising and competent recruits are admitted. And you? One look at you and it is clear that you don't belong in such an elite circle. Don't even concern yourself with the idea. Leo, Walter and I will reap the benefits while you and Johnny swelter in the Sahara."

"You listen to me, I'm as tough and capable as any of you. If that weren't the case, I wouldn't be wanted by the cops halfway around Europe. You think I'm the kind of guy who's afraid of his own shadow? Not me!" His chest swelled, "I'll have you know that I'm as much a gentleman as any one of you. Hell, I broke into their homes exclusively! And just to prove that all this is not just talk, I'm gonna volunteer too."

My ploy worked, and now only Leo and Walter were left to convince. Both mumbled for a while, wondering if it was worth it, and whether they should risk breaking their necks. Their decision was settled by the promise of freedom from CP-3, and four out of five joined the line.

The encouraging speech failed in its intended effect; of the entire group, less than a third or perhaps sixty men chose to take the gamble. Three rooms, isolated from the rest, were set aside for our occupation.

"See, Little Angel? We're singled out already. You just watch. From now on, we're going to be accorded the respect a gentleman deserves."

Little did we know that we had been placed in isolation because of the many vaccinations against yellow fever and malaria that were needed. The third shot made us so sick that we were crawling the walls in pain. Our wails and groans resounded throughout the complex. We suffered almost every conceivable side effect including fever, stomach sickness, swollen limbs and dizziness. Not so much as a gulp of water was permitted to alleviate our maddening thirst.

"Is this what you mean by discrimination? This is how they treat gentlemen?" roared Little Angel. "I get the message. You just wait. If I ever get out of here alive, I'll show you the meaning of discrimination. You're not going to forget it as long as you live. And that won't be for long because if you leave this place at all I assure you, it's gonna be in a coffin."

After twenty-four hours the fever subsided and we were allowed a mouthful or two of water. Our wretched condition persisted for two more days, and three days after the shots, the group gathered and equipment was distributed. The sheer quantity of equipment was so astonishing that we didn't know what to do with it all. We proceeded straight to the CP-1 building and I felt like a free man the moment the iron gate slammed shut. We met others like ourselves, men who were a world removed from novices but who had yet to experience the bitter life of a legionnaire. Even so, that recognized symbol of the Legion, the white cap, was already perched upon their heads.

A week was filled with fittings and preparations. The next destination was Nouvion, where we had training in long distance marching to look forward to.

Chapter Six
Nuovion

Nuovion •

A L G E R I A

August 23 – September 11, 1948

The hours dragged while the train sped across the barren and desolate landscape. The heat was intense and most of the men were close to fainting by journey's end. Then our train stopped somewhere and we were ordered down. This was it?

"Hey Walter! Where's the town?"

"Darn if I know. Never mind the town, I can't even see a train station."

"Seems to me they're afraid to take us into town, in case someone tries to escape," said Leo.

"Where could we go?" asked Walter. "It would be foolish, to escape here. There's no trace of life anywhere."

"What kind of paratroopers are we anyway, trampling through the sand like this?" growled Little Angel.

"Quit your grumbling. If we weren't paratroopers, we might have to trample through sand for five years instead of three weeks," I retorted.

Several trucks appeared, from where I don't know, but we boarded and we departed. The hot air and sand churned up by the vehicles burned our throats, and Nuovion soon rose in the distance.

Good God, this is *Nuovion*?! When they informed us of our forthcoming posting, I had visualized a barrack within a small town. I didn't think that the barracks would be as lovely as those in Sidi-Bel-Abbes, but I never dreamed that Nuovion would be nothing more than a solitary fort on top of a mound of sand in the middle of the desert. Legionnaires had the exclusive right to be stationed in a place like this, for if a hell on earth truly existed, this was it.

Once inside the fortress, we were greeted by a scene similar to that in Marseille. A large courtyard enclosed by walls and buildings, with a water well and trough in which to bathe, in the centre. The attitude of the officers and NCOs was, however, a pleasant surprise. They were so friendly that I refused to believe I was actually in the Legion.

A friendly word of warning was issued before we slept: "Turn all shoes and boots upside down first thing in the morning and shake them out. Any object under your bed, but footwear in particular, is a favorite hiding place for scorpions. Those who overlook this ritual will suffer the consequences."

The heat made it almost impossible to sleep and I was awake before reveille. I thought I would use the time to take a bath and a better look around. While standing in the doorway wondering which to do first I was confronted with a mirage-like image.

I ran to Walter's bedside, dragged him out – a feat in itself, and shoved him toward the door with as much speed as I could muster. I asked him to tell me what he saw. He almost fell flat on his face.

"Scout! Do you see what I see?"

"Why do you think I dragged you out here like this, you fool? I want you to tell me what you see."

"My friend, I see a naked woman standing by the water trough."

"Good. That means I didn't get sunstroke after all. She's not a mirage. Let's go get acquainted."

Just as we were about to go, the Corporal woke up. He was surprised to see us awake before reveille and wondered what was going on. Leo was also awake and was staring at the woman.

"What the hell is this? Where are we anyway? Is this the Legion or Prostitute Alley?"

"Both," said the Corporal. "It is important that a man's needs be met in all respects when he resides in an isolated fortress. The government employs prostitutes who are willing to offer their services out here in the boondocks.

The women take their baths very early in the morning because everyone is *usually* still sleeping."

Isolation and the scorching heat aside, life was tolerable. Of course the two or three hour walks for the supposed sake of our health did not top the list of our favorite activities. That a paratrooper was so privileged as to never feel the sand burn his feet was certainly not the case.

"So Little Angel," I gasped while out on a walk, "what do you think of the Sahara? Don't you think it's going to be so much better flying in the cool air up there? It'll be worth the agony we suffered from those shots."

"You're the smartest man on the face of the earth, Scout," he panted, "but quit talking and conserve your energy. I'm close to collapsing as it is."

Nobody was sorry to see the end of the training period. All patiently awaited the day when Nuovion would become a memory. We knew only kindness here; however, we breathed a sigh of relief when, at the beginning of September, the trucks came to take us to the train station. We now journeyed to Philippeville, and the training site for paratroopers.

Chapter Seven
Philippeville
(Skikda)

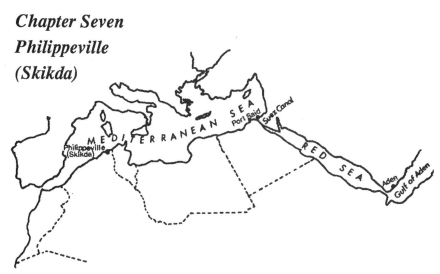

September 12, 1948 – September 20, 1948

Sandy beaches, tepid waters, date palms, orange groves, fig trees and shady forests made for a land of immense beauty. The city was clean and furnished with promenades, bistros, cafes, dancing halls and an army of girls.

The Arab women could not, however, be included in this army. Despite the fact they were completely wrapped in cloth, their eyes communicated hatred. I could not blame them for despising us. We represented a foreign power, an intruder who was strangling their nation and leaving the citizens powerless to do anything about it. I hated the Russians for the same reason. No longer was I the one forced into submission. It did, admittedly, give me a pleasant feeling of power to play the role of the aggressor for a change, but because I knew how they felt I bore no grudge against the Arabs.

Our camp was pitched in a forest six kilometres from the city. The tree branches above the tents radiated fresh sweet air, and the flowers and scattered villas on the slopes of the surrounding hills reminded me of "Rozsadomb" (Rosehill) on the west side of Budapest.

This summer resort would be home for six weeks. I didn't care if it lasted five years.

Training would be initially restricted to the ground and included theoretical instruction. It was imperative that all movements become second nature. This was particularly crucial when jumping in enemy territory, where one or two seconds of hesitation may be all St. Peter needed to open the pearly gates, or conversely, Lucifer to stir his fire.

September 21, 1948

The theoretical portion of the training lasted ten days. We were then permitted a practice flight. The door on the plane was removed to facilitate a drill in courage. Each man was to stand in the open doorway, grasp the handles and lean out as far as he dared. Caution was advised though, since the suction of air may have drawn us out if too much courage was displayed. The stunt was a matter of personal choice, and it is encouraged only to satisfy the curiosity of the instructors who wanted to observe and rate our defiance of danger. Of forty men, only two were not inclined to attempt the feat.

September 23, 1948

Now that we were familiar with flying, jumping was ready to commence. The first jump would take place right after breakfast.

When the head instructor announced this the meal ground to a halt. Swallowing was a struggle, appetites disintegrated and we pushed our food away in disgust. That boisterous group who just yesterday had stood in the open doorway of the plane, was suddenly transformed into a cluster of mice. I hoped for some mechanical defect en route, or better yet, for a complete breakdown of the truck's engine. Anything to prevent us from getting to the airport. The trucks, however, had no intention of malfunctioning and we soon stood in front of the parachute storage area.

Like children engaged in a game of pretend and shocked into silence by the appearance of a real wolf, our mute silence sounded the rude reality of the situation. The only boisterous members were the instructors, who enjoyed seeing us wallow in despair. To watch the learned students experiment with the gear, connect the chutes and adjust them in various ways, one would have thought that we were putting on a fashion show. A detailed inspection of everyone's parachute followed. Orders resounded and standing in single file, we boarded the plane.

The pilot switched the signal light on, to indicate that all were to stand and face the door. We locked our straps onto the rope which stretched down the roof of the plane and waited for the three instructors to jump. If the purpose of this was to instill some courage into the first timers who staggered behind with trembling knees, none came my way. I raked myself over the coals for getting my friends into this mess, and I dared not to think of what they thought of me for it. Little Angel had certainly damned me for all eternity.

From my position near the end of the line, I nervously watched the others inch toward the door. The old Hungarian proverb "If you are a man, then prove yourself a man," popped into mind. The person responsible for coining the phrase had obviously never stood, prepared to jump, in the open doorway of a plane. For lack of any other recourse, I cursed the author with what little strength I had left. I reached the doorway, not of my own free will, but thanks to those behind who were urged to press forward by a couple of none too friendly instructors in the rear. Given a choice in the matter, we would have hid under the benches. An instructor stood in the doorway and encouraged us to bail out with a friendly pat on the back. When I wobbled to the doorway, I chose not to wait for his *kind* shove but simply fell out.

I plunged into the emptiness with eyes shut tight, forgetting to count to three like we had been told to do thousands of times; the parachute opened with a powerful jerk. We had been warned to count to three immediately after jumping, because the parachute opened automatically on the third count and the resulting jerk came as quite a shock if one was not prepared for it.

The sky, sea and ground merged and the frantic convulsions of the parachute relaxed into a smooth and rhythmic sway. The view was breathtaking. A few houses surrounded by orange groves were visible off to one side, while in the distance the blue waters of the Mediterranean Sea stretched into infinity. The open parachutes of those who had jumped ahead of me were a spectacle of gigantic white mushrooms over sprawling green pastures below. I was so mesmerized I forgot to assume the appropriate landing position and touched ground with a thud.

Transformed by the experience, the men were trying to outdo each other in accounting for every moment of their jump. Little Angel, Leo and Walter added to the babble. Little Angel, the man who was at a loss for words in Vienna, was the most talkative of the lot.

Our spirits on the trip back to camp were high. The splendid lunch and several glasses of wine only served to enhance the mood. We assembled in the large tent where our instructors recounted our errors and explained how to correct them. The compulsory French lesson followed. Supper was around five and those without assigned duties were free to do as they pleased. We headed for Philippeville.

The central location for strollers was a large square surrounded by palm trees, bistros and dance halls, and is jam-packed every night. After our first turn around the square, we had our eyes on three attractive, well-dressed ladies who returned our advances with friendly smiles.

"Well," said Chesko. "So much for finding dancing partners. You see Scout? They're already walking toward the dance hall."

"Let's hurry," said Little Angel, "before somebody steals them from under our noses."

"Don't be in such a hurry, you fool!" snarled Chesko. "You'll ruin everything. Women don't like to be charged at. Let them think that we're not really interested. Play hard to get, and they'll fall for us just like that, you'll see."

"Let them fall for us after the dance. We'll hold their waists first and the rest will come later," replied Little Angel.

We were four or five steps away from the girls when the eager Little Angel, tripped on the curb and fell straight into the arms of one of the girls. He tried to grab hold of something to break the fall, and for lack of anything else, he snatched her blouse, ripping it all the way down the front. Not a major catastrophe in itself, except that along with the blouse came the bra.

The young lady was screaming and desperately trying to cover herself, while also trying to slap Little Angel who lay on the sidewalk before her. Her screams attracted a throng of men who commented on her lovely white, firm breasts, exposed for all to see. One of the girls gave her half-naked friend a sweater while the other administered a thorough beating to Little Angel. Little Angel was still lying on the ground, eyes slowly beginning to swell, and holding the blouse and bra when the girls fled.

Seeing that the girls had taken care to give him what he deserved, we assured Little Angel that he was off the hook on the condition that he vanish at once. He did not stick around even long enough to hear the tail end of the warning, for he took the threat to heart and was racing for the jeeps.

We resumed the hunt only to discover, much to our bitter disappointment, that we were outcasts. Every single advance was rebuffed with a sarcastic smile.

"Let's try again tomorrow," I suggested.

"Tomorrow is too soon," answered Leo. "The incident will still be fresh in everyone's mind. Let's explore the area around camp instead."

September 25, 1948

Near the camp was an orange grove. Its guardian likely never suspected that the day would turn into a bleak one for him. Better for him, if the entire twenty-four hour period were wiped clear from his memory.

Since jumping was scheduled on alternate days, today was set aside for sports and theoretical instruction. The results from all of the marching, obstacle racing sports of all kinds, fresh air and good food were obvious.

We set out after supper as planned to explore the area. Little Angel came along too, but we made him beg for forgiveness. We did not want to give the impression of being soft-hearted morons who quickly forgot his dastardly deed. We strolled beside an orange grove which grew down to the side of the road. Its ripe fruits, gleaming between the leaves beckoned to be picked. We disregarded the taboo of picking fruit from a grove, and took the fruit lying closest to the road. Nothing would have come of it but the guardian caught us in the act. He came charging over, waving a menacing stick and intoning the name of Allah. He must have presumed that the stick and Allah would force us to drop the oranges and flee, but he was wrong.

We waited for him to come close, tried to explain that we had nothing to do with Allah, were not at any rate on good terms with him; therefore, intoning his name was in this case an exercise in futility. We had picked a scant dozen oranges, selected from only the very ripe ones, and were willing to pay for them if he was going to make a federal case of it. Leo was the careless one who offered payment, but the guardian was not inclined to cease his irritating ranting and raving. Walter lost control, and kicked the guardian in the behind with such force that he landed under the nearest tree.

We considered the case was closed. The guardian did not. He leaped up, and with a powerful left hook to the jaw, took Little Angel off his feet. Little Angel's cap flew off and the forbidden fruit he was holding scattered.

"Why me?" wailed Little Angel, with eyes still swollen half shut from the previous evening. "I never laid a hand on him," he said, wiping the blood off his lips.

"You have a mug that makes the fingers itch the moment anyone looks at you," I teased.

We told the guardian that to strike a legionnaire was not a matter to be taken lightly, especially considering that odds were four to one. The point was made, and we left him bruised and battered, and lying under a tree. We then helped ourselves to another dozen oranges.

September 26, 1948

Jumping resumed at the usual hour next morning. Spirits were much improved this time around. The second jump transpired smoothly for all except Little Angel. With his swollen eyes, he miscalculated his landing and tumbled straight into a cactus patch. This on top of his two beatings, subdued him for awhile.

As we returned to camp we noticed our friend the guardian was stand-￼ng before the Commander and raging like a madman. Best to do a disappearing act before roll call, I thought. It was a minute too late and we were forced to stand in line for inspection. The guardian paced up and down the line peering through eyes so swollen that he would not be able to recognize his own mother, let alone someone he had seen only once. The Commander lost his patience, and turned to the guardian warning him that he had five minutes to find his attackers, and if not, he could get the hell out. He walked passed the line up one more time, but could not establish our identities.

Plans for the evening, since it was our night off, included a renewed attempt at womanizing. Little Angel with his swollen eyes was not exactly at his most seductive, and given his physical appearance, we wanted to leave him behind. He begged, cajoled and pleaded until we relented, but only on the condition that he remain twenty paces behind at all times, and should he cause trouble again, he would spend the day after in a coffin.

We paced the square, but no luck. We kept an eye out for the three ladies from the previous evening, thinking that they were responsible for luring others away, but they were nowhere to be found. Weary of the futile wandering, we stopped in front of a bistro as two angry legionnaires were leaving.

"I wonder who they're so mad at," said Leo. "Can't say I'd like to be in that person's shoes."

After waiting over half an hour, a small group of girls showed up and our hopes blossomed. Considering that the events of the other day had started out the same way, our advances were more cautious this time.

The dance hall was beautifully decorated with couches and subdued lighting. The band was the middle of a soothing tango when an explosion jarred the building's foundations. The uproar subsided, and the musicians were nowhere to be seen. Not only had the musicians disappeared but so had our dates. We stood staring at each other, trying to fathom what happened. First Little Angel and now this. The evening was ruined. We were obviously not destined for success in the realm of dance halls.

We later found out that the two angry legionnaires were responsible. They were infuriated with the manager who apparently had refused them service and barred them from the premises claiming the two had refused to pay their bill. They were deeply insulted and had gone back to camp picked up a hand grenade, and hurled it through the window.

Leo had been right. To be the object of their revenge was not desirable.

"Forget about parks and dance halls. Let's go to the beach. The mild, blue water of the Mediterranean is sitting right under our noses. Let's trade women in skirts for women in bathing suits. Just think of the advantages! Without our uniforms, women who might not be particularly fond of legionnaires will not be scared off, and we'll be in a better position to stake out the available 'merchandise'."

My proposal was unanimously accepted.

October 2, 1948

We had pinned our hopes on the excursion but returned dejected. There wasn't a soul on the beach, save for a toothless old crone. The private beaches on the other hand were jam-packed but off limits.

The following day was consumed with sports and detail-work again. What luck. Twice in three days. The next day we made another jump and had the remainder of the day off.

To the beach: Charge! At long last, lady luck bestowed her graces upon us. Leo was the first to make the acquaintance of a gorgeous half-European, half-Arabian girl. She introduced us to her friends. A man could not afford to be choosy when he had just three weeks to spare; besides, I had absolutely no reason to complain about Chantal. She was a gift. A near perfect creation with a beautiful and slender body. Her revealing bathing suit outlined her alluring curves which teased and excited. I was drawn to the gentle sway of her waist and ever so gently circled my arm around it. I did not wish to appear aggressive or forward – I did not want to frighten her away. The first hurdle was overcome. She accepted the gesture with a flirtatious glance and a smile before she gave me the slip, and ran for the water and swam away from the shore.

Chantal's swarthy skin tone against the turquoise water was lovely to see. She waited for me to catch up. And when I tried to catch her, she slipped out from under my fingers like a fish. That she was a competent swimmer was clearly apparent, and if I wanted to catch her it would require a lot of hard work. I caught her off-guard and used the moment to dive underwater and pull her down by the thigh. I was no match for that muscular body. She quickly wrestled from my grasp and swam back for shore.

It was dusk as we dragged ourselves out of the water. The beach was nearly deserted, and the last trace of sunlight was fading behind the orange grove in the distance. We stretched out on the soft sand under a palm tree, under millions of twinkling stars, to watch the moon above ascend in majestic glory. As it climbed with great speed above the tree line its glow diminished, its largeness wilted and the night was left bathed in its subdued, silvery light.

We lay there clutching each other tightly and only rarely speaking. There was no need for words. Profound feelings of endearment more eloquent than any words could express passed not through lips, but between heart and soul.

The quiet and gentle music filtered down to the beach from the dance hall. Swaying palms, romantic songs, a moonlit evening by the sea, and a warm-blooded woman. What more could a man ask for?

Life is but a moment, I told myself; but into the moment fit countless experiences if we allow ourselves the openings.

It was almost eleven p.m. when I remembered that the last jeep back to camp would leave soon.

"I have to go back to camp now, Chantal."

"What camp?"

"I didn't even think to tell you that I'm a legionnaire."

"You? A legionnaire? That can't be true. I know legionnaires; they are aggressive, rude and vulgar. You, you are none of these things. No! You can't be a legionnaire. I don't believe it!"

"But I am, Chantal: whether you believe it or not. And you are wrong to think that all legionnaires are like that. Too bad that you've only met the worst, until now. You have to believe me, most of us are exactly the opposite of what you think. You have only seen the bad ones, and yet, make judgements on all legionnaires. I know only too well that many legionnaires are troublemakers, but please don't write us all off on that basis."

"Two days ago, one of you threw a hand grenade through the window at the bistro. And after something like that, we're supposed to think well of your kind? And that wasn't an isolated incident. Who knows how many other rotten deeds you guys are responsible for. And then, you want us to fall into your arms just like that? You think anything goes, just because you're a legionnaire? What kind of people do you think we are anyway? Slaves, whose duty it is to be at your beck and call? I can't understand legionnaires, never could. I avoid them like a plague. And it's not just me, Yvette and Fatime hate legionnaires just as much. Had we known that you were legionnaires, we wouldn't have even come near you!"

She took a moment to catch her breath, then continued: "Now I don't know what to do. If my parents find out about this they might kick me out of the house."

"If that's the case Chantal, then perhaps it's best that we don't meet again."

"But I want to see you again, I like you!"

It was spoken with such sincerity that I was momentarily stilled. Her honesty surprised and confused me. What did I want, but a casual affair for a couple of weeks, an easy parting of ways and pleasant memories for both. The initial meeting had been so easy, the attraction so instant and mutual, that not for a moment had my thoughts ever extended any further. This, I had not planned on.

"Look Chantal," I said, after gathering my thoughts. "I'll be gone by the end of three weeks. That's how long the paratrooper training program lasts . . ."

"Was that your group out jumping this afternoon?"

"Yes."

"And you were among them?"

"Yes."

"Then I'm glad my wish did not come true."

"What wish?"

"That you would all plunge to your deaths!"

"Chantal! Did we do something to hurt you?"

"You are strangling all of Algeria!"

Of course, I thought. They despised us as I despised the Russians, and for the same reasons. No fate less than death was satisfactory as a wish in both cases.

"If you hate us so much, Chantal, why is it that you're attracted to me?"

"Why? Because you are a kind, gentle and affectionate soul. Because when you hold me in your arms, you are not fresh or pushy. If you were I'd be long gone by now."

Thank goodness she didn't know what was really on my mind, nor was she aware of all the self-control I had been exercising.

"Like I said, Chantal, in three weeks I'll be gone and I don't see much point in risking your relationship with friends and family over such a short length of time. It wouldn't make any sense, and I don't want your parents to be upset with you on my account."

"What a shame that you're a legionnaire, Scout. You are such a warm and kind-hearted person."

I felt sorry for her because she was filled with such sadness. I was starting to regret that we had even met. She was not the easy pick-up that I had envisioned, that's for sure! But then, why were we so drawn to each other?

So here I was with a mysterious woman. Well, maybe not so mysterious. Did she not openly admit her feelings for me? No question she was young and beautiful and with a figure that made me go wild. But like a puppy who finally caught the bird he was stalking, now that I had her, I honestly didn't know what to do with her.

That she was attracted to me, an eligible European, maybe she was thinking that something might come of it, that a serious relationship with me might be possible. She conceivably had blown this silly thing out of proportion with unrealistic hopes of marriage. If so, now that she was aware of my status, her dreams lay shattered. I felt very sorry for her. Damn fate, for this burden on my path.

She broke my thoughts.

"Please come by again tomorrow. But wear your bathing suit, that way nobody will know that you are a legionnaire."

"Okay. I'll be here tomorrow at the same time. But I must run now or I'll miss the jeep and have to walk back."

I ran to the jeep like a bat out of hell and thanks to Walter and Leo, who had persuaded the driver to wait, I was spared the humiliation of walking back to camp bare foot and in a bathing suit.

"Did you guys tell your dates that you're legionnaires?"

"No."

"I did. Chantal was terribly upset. She said that had they known, they would have walked the other way."

"What's her problem?" asked Leo. "You'd think that as a half-breed, she'd be more understanding of prejudice."

"That's not fair. At any rate, she wants to meet with me tomorrow."

October 3, 1948

A day off. After theoretical training and exercise, the day was ours. We got to the beach on time and hung around. Today, the beach was almost deserted. Chantal was nowhere to be seen.

"I think we've been had," said Leo.

"I doubt it. I suspect they're in trouble at home. I think their parents somehow found out that they spent the evening in the company of legionnaires."

"Here they come!" yelled Water. "Hey look. They're not wearing their bathing suits!"

They came strolling across the sand merrily conversing and with their shoes dangling from their hands. The skirts of their sundresses billowed in the ocean breeze and the skin tight bodices outlined the girls' every contour.

"What the hell is this?" I asked. "Do they want to go dancing or what?"

"Well guys, this is it. Either we get what we came for by tonight, or I'm gonna look for it somewhere else. I'm sick of playing nurse to such a gorgeous young thing."

Leo wanted to add his bit, but there was no time; the girls were here.

"Hello Chantal."

"Hello, Scout. Have you been waiting long?"

"Only about ten minutes. Why aren't you wearing your bathing suit?"

"Because I'm not interested in swimming today. I want to have a talk with you."

Well then sweetheart, you're about to be dismissed I thought, as arm in arm we strolled down the beach.

"You know Scout, you're a decent kind of guy. Last night you behaved like a gentleman. Your friends too, except for the dark-haired one who was a bit pushy with Fatime. But don't think for one second that we are blind to your intentions. We know you want more than just talk. And I wanted you to know, that we are not willing to go that far. We're simply not available for that. Just because we got along so well does not mean that we will go all the way. I admit that it felt good being in your arms and lying close to you, but if you had tried anything more, I would have left at once. We're not the kind of girls who go to bed with just anybody. And if that's what you were thinking, you thought wrong."

"But . . ."

"Don't interrupt, I'm not finished! My father is French and my mother is Arabian, and I, as a half-breed, want a European husband. That is why I was so willing to make your acquaintance. No offence Scout, but I see no point in meeting anymore. I do not wish to be seen in the company of a legionnaire. And please don't misunderstand, this has nothing to do with you personally. If you weren't a legionnaire, I wouldn't let you get away, but your uniform puts an immeasurable distance between us and the bridge cannot be crossed."

How ironic that after thinking about how to drop her, she was rejecting me.

"I guess you're right. There really is no point in seeing each other again. You see me as a potential husband, and that's simply out of the question. You see, in one month I'll be in Indochina. You're very kind and honest (and a waste of time), and your company has been delightful. I'll always remember the few hours we spent together with a great deal of fondness."

The conversation then turned trivial and we parted.

After the girls were out of ear shot, Walter spoke,

"Hey Scout, did Chantal see a husband in you too?"

I laughed, "Yvette and you – same thing?"

"What luck," sulked Leo. "One extreme to the other. From total failure in the dance hall to almost married."

"I think it's time to get drunk, boys! Let's go back and change. Let's drink to fortune, and give thanks that our little escapade did not finish with a jaunt to the altar."

And get drunk we did. So drunk, that next morning we had no recollection of how we got to camp or why we were now in confinement. We were charged with beating two Arabs half-to-death, ransacking the bistro, and destroying four chairs and two tables in the process.

We pleaded with the Commander. We swore up and down that we did not lift a finger, *a chair maybe*, but he simply did not believe us. We did succeed, however, in receiving a sentence that was relatively light: three days in jail and three nights of guard duty.

October 10, 1948

Little Angel's eyes were completely healed by the time of our release, so the hunt for women resumed. Ours was a noble profession, at times crowded with success and at times not. We would soon bid farewell to this little Garden of Eden. We would soon be on our way to Indochina.

October 19, 1948

It was the last day. The regiment gathered in the square, the military band played, and the Commander with his entourage, ceremoniously awarded the badges for the paratroopers along with the insignia badges of the battalion. The Commander raised a glass of wine, toasted his subordinates and staff, and prayed that God bless each and every member of his troops. The Legion's march sounded to mark the conclusion of the graduation ceremonies.

Now that the First Paratrooper Battalion of the French Foreign Legion was officially established, its graduates were assigned to various squadrons before continuing on to Oran and the four Hungarians were separated. Little Angel was the most upset, "I've never had such good friends in my life, and probably never will again." He abruptly turned and left. I never saw him again.

My new posting was in the second section of Company Two, and in it were five Hungarians. The first was Charles Red, a tall and lanky corporal. Second was a gypsy, and so nicknamed. Not only had Gypsy dared to *enlist* in the Legion, but once inside, he had volunteered to become a paratrooper. Then there was Julius Mole, who bearing a slight resemblance to Walter, was blond, blue-eyed and good-natured. Alexander Bofort reminded me of Godfather, who I imagined at this moment to be trampling the sands of the Sahara. Last was Joe Bristle who not too long before, had lived a sheltered life on the banks of the Ipoly River in northern Hungary.

The evening train to Oran left Chantal, her slender figure; the orange grove with its jilted guardian; the seaside, the palms, the walkways, the bistros, and the enchanting moonlit evenings to memory. We arrived in Oran the following evening after a most uncomfortable journey.

October 20 – 22, 1948

Visits to the city, we are lodged in an old fortress, are not permitted on the pretense that the ship might dock at any time. In truth, the prohibition was put into effect to deter attempts to escape. No legionnaire had any money, and considering this, the thought of escape was ludicrous. The higher authorities, however, didn't see it that way and we were forced to watch the sea and the bustle of the city from high atop the walls of the fortress.

October 23, 1948

The *Pasteur* docked, but most of the space on it is already occupied by men travelling to Le Havre and Marseille. Before it became a conveyor of military personnel, this thirty-five thousand ton monstrosity sailed as a passenger liner.

It was intriguing to watch this mass of steel, its presence was at first broadcast only by a narrow column of smoke which, as it broadened and swelled, rendered the body of the vessel visible. My anxiety increased as the ship grew larger, I knew that it would take me to Indochina, to a land from which very few returned. for many legionnaire's, this journey proved to be the last of their lives. Only a fortunate few ever made it back.

Orders were given and the mass of soliders, spiced with a number of nurses, fell in line and crowded forward. I knew that this ship would take me to Indochina, a land from which very few returned.

October 24, 1948

The ship left the harbor at 10:30 a.m. Officials of various rank and an one hundred and twenty piece military band were on hand to send us off. A tugboat towed the *Pasteur* to open sea, and the figures, fort and harbor shrank to a speck, then vanished. I dreamed about the future and hoped to one day to return to this port.

Had all gone according to plan, I would be listening to the sea from the shore in Brussels and not aboard the *Pasteur*. What else did the future hold in store for me? A few weeks ago I was a mere two hundred kilometres from Brussels, from the security of my sister and her family. Now I was halfway around the globe and heading still further east.

Our living quarters on board the ship were neither unbearably crowded nor especially comfortable. As legionnaires we were lodged in the shabbiest corner, directly under the lower deck. We tried to spend as little time as possible in our cramped hammocks, as they were not at all conducive to a good night's sleep.

October 27, 1948

I heard a rumor that some legionnaires had thrown a sergeant overboard during the night. It was also rumored that this was the officer which Little

Angel had beaten in CP-3. If this is true then I feel no sorrow. The man was a barbarian who had it coming to him. Although the rumors may be false, it is fact that in Indochina, some officers did perish in the hands of legionnaires who were weary of their brutal dictatorship. Such officers presumed that a rank and title gave them the right to rule over life and death itself.

October 28, 1948

The *Pasteur* arrived in Port Said and we novice travellers crowded the deck so not to miss a thing. The merchants were not deterred by the early hour and swarmed around the ship in tiny boats brimming with wares.

The merchants carried baskets to which ropes were tied. They hurled the rope high in the air, a prospective customer would catch it, the merchant displayed his wares and the customer would make his selections. Then came the bartering. The merchant began the bidding with a price that was at least ten times what the item was actually worth. For example, if the merchant demanded seventy rupiers, the buyer offered ten, the merchant reduced his price to fifty, the buyer increased his bid to eleven and the item sold for fifteen. The customer was satisfied and convinced that he had gotten a deal; the merchant was satisfied and convinced that the sucker had been cheated but good. This sort of thing was new but after several hours of trying to catch the rope I coincided defeat and stood back to watch.

I tried to find something else to do for entertainment. But what? I was bored with chess, tired of the library, there weren't any movies showing this early and visits to the city were not permitted.

I managed to catch a few winks in a quiet corner of the upper deck, and I was woken by the starting jerk of the ship beginning its haul toward the Suez Canal.

My imagination had conjured a very charmed picture of this area, something much more attractive than what I now saw. The canal was little more than a ninety metre wide ditch. On either side were sandy shores which were bare and devoid of life. The three lakes between Port Said and Suez constituted the only exception. The largest of these was a point of detour where one fleet of ships waited to allow others to go by. The villages which surrounded these lakes were the only sign of life. Beyond them there was only desolation.

Each hour grew hotter. If I thought that Nuovion was hell on earth, then what was this?

October 29, 1948

We docked in Suez. Port Said had been a metropolis in comparison. Suez, however, was superior in beauty. Villas of European architecture, paved roads, groomed lawns, palm trees and beautifully tended gardens ornamented the landscape.

The loading and unloading went much faster this time, and we continued on to Aden before midnight. The boredom was killing me. I went inside the cabin, then turned around and walked back out. The place was like a steam bath. The swifter pace of the ship on the open sea stirred up a soothing breeze. I lay down and stared at the swaying masts. My thoughts sped home to memories and familiar faces as I drifted off to sleep.

November 1, 1948

When we arrived in Aden, I found it much the same as the previous two harbors. Sick of all the noise and people, I fled to the library. In a few hours the ship moved on.

November 2 – 5, 1948

As the ship passed the northeastern tip of Somali, we waved to the natives who had rowed out only to say hello, and, thank goodness, were not selling something.

The ocean was magnificent with barely a perceptible ripple and colored in a unique shade of blue unlike anything I had seen before. Suddenly, hundreds of jelly fish appeared from the depths. A riot of color representing every spectrum of the rainbow exploded and danced on the surface of the water. This abundance of color was lost all too soon as the ship surged on. We reached the Indian Ocean and began the most boring part of our journey.

Only in rare instances was the monotony broken by a school of dolphins emerging to chase each other and disappearing as suddenly as they came. While watching the dolphins, a flock of low flying birds distracted my eye. A sign that Ceylon (Sri Lanka) can't be far away, I thought. We're bound to reach Colombo soon, and the harbor will at least provide for some diversion. I followed their route, only to find that they were not birds after all, but flying fish. My hopes were dashed and I continued to pace the deck.

It was the nurses who came up with a brilliant idea to relieve the monotony. They planned a variety show, and advertised for promising actors and singers. Charlie and I were among the chosen who were asked to sing something. Halfway through our song the curtain came crashing down: these people obviously had no taste.

One day while loafing about the deck I bumped into Walter and Leo. We were thrilled to see each other, especially since they were just as bored as I was. It was fun to talk about the good old days in Philippeville. The days were now better spent in the company of old friends.

November 6, 1948

At long last we arrived in Columbo, the capital of Ceylon. The ship was anchored away from the dock, and we were deprived of the harbor's merchants and their frantic tirades. After a few hours of rest the ship turned its bow toward Haiphong.

We sailed past the northern tip of Sumtara, maneuvered around many small islands and passed through the strait bound by Sumtara and the Malayan Archipelago before docking in the Singapore harbor. I did not miss the merchants who were absent among the hustle and bustle on the loading dock. Twice was more than enough. The ship's stores were replenished and I was forced to seek shelter as rain started to pour. I wanted to find Leo and Walter again, but that was impossible.

I then remembered that there were a few dozen nurses on board. Might be a good idea to try and get to know one, I thought. My dislocated arm should be as useful a ploy as any. I decided that it was still causing me pain and that I needed something to relieve the discomfort. Nurses were the only people allowed to dispense medication. Entry to the nurses' station was not easy. The area above the walkway was off limits and guards were posted to enforce this regulation. I, however, was bound and determined.

I sauntered toward the guard, and when certain that he had his eye on me, I feigned a fainting spell. He rushed to help and took me to the infirmary without any questions. I could hardly contain my laughter as the guard struggled and strained to drag me up the stairs.

Once in the reception area I revived, so to speak, and turning to the most attractive nurse, donned a tortured expression and complained about my arm. Her reaction was doting and motherly, and with her arms around me, she led me to a bed. How baffling that I tripped on something, fell on the nearest bed and dragged her down too. No big deal had we been alone, but much to my despair, two other nurses were witness to the mishap. One placed a disgusting smelling substance under my nose, and within a fraction of a second I felt healthier than ever before. The stuff cured all my aches and pains, but at the same time the nauseating odor turned my stomach. Wanting to avoid public embarrassment, I raced for the nearest toilet and arrived just in time to rid my stomach of its last three meals.

The three nurses laughed at me when I returned. My idea had not been so brilliant after all. It seems that many others had tried the same trick. Despite this, an inkling of compassion stirred the pretty nurse and she asked me to join her for a cognac, insisting that it would soothe my stomach. One drink became two and then three. Around midnight we checked out the stars and I told her that I felt wonderful and that my stomach was well on the road to recovery.

"I hope so," she replied. "My prescriptions are always effective and if you should ever need another painkiller, please don't hesitate to call."

November 9, 1948
I spotted the shores of Indochina. We would soon reach Cape St. Jaques

where troop carriers were ready to take the majority of the troops to Saigon (Ho Chi Minh City).

During the next few days I saw little of Walter and Leo as I took advantage of the nurse's offer almost every day and was preoccupied with treatment. When I did see them, I explained the ploy, and I suggested a similar course of action, if they didn't want to crack-up from boredom.

Over half the troops disembarked in Cape St. Jacques and were picked up by the long line of carriers waiting to take them to Saigon. In another three days the rest of us would reach Haiphong. I could hardly wait, not only to feel solid ground beneath my feet, but to see those beautiful Indochinese women whom I had heard so much about and who supposedly walked the streets clad in nothing but transparent white silk kimonos.

November 12, 1948

The shallow waters of Haiphong's harbor did not permit large ships to enter, and carriers were needed to transport us to land. Before we changed vessels, we were warned that our forthcoming route passed between numerous tiny islands and chances were that the Vietnamese (or Vietmins as we called them) would mount an attack. We were to stand-by, ready to counter the attack if need be. They also mentioned a general by the name of Giap was rumored to be actively gathering his forces in this area, and we could anticipate at least one surprise attack.

Well, this was certainly a warm reception! They were scaring us half to death before we had even left the ship.

Chapter Eight
Haiphong

November 12, 1948

A large military band and a score of high ranking officials provided a reception that was similar to Oran. I, while trumpets sounded and gilded dignitaries saluted, summoned up all my courage and laid foot on the soil of Indochina. The features of the Vietnamese girls were a stark contrast to the Arabs of Oran.

Well, my boy! You have to case this joint as soon as possible and carry into effect such an expert plan of attack that the target will be forced to surrender unconditionally. Had the choice been mine I would have put my military tactics into effect without delay, but I was hindered by two generals, several dozen colonels and a ceremonial procession.

Assembly was called, yet again. Had we been captives at sea for twenty-one days only to be ushered from one lineup to another? There was no need to leave Philippeville to end like this. I ploughed my way through piles of wreckage and stood in a line which lead to several trucks from which cotton stuffed mattresses and folding cots were being flung. Those who ventured too close found themselves buried under what was to be our *bedroom furniture.* We lugged the stuff to the allocated areas with the intent of assembling our beds and moving in, but another roaring call to assembly interrupted our task.

Street scenes in Haiphong

Sanitation Maintenance   *Rickshaws in front of the theatre*

An open banana market

This little charade was starting to get on my nerves. Six lineups after less than four hours in Indochina. This particular call turned out to be for supper, a worthwhile cause at last. After the meal I met a sixteen month veteran of Indochina. He had much to recount about local customs and living conditions. After listening to his stories I felt a strong impulse to gather my gear, head for the harbor and catch the next ship sailing for Marseille.

November 14, 1948

My twenty-eighth birthday. I sought out the Viennese and told them that it took some courage on my part to be born, and barring any objections, it was just cause for a celebration. They agreed, and we purchased the appropriate liquids. We returned to our rooms with at least a dozen bottles. Chances are that we wouldn't have partied all night had we suspected what the next day had in store for us. But today was still my birthday, everyone was still in a good mood and there was no reason to quit. Besides, we still had a few bottles of wine left. Another line-up brought the party to an end. Its purpose this time was to announce our departure for Hanoi the next morning. The entire battalion stood in a half circle while Commandant Duvallieux spoke. The meeting might have finished in the same orderly fashion it began, if not for our birthday celebration. While the rest of the men stood still, we swayed back and forth like reeds in the breeze. If only we had been standing in the very back row! But no, we stood in the third row where Duvallieux could clearly see us. I expected him to say something, but he proved to be a reasonable man who tolerated our condition just so long as we remained quiet and did not disrupt his speech. Alex, however, let out such a powerful belch it sounded like cannon fire.

Duvallieux's face turned flaming red and for an instant the words stuck in his throat.

"Who was that?" he bellowed.

An officer grabbed Alex and took him to Duvallieux. Alex tried to defend himself, but under the nervous strain he spoke in Hungarian instead of French. He could have spoken in Chinese for all that it mattered, because his knees gave out and he sprawled out under the table like a trampled frog.

Alex was immediately removed and Duvallieux continued as if nothing had happened. I wanted this gospel to be over with as quickly as possible. I wanted to find Alex. I imagined him to be confined in the *tombeau* for it was unlikely that he got away with anything less.

Of the various modes of punishment used by the Legion, the *tombeau* was one of the most severe. A hole, or grave as it was affectionately referred to, was dug to a depth of a half-metre. The offender was laid inside the ditch and covered with a wet blanket. The guilty party was forced to stay within the pit it for a prescribed length of time – fifteen minutes at the most. This might not sound all that bad, but the ditch was dug in a spot where there was no shade. Imagine the torture of 110° Fahrenheit under a wet wool blanket.

Alex was spared the punishment. I found him under a tree where two legionnaires were pouring bucket after bucket of water over him.

November 15, 1948

Reveille was at 5:00; and it took a few seconds before I remembered where I was. There was no way I could get up and pack with this hangover. Anything, instead of having to get up and pack. The other party-goers were in no better shape, Alex, in particular, looked like a sheet of crumpled newspaper. We somehow managed to make it to the station on time.

The train was ancient and in wretched condition: broken windows, cracked plaster and sagging roofs. I couldn't believe that such an elite regiment would be forced to travel on a dump like this. I was disgusted and infuriated that the Legion was too cheap to waste their precious airplanes on us.

We stood in single file and boarded. No one was allowed to enter once the available seats were filled. The car filled to capacity just as I was to board, and I became separated from my friends despite my efforts to sneak by. So much for a little post-birthday celebration. Sergeant Mortier tolerated no provocation and ordered me to the next car. The tiny windows allowed no air circulation and within half an hour I was nearly suffocating from the dense cloud of cigarette smoke. I went out on the platform to get some fresh air. The monotonous clanging lulled me to sleep as I sat on the stairs, but I woke with a start as the train came to a sudden stop. The conductor got off to inspect and oil the wheels, and the train struggled on moments later.

My tranquillity was again shattered barely fifty metres down the track when an explosion filled the air with wood and iron splinters, and the screams of the injured. The explosion originated from under the car my Hungarian friends were in – the car I had been banned from. After the initial chaos, the uninjured began carrying out the dead and wounded. Steve Maro was the first. The explosion had almost severed one of his legs, and the rest of his body was riddled with large splinters. Julius Mole was crippled by his leg injuries. Two others were badly wounded and three were dead.

The wounded were housed in the last train car after first aid had been administered. Leo humbly volunteered to help out with the medical emergency. He lent an able and experienced hand. It was thanks to this that Leo was assigned to the infirmary, and soon after, promoted to a sergeant's rank.

The conductor, a conspirator in the explosion, tried to escape during the first few minutes of panic. He, however, was caught and placed under armed guard until the train reached Hanoi.

Thanks to this cordial reception by the Vietmins it was almost dark by the time we arrived in Gia-Lam.

Our quarters consisted of three long single storey dwellings without doors, windows or electricity. There was a grassy area in front of the buildings, a highway on its opposite side, a large and shallow lake and finally the airport. Behind the enclosure a long and narrow lawn, a canal five metres wide and a raised railway embankment.

There was little to do so I tried to fill the hours with writing letters to home. The sentries, however, took their duties more seriously, and while we were having fun fishing, swimming and writing letters; they remained alert and ready to halt any attack. There was nothing to worry about during the day, but we did not wander off into secluded areas beyond the eyes of the patrol. The night, however, was another story. Indochina was ruled by the French during the day, but at night, the Vietmins governed. It was during the night that they went about the task of planting bombs and mines in the surrounding fields. Their very presence, even in the absence of offensive warfare, made a psychological impact.

November 20, 1948

I saw the third section preparing to go somewhere.

"Where are they going?" I asked Mortier.

"On patrol."

"Too bad. I wish it were my section, I haven't done a blessed thing since we've been here. Do you think I could go along?"

"Ask the Commander. If it's okay with him, it's okay with me."

The Commander gave his permission and along I went. I was very curious to see what a jungle looked like. With great anticipation, I packed all the necessary items including food, ammunition and so on into my backpack. I hooked a jungle knife to my belt and was ready to face the jungle. Little did I know that I would curse this "green hell-hole" and never want to lay eyes on a jungle again, but for now it was a novel experience.

To reach the jungle we made a ninety minute truck ride followed by a two hour hike. There, however, was still no jungle in sight. Instead of a jungle, we endured 110° heat, waded through waist deep rice paddies, marched through eye-level razor sharp blades of grass and encountered millions of mosquitoes. There was no sign of the abundant vegetation that characterized a true jungle, the odd palm tree did not exactly meet my specifications. The march seemed to have no purpose.

Go ahead and volunteer next time too, you stupid fool. You really need the exercise, I thought while also trying to justify my volunteering by telling myself that as the only Hungarian, I was representing my country. An admittedly poor excuse.

Supper was over by the time we got back to Gia-Lam. But I didn't care and collapsed into bed.

November 21, 1948

I woke at dawn to now dry, sweaty clothes which were omiting a less than desirable odor. I grabbed my fragrant clothing and went down to the lake to do laundry. It was well before reveille, and the camp was still sleeping. I relished the solitude. The tepid water and crisp morning air were rejuvenating.

After breakfast I sat down to continue writing in my journal, and was attacking the project with fervor when someone yelled.

"Tonue Combat!"

The signal to prepare for combat. I couldn't believe my ears. The march yesterday had left me more dead than alive, and my clothes were still soaking wet. I turned to Mortier and pleaded my case.

"The entire company is going. No exceptions!" he replied.

Half an hour later we rolled out of Gia-Lam. I didn't mind the wet clothes because they kept me cool, but I did promise myself never to volunteer for anything else again.

The trip was much like yesterday's.

"Charlie! What's the point of wandering around like this?"

"That's what I'd like to know!"

The answer appeared an hour later when in the forest clearing ahead appeared a village. What surprised me about the village was that the bamboo huts were built on stilts. Livestock occupied the lower level and the family the second floor. It had come to the attention of our intelligence service that the Vietmins were plundering this village, and our job was to stop the ravaging and capture those responsible.

The notion was absurd. Our company had caused such a ruckus along the way that any Vietmins in the area had long since fled. And had they been so inclined, they easily could have wiped out half of our troops while we were stumbling across the open rice fields. We reached the village in one piece only because the Vietmins had thought it best to retreat into the safety of the dense forest and avoid a confrontation. I was appalled at the Legion's lack of precautionary measures and poor organization. At the time I did not understand that it was considered no big deal if only half of the troops returned after any given mission; the Legion didn't care.

We ignored the questioning inhabitants and surrounded the village. We did not retreat until everything in the area was turned upside down. We had hoped to find concealed weapons or enemy troops in hiding, but we had only one outdated handgun to show for our efforts.

November 30, 1948

The order came near the end of November: Company Two would be transferred to Lang-Son, a city approximately one hundred and fifty kilometres northeast of Hanoi and close to the Chinese border. General Giap and his freedom fighters were most active in this region. Attacks of varying proportions were most frequent along this line and reinforcements were needed. I went to the canteen to bid farewell to Leo, Walter and the others, then went to the airport and flew off feeling alone and dejected.

Lang-Son come into view after an hour's bumpy ride. The city was much larger than I had imagined, and similar to Hanoi and Gia-Lam in that it was divided by a narrow river. On one side lay the city of Lang-Son and on the other the suburb Ky-Lua. The plane circled once or twice over the city before touching down at the airport of my new posting.

Chapter Nine
Lang-Son

December 2, 1948

A fortress in Ky-Lua proved to be our final destination. To make sure that we did not feel like complete strangers, the facilities had no doors, windows nor electricity. In addition, the Legion's labelling our residence a fort was stretching things a bit. The protective walls that traditionally encircled fortresses were lacking and the entrance facing Lang-Son was protected by neither fence nor gate.

The space in the living quarters was usually shared, but I, again, lucked into a private room. To deter anyone from moving in, I spread what little belongings I had all over the room and rearranged the scant furnishings. I set out on a shopping spree to find more furniture and *acquired* a battered table and two chairs from the canteen. My next find was a smoothly finished plank from which I fashioned a shelf. My room began to acquire some character. I solved the problem of my bare windows by *borrowing* a large section of rush matting from the kitchen, hoping that it would be awhile before the cook noted its absence.

I was proud of the result. My little room looked lovely and everyone else was so impressed that they wanted to claim it for themselves. I, however, would not give in and protected my empire at all cost.

The entrance to the fort

In the courtyard of the fort

In front of a park in Lang-Son

December 3, 1948

"Tonue Combat" resounded at 3:30 a.m. It was no easy task to get ready fast in the absence of electricity, and thus light, but we surmounted the dilemma and filed into the courtyard, where corps, who were roused out of bed an hour and a half earlier stood-by. I gathered that this was no drill but a serious call to action. A vast amount of ammunition including two cannon, trench mortars and machine guns were being loaded into the trucks.

The trucks rolled out of the fort around seven, passed through Dong-Dang and turned toward Na-Cham. Ten kilometres later we stopped, hauled the cannons atop a small hill and aimed the nozzle in the direction of the mountain we were about to climb. I had no idea how the hell these inferior cannons were expected to hit a mountain almost two kilometres away. The mountain was high that I had fears of becoming a grandfather by the time we reached the summit. Presuming, of course, that I married first, the prospects of which were nil at this moment.

Up the mountain, down the mountain we marched, the weight of the ammunition growing heavier.

Several hours later we stopped above a wide valley rich in forest; a perfect camouflage for the enemy troops. The plan was to descend into the valley and capture the Vietmins. The men divided into two groups, one crossed to the other side of the valley and fanned out across the mountain. My group stayed behind and waited until the others reached the designated area before starting our descent into the valley.

Halfway down, machine guns began blasting away at us. Yes! The Vietmins were hiding down there, but their aim was poor and the shells missed their mark, and hit the trees above. We returned fire.

After twenty minutes the shooting suddenly stopped. It was the Commander who realized that our allies across the valley, had mistaken us for the Vietmins and we had been shooting at each other. If the precision of the aim, was noticed by the Vietmins, they would surely breathe a sigh of relief.

After the truth was straightened out and we combed the valley to no avail, we regrouped and were returning to the trucks when we discovered a village of eight huts. There wasn't a soul in sight, though all indications led us to believe that ten minutes ago the inhabitants were still here: open fires burned in almost all of the huts and the pots were still hot. There was only one explanation, we had stumbled into an enemy hideout.

"No doubt about it. This here's a Vietmin camp," I said to Mercier. "I'm willing to bet that they're watching our every move this very second."

No sooner had I finished the sentence when shots came flying through the forest. We retaliated, burned the village and kept hiking.

The path cut through a dense forest that miles later opened into a field of rice paddies. The sun was intense and mosquitoes by the thousands feasted on our blood. We walked along the heaping mound of dirt between the paddies and took turns sliding into the marsh below. The effect in the heat was soothing, and nobody seemed to mind that we got slathered up to our waists in mud in the process. Exhaustion was taking its toll and rest periods increased in frequency. Lieutenant Mercier was well-aware of my fatigue and relieved me of my ammunition for awhile. We shared the burden and continued to trade off. Twelve kilometres to go and by the looks of the company, perhaps half would be strong enough to make it back to the trucks. If a squadron of Vietmins attacked now, no one would be left. We reached the trucks around seven in the evening.

The next day the bulk of the squadron was assigned to escort a truck caravan to Cao-Bang, while I, along with twenty others, stayed behind to protect the fort. I used the day to clean my room, something which took all of about fifteen minutes. For lack of anything better to do, I went outside to watch our dogs massacre the volumes of rats racing around the fort.

December 13, 1948

We spent the morning making preparations and to leave in the early afternoon for three days in the bush. Scaling the terrain was no easy task even without the weight of equipment we were forced to lug on our backs. After thirty kilometres by truck, we continued on foot. Why the hell we even bothered to go through all that training as paratroopers was beyond me.

We ascended a steep mountain through wilderness to our destination fifteen kilometres away. I brought up the rear and watched with fascination as the long line of men snaked upwards, through the misty twilight of the foliage. Branches fashioned a canopy, blocking out even the stars and ensuring that travel by night was certain to be impossible. These giant trees made me feel tiny and inconsequential. I was overwhelmed and completely forgot the purpose of our presence. Nature, in all its intricate loveliness brought man closer to God than any church was capable of. The jungle with all of its colors and species able to co-exist peacefully, while man claiming the right to dominate, had the audacity to kill without reason. Deep in thought, I was not aware that we had reached our destination, a fort built on the very top of the mountain. In my opinion, a hovel was more apt a description but if the Legion chose to christen it a fort, so be it.

The fort was pieced together to discourage the Vietmins from attacking. No doubt about it, the locale did offer natural protection; nobody in their right mind would risk the climb on a hunch. Whoever had the bright idea to build the fort had foresight, because not a single Vietmin had been sighted since the fort's existence.

The fort was very small and each man settled in whatever vacant spot he could find. In an effort to avoid the dirt which was dropping from the ceiling and on to my face, I moved into the yard, arranged my sleeping bag and quickly fell asleep.

I was roused at 3:30 a.m. with a harsh kick to my side. I leaped up, grabbed my gun, presuming the culprit to be the enemy but discovered it was only Mercier making the rounds and heralding reveille. The luxury of sleeping in just once was obviously something we could not count on. It was beyond me why the hell every damned operation had to commence at such an ungodly hour. The crisp morning air was refreshing and quickly brought me to my senses, and I cursed myself for sleeping outdoors. I had completely forgotten that we were at least eight hundred metres above Lang-Son and my clothes were soaked from the morning dew. I raced to the kitchen for some hot coffee, I filled my thermos, grabbed a bit of breakfast and headed out to witness the view.

The clouds had descended and formed a satiny tablecloth which spread to the horizon. Here and there the surrounding peaks pierced the milky whiteness. From the darkness of the sky the shining stars shed a mysterious light over it all.

I was startled back to reality by Captain Plessiner's commanding voice.

"Would you care to join us, or are you going to stay here and wait out the end of the world?"

"I'm not exactly waiting for the end of the world, but a platoon that moves at a snail's pace and a captain to go along with would certainly be nice."

I regretted the sarcasm at once. Thank goodness he was still bleary-eyed and my remark escaped him. He merely mumbled something along the lines of, "I don't think you'd be in much of a hurry either if you had stayed up playing poker all night."

The path that we had climbed yesterday had turned treacherous overnight. It was almost impossible to grab a foothold. Many solved the problem by sliding down on their bums. The odd cry of pain sounded, however, when their sensitive anatomies hit a protruding rock. I too mumbled profanities whenever someone slipped and used my body to break their fall. On such occasions both involved tumbled to the ground, and inevitably I was on the bottom.

We reached the perimeter of the forest and deliverance from obscurity. What a relief. We looked like drenched rats. Our teeth chattered from the cold, cramped fingers clutched our weapons, but at least we could see our way and stopped falling.

The village which stood before us was probably full of Vietmins and had to be investigated. The approach was somewhat complicated because of its distance. We would be completely exposed if we tried to cross the field. However, the forest on either side of the field provided perfect camouflage, and we tried to encircle the village. The Vietmins opened fire before we were halfway to the village. My group stormed through the remaining two hundred metres of dirt and slime, but all of our efforts had been wasted on one Vietmin and a swarm of flies. The only remaining hope was to search the immediate vicinity and perhaps uncover some of those who had taken flight. Our hunt was in vain, the task was hindered by such dense vegetation that it was a lost cause.

Thanks to the giant cliffs and crevices overgrown with vegetation my group fell behind and headed off in a different direction than the main group. We got out of the maze, reached an area with sparser vegetation and found another settlement. Our arrival was unexpected and the inhabitants stared at us in astonishment. The surprise of our arrival enabled us to find six Vietmins, eight machine guns and a load of ammunition. Considering our track record this was a significant find, and for once, we would not return empty-handed.

The company unexpectedly regrouped around noon and we headed back to the trucks laden with loot and prisoners. Admittedly, my group was outdone because the others had twenty-four prisoners and a vast amount of weapons and ammunition.

We reached the trucks in the late afternoon, only to discover that the limited space could not accommodate thirty extra people. My group elected to stay behind, but we soon grew bored and tired of waiting, and headed down the road. It was now dark and we were itching to get back to Lang-Son after such an exhausting mission. We could not afford to take any chances and one never knew which tree, bush or corner possibly shielded a couple of well-directed machine guns. Our rubber soled boots tread silently on the paved surface, and conversation was scant and subdued.

We did not, however, manage to avoid gun fire. The ensuing volley may have been anticipated, yet it still shocked. Lucky for us the adversary could not judge the distance properly and the first round whizzed over our heads. We were at a similar disadvantage and were forced to guess their location, guided only by the sparks from their guns. Their aim improved dramatically, and if not for the ditch, we would have been shot through like a sieve. After two hours of exchanging fire the enemy was close enough to be identified.

Inside a pagoda, by the sacrificial table

A restaurant on the sidewalk

An open market square in Ky-Lua

A legionnaire's funeral in Lang-Son

In Na-Cham (author, far right)

A Chinese funeral in Na-Cham

A band of partisans were ordered to patrol the road and protect the trucks while we had been marching in the jungle all day. After the first transport returned to Lang-Son they too were left behind for lack of space and to guard us. They were informed as to our whereabouts and had not counted on our leaving the post. We, in turn, had no knowledge of their presence. It was only natural that they open fire on approaching shadows. Had we been any closer when they decided to open fire, the situation would have been tragic.

We untangled the whole mess and continued down the road to meet the trucks. It was almost dawn by the time we reached the fort.

The mission had been completed in two days instead of three. Two days was more than enough and we were given the next two days off to rest after the strain of the journey.

December 16, 1948

These two days were spent loafing without interruption. If not for the missions, and if only we could forget about personal safety, life in Indochina was very agreeable. Yesterday we received our salary, and if we considered that all our material needs were provided for, a man could save quite a bundle here. That is, if he was sure of getting out alive and the chances were not very promising. We accumulated small fortunes between our forays into town and squandered it all at once.

December 18, 1948

Lang-Son was not a sprawling metropolis, but in all fairness, neither was it the kind of place where a man was bored. It had much to offer but before I could take advantage of any of it, it was necessary to check out the surroundings. Finding a tour guide was not an intricate affair, finding one that was uninhibited and inclined toward seeing past the Legion uniform was.

I strolled aimlessly and strayed into the market district where a crowd of shoppers were gathered despite the midday heat. I was content to observe them with curious interest. While looking through shops and watching the craftsmen it suddenly dawned on me that I, as a solitary legionnaire, was gallivanting around the most dangerous part of town. Spurred by a few threatening glances, I hurried out of there to find a safer spot. I sighed a breath of relief after emerging from the district intact, and to vent my sudden attack of fright, I settled down on a shady park bench to watch the afternoon traffic.

December 19, 1948

I spent the entire morning cutting meat and breaking large blocks of salt. The one consolation was that it was too overcast and dismal to do anything outside. These tedious chores helped pass the time and I was not crawling the walls with boredom.

When I returned from hauling the daily water from the nearby river, I saw that the troops were ready to roll out on a mission. In this rotten weather? Are they out of their minds? Not being in a position to argue I jumped onto the truck.

The Vietmins had attacked a lookout approximately thirty kilometres away. One man was dead, three were injured. It was our job to recover the body and take the casualties to the hospital.

The joyride lasted forty-five minutes. The platoon divided into two groups and while one group collected the dead and injured, the other stayed behind in case the Vietmins staged a comeback. We couldn't afford to take any chances and leave the post unprotected, even though the odds were against another onslaught.

I had three hours, there was nothing to do but inspect the surroundings and I was anxious to try the local cuisine. I headed for the restaurant in the far corner of the courtyard. The tables and chairs led me to believe I had strayed into a posh establishment. The host greeted me with a deep bow and a smile as I stepped through the doorway. He invited me to sit down, wiped the table and apologized the soup wasn't ready; but if I wanted to wait another ten minutes it would be.

The soup was thick and hearty, the porcelain bowl was brimming with a medley of noodles and vegetables sprinkled with small chunks of meat. I told the gentleman how tasty the soup was and without my ordering it, he produced a second helping. Inquiring about the soup I asked,

"Is it not a common practice to fatten pigs before butchering? Or is it just that you take special care in trimming off all the visible fat?"

"You're not eating pork, you're eating dog meat."

My hand holding the spoon stopped halfway to my mouth.

"That's absurd."

The man maintained that it was dog meat and not pork. I finished the soup, meat and all. I praised the old chap again, gave him a generous tip, and left him with the blessing of Buddha.

December 20, 1948

My platoon went on a mission without me. No word arrived, though they should have been back by now. I considered myself lucky to have been left out. I was, however, included in a campaign organized by those left behind. The plan was to scour the surrounding area, and thus deter any potential attacks. We marched out for all to see, proof for potential troublemakers and undesirable Vietmins that despite the approaching Christmas holiday we maintained a guard.

I was assigned a narrow winding alley with hidden nooks and corners at every turn. Not that I was afraid, but to patrol such a lane alone was asking a bit much. I understood that the life of a legionnaire was not worth two cents, but in pairs we could at least support and encourage each other. I am not one to flee from my own shadow, but when I stepped into that alley alone, maybe I was a little afraid.

With a loaded gun in hand I quietly inched my way into the passage. Curious eyes followed my steps from every window. I reached the end of the alley and headed back just as slowly.

Nearing the entrance I saw two girls standing beside one of the brick walls, struggling to uproot a small bush. Seeing that their efforts yielded no result I set out to use all of my strength. With one pull the bush flew into the air, propelled me backwards into the girls, we fell into the ditch and my gun discharged. We were not hurt, but the gun shot was deafening.

There was only enough time to dust myself off and for the girls to disappear before the entire platoon appeared in the lane. I hurried to meet them and excitedly stated that I had spotted a Vietmin, had ordered him to stop but the man ran and I fired. A search for the man ensued, but not a trace of him could be found. After an hour of searching, the platoon abandoned all hope of finding the Vietmin and departed with orders that I was to shoot if he showed himself again.

Weary from all the excitement, I sat on the spot where I had uprooted the bush. The two young ladies came back, a bowl of soup in hand as a show of gratitude, but intuition warned me to refuse the food.

Lying in bed recalling the incident, it suddenly struck me that the shrub had not been firmly embedded in the ground after all, that the two girls could have easily removed it and they had been faking the whole thing. To shoot me would have caused too much noise, stabbing was risky because I might scream or shoot in defense. Poisoning was the simplest and quietest solution. And, since the poison would take effect a few hours later, they could escape suspicion.

December 23, 1948

I woke up with an excruciating toothache. I took aspirin and drank cognac but nothing helped. By the afternoon I had had enough and went to see the dentist. He gave me painkillers and instructed me to take one, and only one, every two hours. I went back to the fort and took three. What did a dentist know about a toothache? If he said one, that meant three at least, and to maximize their potency I washed the pills down with a glass of cognac. I passed out in seconds.

December 24, 1948

I was shaken from my dreams around one p.m. Joe said that they had been trying to rouse me since 9:00 a.m. and worried that I was suffering from sleeping sickness, Charlie had gone to fetch the doctor.

Maybe I did have sleeping sickness but on the other hand, my toothache was gone.

It was warm, warm enough to be outside in shorts. The sun was shining, all was fresh and green, the flowers were blooming, and birds were singing. Back home, bells were tinkling as sleds laden with gifts and people glided across the fresh bed of snow.

We cleaned everything and decorated every corner of the fort with flags and colorful streamers, and then I tried to give my own room a taste of the holiday spirit. Somehow, somewhere, I managed to find two pine branches, set them against the wall on the shelf above my bed and placed a candle on either side. By adding tinsel, family photographs and religious pictures the setting was complete, and most important, I had the Christmas tree that meant so much to me. I lit the candles and prayed for my parents in Hungary, and for my sisters in Brussels and Ankara.

We built a huge bonfire in the yard, set-up long tables on either side of the bonfire, and draped sheets over our Christmas gifts from the Legion. Everyone received a gift. The gesture meant a lot to each of us and even if the gift was only a handkerchief or lighter, it was gratifying to know that we were not forgotten. The Legion was well-aware of our feelings of separation at this time of year and did its best to make us feel at home. If not for the officer on duty who reminded us that lunch was ready, we would have forgotten to eat. We gulped down a few bites, careful to leave room for the two suppers that lay ahead.

After the presentation of gifts we stood around the bonfire and sang *Silent Night, Holy Night*. The effects of the wine were soon apparent and by midnight few men could stand. The Hungarians gathered under a large tree and spent the rest of the night singing Hungarian Christmas carols. The wine ran dry before we were ready to retire, so off we went to purchase more and returned ready to continue the party.

In spite of all of the excitement, the highlight of the day was the two letters from Ankara.

December 25, 1948

I woke up at 9:30 with a terrible hangover. My head felt as big as a barrel, and my mouth! On my way to the kitchen I glanced in the rooms; everyone was still snoring and the air reeked of alcohol. I washed four croissants down with a gallon of cocoa, and then immersed myself in a wash barrel to no avail. I filled a pail with cocoa, grabbed a tray of croissants and took the food upstairs, thinking that it might help revive the others. My efforts were lost on all but Charlie and even he had barely enough strength to open his eyes. Leaving the breakfast behind, I returned to my room and set down to answer the letters from my sister in Ankara.

When not on patrol, we played cards from morning to night – exempting those hours which we filled with argument. Charlie and Gypsy's fist fight is a perfect example. I was but an innocent bystander who observed, from a distance, as they shattered my already frail and battered table. There was no way that I could get another one from the canteen and now there was nothing to write or play cards on. I brought the issue up when I bumped into Charlie the next day.

"Charlie, you know that I came by my table with great difficulty, you guys went and broke it, and now I have nothing to write on. If you want to fight do it anywhere but not in my room, and leave my table out of it!"

"Don't make such a case out of it. 'Great difficulty' and 'obtained' indeed. Everyone knows that you stole the stuff from the canteen!"

"Excuse me, but I did not steal. I found."

"All right, big deal, you found it. What's the difference? It's not worth shiting you pants over. I will steal another one for you tonight."

Charlie and Gypsy did bring my replacement that night. Heaven only knows where they got it, but it was huge, and they dumped it in front of my doorway.

"My dear old chap," said Charlie, "we broke your table and you demanded another, so here it is!"

I was outnumbered and Charlie had a look of provocation on his face. Had it been otherwise I might have vented my anger, but I kept it bottled inside and fumed quietly to myself.

I now had a table, but I didn't know what to do with it. My room was barely three metres long by two metres wide and already crammed full with a bed, two chairs and a clothes rack. Those two had pulled a fast one on me. I was not amused. I was still mad when Charlie led the entire Hungarian contingent in and made a public spectacle of the table. Each man commented with mock admiration at the beauty of the table and their remarks infuriated me even more. Joe suggested that I build a room around the table. Alex proposed that I hold a rummage sale on it. Gypsy praised it to no end.

"Now this is what I call a table! Fit for a king. Now all you have to do is get it into your room."

At this my temper gave way and I kicked Gypsy in the rear with such force he went flying head first into the wall.

"You son of a bitch! You're the one who started the fight yesterday, and it's your fault that my table was broken in the first place. Charlie almost made mincemeat out of you and I'm gonna finish you off unless you find some tools and help me cut this thing down to size."

I had barely finished my threat and Gypsy leaped at me like a cornered tiger. I ducked to avoid the oncoming blow, and his fist whistled past my ear. The momentum threw Gypsy off balance and against the table. The others remained off to the side and enjoyed the show. For me the entertainment value thinned as it became obvious that Gypsy was serious and harder to deal with than I had thought. He was, after all, the same man who had attacked Charlie. I should have thought about that before acting. Gypsy jumped on my back and was squeezing my throat with both hands. I tried to shake him off but slipped on the damp tiles and sent both of us tumbling headlong into the wall. I was able to lessen the blow but Gypsy, who had his hands around my neck, caught the full force of the impact and smashed his head. Gypsy lost his senses long enough to release his hold on my neck and fall off my back. I took advantage of the moment's hesitation and twisted his arms behind his back. He fell flat on his face and dragged me down with him. He on the bottom and I on top.

"Gypsy, if you swear that you'll find some tools and help me fix the table, I'll let you go. If you don't, I'm gonna beat you to a pulp." And to prove I wasn't kidding, I gave him a clout on the back of his head.

"Drop dead, you son of a bitch! You have some nerve sittin' on top of me and shootin' off your mouth like that. I'd teach ya a lesson you won't soon forget if I had you pinned down. Damn you anyway, and let go of my arm before it breaks."

"I haven't heard you promise me anything yet. What's it gonna be? Are you gonna get me those tools or not?" I asked while putting pressure on his arm.

He winced and cried out in pain.

"Okay, okay, I'll do what you want."

So thanks to the slippery floor and the wall, I ended up with a splendid table that was sturdy enough to withstand another difference of opinion.

December 27, 1948

The rotten fog did not show signs of lifting. Everything was damp and soggy, and since I was already soaked to the skin I thought to hell with it all, and decided to brave the weather and headed for the canteen. Along the way, my ear picked up the sound of gypsy music. I stopped to listened. No doubt about it, someone was wailing away to the accompaniment of a violin. As I got closer, the sound of the fiddle and the howling voice grew louder.

I entered and saw that it was Charlie, leaning up against the bar with a bottle of rum. He was singing, and I use the term loosely, a Hungarian folk song whose lyrics begin with "A golden canary lies nested atop a poplar tree. . . ."

It was Plessiner who was responsible for rounding up the records and something to play them on. And, on top of it all, he had gone out of his way to secure albums that were representative of the various nationalities in the camp.

December 31, 1948

We raised glasses, toasted each other and the New Year, shook hands and drank to each others' health. Plessiner spoke a few words in honor of the occasion and the cannon fired a round in salute to the end of the year – 1949 had arrived.

Our captain did everything in his power to make our stay here more tolerable. He did his best to capture the spirit of the holiday and create a mood of optimism. He meant well, but despite his best intentions, the memories lingered. As I reflected on the events of the past year and could scarcely believe all the things that had happened to me.

January 2, 1949

New Year's Day was all but forgotten and everything returned to the same old routine. My section was assigned the distinctive privilege of constructing a coop for the geese and chickens. The question was from what? There wasn't a spare board or single nail in the entire compound, not to speak of meshing. That we did not have the raw materials at our disposal was not only irrelevant, but considered a given for the Legion.

The fact that by nightfall we had obtained five thick bamboo rods, counted as a gigantic accomplishment in light of the fact that only twelve men had been entrusted with this noble mission. The rest of the company, thirty bodies, were held responsible for preparing the area in and around the supposed coop. Julius and I were assigned the task of finding nails. Since we could not track down a blessed one in the entire fort, we decided to try our luck in Ky-Lua.

We had scarcely covered fifty metres of the four hundred metres of meadow between the houses of Ky-Lua and the walls of the fort when Julius started complaining. His feet hurt, and needed not only rest but a painkiller. I, as a devoted scout and aware of my responsibilities as such, suddenly remembered my pledges and the section referring to "assist your fellow man in times of need." I sat Julius down beside the ditch, then hurried back to get some aspirin from the medical centre. Finding it locked, I headed for the nearest "pharmacy", the canteen, and returned with a bottle of cognac. For lack of aspirin to ease the suffering of my neighbor, it was the next best thing. The cognac proved to be more than adequate medicine. Before Julius had drank even half the bottle, he declared that the pain had subsided and we could continue on.

We did not get very far before Julius started complaining again. This time I grabbed the martyr, and pressed the bottle of medicine into his hands before he could finish his sob story. He was a generous fellow who did not want to consume the medication alone and insisted on sharing it with me. And so we both reaped the benefits of the cure. We left the empty bottle in the ditch and continued toward Ky-Lua. When we arrived, we promptly sought out a bistro where nails were not for sale but cognac was.

Several hours and two bottles of cognac later, we came to the sad conclusion that there was not a nail to be had in all of Ky-Lua. To compensate, we found a bunch of candles among the many barrels in one of the Chinese stores and bought two of them. We couldn't very well go back to the fort empty handed, now could we!

We lit the candles and headed back, singing a folk song called *Molly Is Cooking Beans* at the top of our lungs. Ky-Lua was behind us when sensing that something was very wrong, I looked at Julius and saw that his gun was missing.

"Julius! Where's your pistol?"

"What pistol? You're confused. I never did have one."

"Not your own, but you borrowed Charlie's, remember, because you didn't want to drag your gun along. That pistol! Charlie's! Where did you lose it?"

What a rude awakening! Never in our lives did we sober up so fast.

We ran back to the Chinese store remembering that the pistol was still in Julius' possession at that point. The pistol was still there. We found it as we had left it, leaning up against one of the barrels; the barrels camouflaging the pistol almost completely.

Our brazen mood had vanished when we headed back a second time, it was in silence. Supper time had long since passed by the time we returned and we had no nails, only candles to show for the effort.

January 3, 1949

Charlie's screeching voice woke me at 6:00.

"Tonue Combat!"

From the sound of his voice, one would have thought that the bulk of the Vietmin army was standing at the gate. It was about time for a little action. All this sitting around suffocated a man with boredom.

The Vietmins must have caused quite an upheaval. There could be no other reason for this senseless blundering; everyone was running around, blocking traffic, tripping over each other, curses flying. Charlie went racing from one room to the next driving us out. I could almost see the whip in his hand. Despite the confusion, we were all on the trucks and ready to go by

6:45.

After all the fuss they tell us that it was not a call to combat at all but that we are escorting a convoy to Cao-Bang. Couldn't they have told us as much last night?

We were ready to leave as soon as the convoy arrived, but the convoy, which was suppose to arrive any moment, pulled in four hours late at 11:00. We cursed the higher authorities to no end. And as for Charlie, we strongly advised him to remain out of sight for several weeks.

"My friend, please have some heart," he pleaded. "What could I do? I had my orders!"

"Fine, but there was no need to howl like a hyena in heat," retorted Joe.

"But . . ."

"Don't try to get out of it," I told him. "I saw you kick Gypsy in the ass."

"But that was only because he stepped on my corn."

"Like hell I did! You kicked me just because I was in your way. You just wait Charlie, you're gonna pay for this!"

We waited another fifteen minutes for the Lieutenant, and the trucks finally rolled out of the yard at 11:15. The section was divided into two groups, one group advanced to guard the front while the second brought up the rear.

The infamous Route Colonial 4 Passageway wound its way through the jungle. Its countless blind corners and steep turns served as perfect ambush hideouts for Vietmins who, following the guerillas in China, were waiting for the opportunity to swoop down on any passing caravan.

We passed through Dong-Dang, Na-Cham, Lich-Son and That-Khe, only Dong-Khe remained and after that, Cao-Bang a mere thirty kilometres away. An unprovoked assault could come at any time, and from any direction. The superb camouflage of the jungle made the first, and quite often the second and third assault the Vietmins'.

January 4, 1949

We headed back to Lang-Son after breakfast. It was raining, cold and foggy. Gloomy and dejected, we sat in silence and listened to the monotone humming of the engines. Where the trucks had to slow down, many of us jumped off and hiked in an effort to ward off the chill. We were not afraid of being attacked, the Vietmins were in no mood to start shooting in weather like this. It was late afternoon by the time we arrived back home. A cup of hot coffee and rum would taste mighty fine right now, and I hurried to the kitchen to see that fifty others had the similar idea. By the time I got to the urn, the coffee was gone and I was obliged to drink my rum without it.

Quite a few of the men kept pets at the fort, myself included. My monkey was wonderful company during night watch, and was alert to even the slightest disturbance. I could doze off without worrying about surprises because he would wake me up with a tug and a bite on the arm.

January 6, 1949

I think the whole fuss of our celebration of Epiphany was Plessiner's idea. The cook baked a cake in which four beans were concealed. After supper everyone was handed a slice and a king and queen were chosen from the four who found a bean in their slice. Absolute power to reign over the fort for an entire day was granted to the winners. Charlie was the lucky one chosen King, and when Plessiner introduced the Queen we rolled with laughter. Her Highness was led into the canteen on Plessiner's arm with a veil of colored streamers ten metres long. A rusty pot served as crown and her face was smeared with red, blue and white paint. Her Majesty was ushered into the throne room where His Majesty was patiently waiting on his throne.

The King was allowed four wishes. His Royal Highness' first wish was to demand the release of the prisoners from the jail. Then, he drilled one of the sergeants, ordered two barrels of wine to be brought for his subjects and finally, forced the cook into eating a huge piece of cake. After this he put his subjects on parade for military review. And only after, were we allowed to tap the barrel.

January 7, 1949

My platoon adopted a five-year-old boy. We christened him Bep (Battalion Etranger Parachutiste) after attempts to discover his name led nowhere. We hired a tailor and had a complete paratroopers outfit made for him. Little Bep was terribly proud of his new belongings, especially the shoes and the insignia of the regiment.

He was pampered and spoiled by everyone in the company. We got a puppy for him to play with and at morning assembly we stood him in front of the line; at meals, we gave him the best of everything and in the evenings, ten of us were on hand to put him to bed. We furnished a separate room for him and provided him with everything that we could. He would often burst into tears as he was passed from one pair of hands to another. I suspect he would have been happier with one daddy instead of one hundred.

Since we had no bathroom, we found a large washtub to bathe him in. It did not go smoothly, however. Every attempt called for hand to hand combat before we were able to stuff him into the tub, and by the time we got him in, he would cry for his puppy. We would leave Bep alone to search for the dog, who had run for cover, and taking advantage of our absence, Bep would make his own escape.

Time slipped by with tedious monotony. We wallowed in free time, played countless games of cards stopping only when we were no longer able to distinguish an ace from a deuce. The depressing weather kept us inside.

January 16, 1949

The rain had stopped, a thick fog saturated everything and 5:00 reveille sent us scrambling to board the trucks to escort another convoy to Cao-Bang.

It started to rain again after we passed Dong-Dang. The miserable weather made us short-tempered and many words were muttered while pulling our raincoats around us even more tightly. The rain stopped periodically and after Na-Cham, the sun even showed itself. By the That-Khe bridge the sun was shedding its warmth without disguise. A tall hill rose beside the bridge and at its summit was an outpost large enough to shelter sixty people. Two guards were positioned in a telephone station here. We reached the town, a mere three kilometres away, and to our surprise, a tank was waiting to escort us to Cao-Bang. According to the Commanding Officer, the Viet-mins were very active in the Dong-Khe area and it would not hurt to proceed with a tank in tow. The feeling of tranquillity melted.

"This is ridiculous," I muttered to myself. All this rumored activity was exactly that, rumored. The evidence was too circumstantial to be true. We had escorted caravans to Cao-Bang many times already and with only minor episodes of violence. If anyone was responsible for a direct hit it was the mosquitoes.

It was early afternoon, the sky was clear and the sun was scorching. It did not matter, rain or shine, we were drenched.

We inched along the steep winding road with hairpin bends. The dense vegetation which grew to the side of the road also obscured its end. The tank, which creaked miserably advertising to any would-be attackers that we were coming, reached the end of the road, waited for the caravan to catch up and as we approached the rattle of a machine gun cut the air. The truck emptied in a second, and the wooden side of the truck where I had been sitting was destroyed. We were very lucky. Of the ten men aboard, three sustained minor injuries and the rest suffered from fright.

The tank shot its cannon and machine gun, but for lack of a target, shot blindly. Those of us in position also fired but discovered after raking the mountain to the right with gun fire that the attack originated from the left. The strength of the enemy seemed to be gaining and the cries of the wounded resounded. In an effort to help one of the wounded, I crawled to the road and just as I reached the back tire of one of the trucks a grenade slammed down in front of me. I flattened against the road, but not quickly enough to escape the flying splinters. My face and neck caught the brunt of the injuries, and as I placed my hand to my face it was covered in blood.

So I was injured. I wiped the blood off my palm, stroked my face again to make sure, and the same result. "So Scout," I muttered, "you have shed your blood not only on the Russian front but on the soil of Indochina too." The fighting continued and I thought it best to stay put rather than risk a run for the ambulance.

When the fighting finally did cease I did go to the ambulance, but only as far as the side of the truck. There I saw the dead and the seriously injured, and turned away in shame for even daring to make make such a case out of a few splinters. A brook ran beside the road, and I washed myself in its waters and that was as far as the first aid went.

The whole encounter had lasted two hours. Our casualties included two dead and four seriously wounded. Many Vietmins must have also died as our tank's cannon had made a direct hit on their artillery. After order had been restored, the French dead and injured were transported back to That-Khe while we continued our journey to Cao-Bang. The rear guard stayed behind to collect the dead and injured Vietmins. The Commander's precautions had been right, without the cannon, our casualties would have been much higher.

Equipment aboard the trucks had been blown to bits by the Vietmins. The rest of the ride was no picnic because even the benches had been shredded to toothpicks. I did not envy the driver who, with his chair blasted away, was forced to finish the journey half-squating. After one very uncomfortable hour we arrived in Cao-Bang. Hundreds of legionnaires outfitted to the hilt with weapons were standing at the gate, waiting to take their turn, but both sides had had enough for one day.

January 17, 1949

Since the Vietmins had thoroughly settled the matter of our trucks yesterday, we were obliged to borrow one from the local garrison and by 7:30 we were homeward bound. The ambulance and the tank remained in That-Khe. The injured were taken back to Lang-Son early in the morning, while the dead were buried yesterday. We were fired upon hardly ten kilometres down the road. This time, we did not bother to stop, but dashed ahead with as much speed as possible.

After two days of rest we were told that we had to do it all over again. Only this time, my group was to serve as the rear guard. With our luck, the Vietmins would wait to direct some of their guns at us.

A few of us went dancing in Lang-Son after supper. Contrary to my experiences in Philippeville, I found a partner without delay. This was not surprising as the ladies were employees of the nightclub and dancing was part of their job. I had only to buy a ticket from the cashier and present it to the chosen one.

I woke up to the wonderful news that my section was not to be escorting the caravan after all. I was more than glad to escape the chance of reliving last Sunday's episode. No matter how I looked at it, it was safer within the confines of the fort. I would much prefer guard duty or die from boredom than duck bullets any day.

In the afternoon Joe, Alex, Julius and I went to a nearby spring where one could always find women. We bathed and after put our clothes on the nearby branches to dry. If we could manage it, we would sneak over to the bushes where the women had hung their clothes and steal their clothing. They would run around trying to recover their clothing while we enjoyed the joke. However, once trust had been established (a thin gold bracelet, or a silk blouse made a suitable impression) we, like they, were inclined to be generous.

January 22, 1949

The caravan returned. The convoy had been attacked from both sides this trip and of the twenty-two men who started the journey, only three survived. The attack had occurred in the same spot. General Giap was concentrating his forces in that area and we were suffering the consequences. The terrain was ideal for military action for he could deploy his troops from, and retreat to, the security of the nearby Chinese border knowing that legionnaires would not pursue and risk political conflict.

January 28, 1949

We buried our comrades. Plessiner conducted the ceremony that lasted over an hour. The gesture was fitting Plessiner's character, and proving he valued every human life. The cemetery was lovely and well-kept, but please God, arrange to leave me out of it.

It was announced during lunch that we could look forward to an extended mission. For the rest of the day we conserved energy in preparation for the five days ahead; even card games were dispensed with.

January 29 – February 4, 1949

We rose with the crack of dawn. First on the agenda was to escort a caravan to Dinh-Lap, and then a trip through the mountains on foot.

A guide was necessary because the terrain was unfamiliar. Our commander, along with the guide, put on the pace because, or so they said, a designated spot had to be reached before nightfall. Despite our haste we were unable to overtake time, and the density of the forest only served to enhance the darkness. So that no one would go wandering, we hung on to each other's backpacks. We soon had to stop for the night because it was impossible to advance any further. Mercier did roll call, no one was missing, and we snuggled down to sleep. I, however, happened to stop where there was an abundance of sharp rocks. Sitting was a nightmare and lying down was impossible, so I spent the night standing.

When dawn finally arrived the first thing we noticed was that our guide had disappeared with the night. While feeling our way through the darkness we had deviated from the agreed upon course and now we were hopelessly lost. Mercier had a compass so we could head in a specific direction but had little else to guide us. Turning east would eventually lead us to Dinh-Lap, a northwest route meant Lang-Son, or we could choose a southern route and hope to arrive in Tien-Yen. For all practical purposes east was the wisest choice, or at least the Commander thought so. We set out in hopes of reaching the highway that joined Lang-Son and Tien-Yen.

Our provisions were intended to last four days, and one was already gone. To make matters worse, our absence would not be noted for a few days because our destination had been a remote village where Vietmin activity had been rumored. The road there and back involved three days, not allowing for delays or lost time which could consume another day or so. This meant, that for three and a half days not so much as a passing thought would be given to our absence.

By the third day our food was nearly exhausted. The only advantage was that our load was lighter and it made travel easier. For three solid days we had done nothing but trample through the jungle. We had hoped to come across a village so someone could point us in the right direction, but no luck. One more day of food before we would rely solely on bananas. We hiked all day with no sign of life. The exhausted company didn't care whether they slept on rocks or grass, we slept like logs.

The fifth day and all the food was gone, but there were plenty of bananas. The hours dragged on as we marched and marched, and exhaustion crept over us. The sixth day and the journey became automatic, we rested, marched and ate bananas on cue. We had given up hope of finding our way out when bamboo huts suddenly appeared.

We searched the huts and found an elderly man who trembled with fear as we pulled him from his hiding place under rags and baskets. The others had left him behind when they had fled to the jungle because with one leg missing he would not have been able to keep up. It took a while for him to understand that we meant him no harm. We gave him a few cigarettes to prove our good intentions. He calmed down and sat back blowing smoke rings.

We then tried to explain what we wanted. The Commander produced a map, pointed to Dinh-Lap and with hands and feet tried to explain that we wanted to go there. It was late afternoon by the time our dilemma finally sunk in. Now we faced an even bigger problem – trying to understand what he was saying. The communication took up the rest of the day, but by night we knew that Dinh-Lap was ten kilometres north while the highway to Lang-Son was but one kilometre from the settlement.

The old man offered his services as a guide and set out in the same direction that we had come. We had taken a wrong turn some where before we reached the village. That one kilometre turned out to be a mighty long one, for it was an hour and a half before we actually reached the highway. We thanked the old man profusely, gave him another pack of cigarettes and embarked on the return trek. After six very long days we arrived in Dinh-Lap.

February 9, 1949

It has rained for the past five days, and rest and letter writing have consumed the better part of them. The city offered little to divert my attention, and with only dancing to look forward to, even it became monotonous.

While I thought out the various options of entertainment open, Mortier's voice broke the silence.

"Tonue Combat!"

I glanced at my watch and saw it was 6:30. For heaven's sake was that all? The weather conditions held no promise for a pleasant journey. Damn those Vietmins, why was it impossible for them to cause a disturbance when it wasn't raining? We followed our former course toward Dinh-Lap but the trucks stopped and we continued on foot.

The surface of the road was like a skating rink. Water had swelled over the soil, and after an hour of slipping and sliding accompanied by alternating curses and prayers, we arrived soaking wet and smeared in mud.

The inhabitants were not expecting company and were downright rude when they fled to the jungle. We fired a few rounds to warn them that fleeing was hopeless and escape impossible. We searched every hut and collected two dozen Vietmins, twenty handguns and a small amount of ammunition.

The return trip was even more hellish than the trip there. The rain had increased in intensity and made the road treacherous. I muttered a few curses but the words were lost in the rain. We arrived back home worn out, as usual, and by the time I finished off three mugs of black coffee and rum, my fatigue was gone and even the rain felt soothing.

February 10, 1949

No sooner had I opened my eyes and it was announced that in two days there was to be another five day mission. Intuition told me that some big shot had overheard me complain of boredom. Whoever it was took my concern to heart and made sure to provide for adequate recreation in the form of another mountain excursion. The rain never ceased. I was confined to my room and left to stare at the ceiling or write letters. What else could a lonely and forsaken legionnaire do? Even if no letters were forthcoming, the least I could do was send some out.

February 11, 1949

I couldn't believe my eyes when I woke up – the sun was shining. Intending to make the most of a free day replete with sunshine, we went down to the spring. The girls were there bathing, and together, we had a lot of fun. Preparations for the trip began after lunch. There would be no rummy games today. It was imperative that we get to bed early for it was certain that we would be roused out of it not at three than at four a.m.

February 12 - 17, 1949

My prediction proved correct. We were driven out of sleep at 4 a.m. Why the hell we were harassed so early in the morning? Those damn Vietmins would surely wait for us if we got up at seven instead. And if they were not so inclined then all the better because, we could arrive at midnight. I could bitch and complain all I wanted but it would not change the situation. I really had no right to complain, the trucks were standing in the yard and the poor drivers had been deprived of sleep altogether. We were on our way toward Dong-Dang before five. Somewhere around Na-Cham we got off and proceeded through the mountains on foot.

"Sergeant," I asked Mortier "Why are we crawling so slowly? Where are we going anyway?"

"We're not going anywhere," he replied. "We are to disperse somewhere around here and wait for the Vietmins. It's our turn to organize an ambush and grab them first for a change."

"Who the hell wants to get them?" I protested. "Let's get out of here as fast as we can, before we actually do clash and witness a battle unlike anything we've seen."

My objections were not heard. We soon stopped and scattered, superbly camouflaged, to await the inevitable collision.

"Oh God, please lead those Vietmins in some other direction, I am in no mood for warfare."

Somebody up there heard and heeded my brief supplication, or so it seemed, because we lay for hours without so much as a dog passing through. The night was spent at a nearby outpost. Partisans served as the guards of this large and comfortable bamboo fort which was surrounded by not one but two protective barricades.

Reveille was at 3:00, and by 3:30 we were on our way. We reached a steep mountain and stopped. Our commander told us that on the other side was the Chinese border. Immediately alongside the border was a settlement, and our mission was to capture and return with the group of partisan deserters and Vietmins who made their hideaway there. This was the retreat from which attacks against caravans and outposts were launched, and why their capture, or elimination, was imperative.

Once we reached the top of the mountain we formed two groups. The smaller group was to stay behind and function as the rear guard while the others attacked. I was with the rear guard. Everyone took their places as the larger group headed for the village. We stayed above waiting for something to happen. The crackle of weapons snapped me out of my dream world and reminded me where I was.

Judging from the sounds of the skirmish, one would think that two regiments had clashed. The combat did not last long and soon we heard our troops forging ahead. Chances were that they did not hit a jackpot after such a short-lived romp. I was right. Despite their best efforts there was not a single weapon or piece of ammunition to show for it and only nine Vietmins had been captured. The trip was hardly worth it.

During the rest period we interrogated our captives and found that of the nine, seven were Chinese citizens. Documents supported their statements, and thus left only two authentic Vietmins. One bore no identification, but the other had a partisan registration card. The seven Chinese were released but the other two were held captive and taken to Na-Long.

The cross-examination of the partisan traitor began after supper, but not one word escaped his lips despite hours of questioning and other means of coercion. The other captive, sat listlessly under a tree. He knew what awaited him. He knew too, that no one could save him. After hours of futile questioning, the powers that be placed a shovel in the hands of each man and ordered them to dig their own graves. It was unbelievable to watch them do so without offering the slightest resistance. The captives were bound to fence posts after the pits were dug. They refused to be blindfolded and looked toward the barrel with defiance.

The marksmen had been instructed beforehand to execute the partisan traitor and to spare the Vietmin. A round was fired and both men collapsed, the partisan from the mortal wound and the Vietmin from the shock. A few moments later the Vietmin opened his eyes, glanced about in disbelief, then fainted again.

Some scare! Thanks, but no thanks.

He revived again. Confident this time that he was really there, he shouted "I live!" His bonds were loosened and he was free to go. The partisan was accorded a mercy round of fire and then buried.

I watched all this from a respectable distance and pondered the reason behind the madness. Why make a public circus out of an execution? What was only an enemy up until now, became, with this act, a mortal antagonist. I knew that he would always remember.

Morning came and as usual, we were up by 3:30, ready to stand on lookout again or rather, lie in ambush. Three of us perched in trees while the rest of the men scattered. Hour after hour we waited, not daring to move or heaven forbid, talk. Even the birds would flee if fifty men chose to socialize. That they made such a row above our heads was a positive sign. A sudden silence on their part would be an indication that people were approaching, and people in this case would mean the Vietmins. There was little to do but lie still and wait out the day and the next one as well. By the third day we grew bored of the futile experimentation and returned to Na-Long with the intention that we would spend the night there and would return to Lang-Son in the morning.

News of a forthcoming Vietnamese gathering greeted us in Na-Long. It was supposed to take place, according to the reports, in the small valley to the right. The meeting was scheduled to take place early the next morning. Our lieutenant did not want such a golden opportunity slip out from under his fingers. After three days on a wild goose chase, here was the chance to corner them at last. He explained that because of the foreseeable dangers only volunteers would be taken. Despite the fact I had vowed never to volunteer again, I was the first to step forward when Mercier called for eleven volunteers. Only a bit of food was permitted for supper because they claimed that a man shot in the abdomen was more likely to survive on an empty stomach. In the wakes of such an enticing prospect, we sat down to finalize details.

The partisans provided us with the same flowing black garments worn by the Vietmins. We were barely able to cram ourselves into them as we were so much bigger. In the long run it turned out for the better because the loose wraps would have gotten in the way. We smeared our faces and hands with black cream so that our white skin would not be visible under the penetrating light of the moon. The final touch was a black scarf around our heads. True, almost all of us had black hair, but if the one or two blondes covered their heads it seemed only right that we do the same. We stood in rank and file waiting for a final inspection by Mercier before departure.

I could almost read the Lieutenant's mind when he looked us over: I wonder which ones will return.

One-by-one we crept out through the watchtower gate. We crawled to the base of the hill, a necessary tactic since the light of the moon was almost intense enough to read by. From there we ran as fast as we could to the mountainside, and we approached the hill in front of the passage into the valley. Our plan was to wait for, and surprise, the Vietmins while hiding in the dense shrubbery.

For all we knew, this so-called gathering was a well-thought-out trap. A few dozen Vietnamese might feasibly be lying in ambush anywhere along the kilometre between the outpost and our destination, and just as we waited for them for three days, so they too could be standing-by, ready to mow us down as we neared.

There was a small pagoda near the front of the hill and the Lieutenant, along with four others, took up position in the area directly in front of it. The pagoda provided excellent protection from the rear and any attack could be anticipated from ahead, or from either side. Four men on the right and three on the left barricaded the only route in and out of the valley. The dense foliage along with our black attire rendered us invisible. We, on the other hand, were able to scan the entire area merely by clearing away any vegetation that obscured our view.

There was a hollow tree stump beside where I lay. The stump had decayed to the point where the side facing me had rotted away, and made it look like a small guardhouse. We waited for two hours but there was nothing. I wondered how much longer Mercier intended to wait? It was obvious that the whole thing was a hoax. The Vietmins had no intention of gathering here. Upon my head I swore that they tricked us into coming here while they held their meeting someplace else. If they had planned on holding the meeting at all!

I was still fuming when from the opposite hillside came the sound of dry twigs and leaves crackling. Voices blended with this noise. They were coming. Mercier had been right after all.

And come they did. With the alertness of a cat beside a mouse hole, we watched and waited for them to reach the meadow where they would pose as a first-rate target. Our weapons were standing-by and aimed in the direction of the meadow. At first they came only from the hillside opposite us, then from the roads alongside the hill and finally, from the furthest mountain. It dawned on us that we were completely surrounded by God only knew how many Vietmins. We could not even budge without being detected.

According to our plans, Mercier was supposed to deliver the first round as a signal for his men to start firing: I hope he doesn't lose his mind. I hope he can see that we are outnumbered by the hundreds. Were all the Vietmins of Tonkin going to gather here today?

Our predicament was not just unusual, it was downright absurd. We had not seen a solitary Vietmin for three days and now I couldn't count them all.

It's no use to dwell on the nerve-wracking strain we were under. Our hiding place was approximately two metres high and protected by steep flanks. The Vietmins could not see us unless a few decided to pay the pagoda a visit. Then, we were lost. Many of them drew so close beside and below me that I could hear the sound of their breathing.

I glanced at Mercier and his entourage and saw them trying to retreat back to the pagoda. The pagoda was some distance away from where I was, so I figured it was safer to hide in the hollow tree stump for now. It proved spacious enough to allow some movement. A total retreat was out of the question. There was no choice but to wait here until the party was over and we could go home. Once inside, my nerves calmed down a bit. With any more courage I might have risked lighting up a cigarette.

I lay there minding my own business when suddenly I felt a sting on my hand. Another, then another. I scratched at it, an ant.

You stupid soldier! You should have known that rotten wood and ants go hand in hand!

The question was, how many? Judging by the growing number of bites, quite a few. The bites were becoming a nuisance and I had to get out of there. I poked my head out to look around and just as quickly drew it back in: a Vietmin was perched on a root protruding from the side of the hill. If I had stayed where I was instead of seeking refuge in the trunk, we would now be eye-to-eye. I put the machine gun down very carefully and readied my dagger. In truth, I had never used a dagger before, but if he ventured up here, there would be no time for indecision: it would have to be him or me.

He was half a metre away, his head in line with the edge of the hill. It's interesting to wonder which of us would have been more frightened had we taken each other by surprise.

My dear God! You have blessed us with more than enough storms and pouring rain in the past, would you be so kind as to suddenly let loose one now? My wish was not His command, and how timely it would have been because the Vietmins would have scattered, leaving us free to make a run for it. For myself a sudden storm would have been especially beneficial, a chance to get out of here and encourage the ants to seek their supper elsewhere. How I cursed the very same bugs I had admired so much yesterday! Thank goodness my clothes were tight and they could not crawl underneath.

After what seemed like an eternity, the bustling and talking ceased.

They were gone.

With great caution I crawled out. One never knew, there may be a few stragglers. I heard Mercier whisper, "Retreat!" We returned to the outpost only after we were absolutely certain that the coast was clear.

February 20, 1949

There was not much point in resting after so many days spent lying in the grass. The twelve of us did suffer from nervous strain, which was more difficult to recover from than sheer physical fatigue.

Yesterday I had some x-rays taken because I had been feeling twinges of pain around my heart. The results were negative.

Today was Sunday and I had nothing to do. The rest of the unit was occupied with a mission that by some miracle I had been excused from. This meant, that until they returned I would be on night duty. I wish I could have gone along instead! Julius stayed home but then, he rarely went out on account of his leg. We did nothing but sit in the shade and mourn over the past. Evening came and off I went to my shift, taking my monkey along to keep an alert eye while I dozed.

February 22, 1949

The unit was back. The mission had been a futile ramble. All the men were exhausted and barely able to stand. Unfortunately, they would have little time to rest their weary souls because tomorrow we had to escort a caravan to Cao-Bang. The men were so short-tempered that I could hardly say a word.

Julius alone was in good spirits. He was finally permitted to join the convoy tomorrow and looked forward to some excitement after the monotony of his existence. During the night he was forever on guard duty while during the day, with everyone gone, he had little to do but loiter about the yard. Based on my own experiences in the same situation, I suspected how boring his life must be.

February 23, 1949

Damn it anyway, I don't believe it, I was left out of the convoy again! I alone of the entire unit and now with Julius gone, I'll die of boredom and no one will give a hoot. I'll be left to guard the fort by myself tonight, but if all goes well for them, maybe the guys will be back before then.

Evening came but the unit did not. Everything was not going well for them after all. I had no choice but to go to my post. As usual, I leashed my monkey to my doucette and dozed off leaning up against a tree. I woke up to discover my trustworthy monkey was sitting on the gun barrel and sleeping too. I guess this meant that I could no longer rely on this faithful creature to cover for me. Fortunately, I had woken before the change of shift and was not found out.

February 24, 1949

The boys were back before lunch. They could scarely believe that everything had gone so smoothly. It was just my luck to be left at home at a time like this, and to be in the thick of things only when we were up to our necks in a heap of trouble.

I had a good day only because I received a letter from my sister – a letter she had mailed on December 16. We were also given a Hungarian newspaper, *News Journal*, dated last September. It had a confusing account of the Legion, such jumbled nonsense that if those at home read it they would die of fright on the spot. It reported in detail of a "human torment and suffering so great that it defied the imagination," the brutal discipline that went past all belief, the "unavoidable dangers which forever threatened life and defined a hellish existence!" I wrote a letter in response and had it signed by all the Hungarians. I addressed it to Dr. Barankovics and asked that it be published in the editorial pages. I never saw the letter.

February 27, 1949

It was Sunday again. Wonder of wonders, there was no mission to go on, no caravans to escort, and my unit was granted a day of rest. It was about time, after playing the role of the protagonist for so long. It was also about time to nose around Lang-Son a little bit. I talked Joe into coming with me to try and make the acquaintance of ladies. There was absolutely no need to reason with him because when women were the topic, he was blind and deaf.

"Let's take our machine pistols," I suggested. "After all, they look better than those clumsy rifles."

"Don't you have any sense of decency, Scout?" asked Joe, indignantly. "Have you ever seen anyone trying to make friends while sporting a machine pistol?"

"The father of my neighbor's daughter did just that. He went to contact his daughter's suitor, because the lad had committed some grave wrongdoing in connection with the girl. He couldn't find a machine pistol and went searching with a hunting rifle instead. And like I said, a rifle is so much more awkward even if you can fold it in half and hide it under your shirt."

"Don't talk nonsense, Scout. The girls will not even stand to talk to us if they see those weapons."

"So who wants them to stand? I know of many positions that make more sense."

"I thought you said you wanted to meet some decent girls. Those kind of girls will not fall for you, or be taken in, at least not right away."

"You see Joe, now you're talking! You are already able to differentiate between good and not so good girls. Carry on the same way and you just might turn out to be a well-bred legionnaire. And if a machine pistol is too imposing for you, then let's take daggers. We can hide them under our shirts."

Having settled the matter we headed out to conquer the boulevard filled with the greatest of hopes. We had to cross a bridge along the way and as we neared it we saw six loudmouthed youngsters on the other side.

"Hey Joe! Don't you think it would be better to wait until those brats get lost? They're going to lay into us for sure if we go over there, and I see no reason to start a senseless brawl; especially when there are six of them and only two of us."

"Don't be a fool! You want them to see you like this, scared out of your wits?"

I was seething and felt deeply insulted.

"Who's scared? I don't see the point of a useless fight, that's all. Especially now when I'm so eager to hunt for women, reluctant or otherwise! If we pick a quarrel with these guys they'll tear us apart and then what? We can go right back to the fort."

"So what, then we'll go back, but I refuse to just stand here and wait. Besides, if we stop here then they'll know that we aren't crossing over because of them. You want to be ridiculed and laughed at? I don't."

We found ourselves walking straight between the gang, three on either side. And as I predicted, a loud and threatening voice called out before we were even in their midst.

"Hey you, legionnaires! Don't tell me that you came to massacre Vietmins empty-handed!"

"Not exactly, but if you don't shut your face then you're in for a fight," I yelled back. "Who needs weapons? I'll grind you to a pulp with my bare hands."

We were now face-to-face, six to two. Instinct warned us it was time to grip the daggers under our shirts.

Others were coming across the bridge during the commotion and drawn by the violent exchange of words, a well-dressed gentleman stopped beside us and he spoke a few words to the boys and within seconds they had made themselves scarce.

"We're very lucky, Joe. Can you imagine the scene if this chap hadn't interfered?"

Then our advocate said with a grin, "Don't be angry with those kids, they did not mean any harm. They are young and were only playing a joke on you. You know how kids are! They want to be noticed. And now that we are brought together like this, I ask you to honor my modest home with your presence."

To simply turn down his invitation was to gain an eternal enemy, but if we accepted, chances were likely that tonight we would be drifting towards China face down in the river. I summoned my most courteous behavior and told him that we felt deeply privileged by his most gracious invitation but must refuse. So sorry, but we are in a hurry to visit our sick comrades in the hospital. Perhaps we will have the pleasure of meeting again and then, by all means, we will pay our respects. He too was sorry we could not go and expressed his regrets. The customary deep and formal bows were exchanged and then, we were free of our benefactor.

"What a smooth talker you are, Scout! I could hardly keep from laughing."

"So what? The important thing is, that we got rid of him. Hurry up! Let's go find a bistro. I'm hungry and I'm dying for a bottle of ice cold beer."

We found a sidewalk cafe that looked good. We found a table that was somewhat shaded, flagged down a waiter and ordered supper and that much desired beer. Then we waited for good fortune to bring us a few beauties clad in silk kimonos.

We finished the first bottle of beer in one gulp and damn near swallowed the bottle in our urgency. The second and third bottles were drank much slower. We took our time over dinner too, but those ladies holding parasols and clad in white kimonos refused to materialize.

"Look, it's quite obvious that we have nothing to look forward to sitting here. Let's go someplace else."

"Let's go to the park!" he suggested. "Maybe we'll have more luck under the shady trees there. It's no wonder that no one is walking around here in the scorching sun."

The traffic in the park was amazing in comparison to the area around the bistro. Now all we had to do was find the two single women whose one and only desire in the world was to melt in the arms of two such athletic legionnaires as Joe and myself. We walked around trying to spot the two single ladies who were prepared for any and all sacrifices, and who should we bump into but our friend from the bridge. He was walking in the cool shade of the trees with his two daughters, two girls who deserved better fate than this.

"Oh, Monsieur! We meet again! How are your dear friends in the hospital? I hope they will recover soon."

It came as such a surprise that we were left speechless. We had counted on anybody but him. Incoherent though we were, we stammered a thanks for his considerate interest and said that our friends were on the road to recovery and soon to return to the squadron. We were desperate to move on and as a lame excuse to get away said that we did not wish to disturb his dear girls any longer.

"But Monsieur, you are no bother at all," and made the proper introduction. They were quite ordinary looking and not at all like the many beautiful women who graced our past.

Their names were Michelle and Chantal. It was a bit surprising that the girls were christened with French names. Since Chantal was prettier, I quickly jumped to her side. Their father repeated his invitation and now, there was no way we could refuse. We found out that the father was a supporter of the French cause whose schooling had been in Paris. Thus explaining his daughters' names.

We arrived at the gentleman's house, feeling somewhat uneasy. The usual stone wall surrounded the house, in this case with a gate boasting decorative Chinese carvings. I stepped through the gate wondering if I might never come back through it. How was I to know if this Francophile was genuine or not? Well, we shall see. I sincerely hoped that this would not be the last thing to see in my life!

Madam Huan-Ching-lee appeared from behind the house as we neared and when she saw Joe and I she lurched in surprise. Well, I thought, she was obviously prepared for any sort of company today except for legionnaires. She pulled herself together and with a wide smile ushered us into the house. A scattered mixture of French and Chinese furnishings lent a warm atmosphere to Monsieur Huan-Ching-lee's large and comfortable home.

We had barely stepped inside when the two girls vanished, only to return dressed in European attire and holding a chilled bottle of wine and glasses. Those same girls who in the park had stood demurely with downcast eyes, too shy to say a word, had transformed into chatterboxes who would not shut up. Their mother, however, was very disconcerted over our presence.

The father was very friendly, saying that when he saw us by the bridge it was clear that we were not the stereotypical legionnaires whom the people at large wrote off as such. This reassured us. Monsieur Huan-Ching-lee declared that he was decidedly happy to act as our host and that the doors of his home were always open to us. This was the last straw for Madame Huan-Ching-lee who stood up, muttered an excuse and left.

After a delightful afternoon we thought it best to start heading back because for us, darkness and danger went hand in hand. And so we took an affectionate leave from the hospitable father and his daughters, and even in our departure they repeated their open invitation. Only the mother, who reappeared from time-to-time, was noticeably absent during our fond farewells. She had obviously been deeply touched by our white caps and did not wish to express a goodbye of any sort, be it heartfelt or heartless.

March 1, 1949

I have been inhaling this humid, putrid and foul Indochinese air for almost four months now. The fourth month! Many more months had to pass before the ship's bow would cut through the ocean waves in the opposite direction. If I would be on such a ship at all! Chances were slim. This northern part of Indochina, the Route Colonial 4, was the worst. Activity was highly concentrated along this stretch of road and the entire zone between Lang-Son and Cao-Bang was the most vulnerable.

The fact that the Vietmins had received their training in China was becoming evident. Their attacks were carried out with every increasing daring. I would not be too surprised to see them invade this entire frontier zone. It's bound to happen sooner or later, but not for another two years, I hope.

It is pouring and blowing again.

March 6, 1949

Loud voices and the sound of men running woke me up at 6:00. The first unit was preparing for an operation. I had just dozed off again when I heard Mercier's voice over the din of fifty men on the go.

"Unit Two, make preparations!"

Naturally! I don't understand why he waited so long to make the announcement. The world might just collapse in ruin should we be excluded from anything.

We were like a nest of deranged ants bustling back and forth in confusion. Mercier and Charlie pressed us on. I grabbed this and that, then made a sprint for the kitchen before anyone else so that I could at least eat my breakfast in peace.

Mortier's voice stopped me before I was halfway there.

"Scout! You will stay home today."

I was ready to burst on the spot. Just like him, to be so kind as to relay this information after I was out of bed. I made such a rude remark that he turned pale. It took him a while to get over his surprise.

"We'll reckon with that after the operation," he hissed, eyes flashing with rage.

"You would have blown up too if the tables were turned. Why didn't you say something sooner?"

"That is none of your business. But when I come back, you will have your answer!"

I did not mind being left behind after I found out that they had gone to gather the dead from two truck loads of men who were attacked by the Vietmins somewhere along the road to Hanoi. Ironically, they had been going to receive their discharge and now seventeen of those poor boys were permanently discharged.

"Charlie, I had a fight with Sergeant Mortier this morning. Did he say anything to you?"

"Yeah, he said that you ticked him off and he would take the proper measures later."

"Measures? Against who? And speaking of retaliation, I can do just the same if opportunity presents itself."

"Don't you dare say that to him, my friend, or you'll wind up in the penal colony!"

"What do you take me for? Of course I won't tell him that."

"The Sergeant, he wants to talk to ya. He wants you in his office, like right now!" interrupted Gypsy.

Besides Sergeant Mortier, our captain and lieutenant were also there. I had never seen Plessiner look so serious.

Well Scout, I thought, You are about to be hauled over the coals. Mortier has undoubtedly already had his say. Perhaps he even saw fit to blacken my reputation no matter how well we got along in the past.

Plessiner began. "Sergeant Mortier has launched a complaint against you for perpetrating an insult against a superior officer."

Good God! Were they going to be so stuffy about this? It is true that I did not choose my words with care when I expressed an opinion with regards to his dear mother but then he should have known better than to take my words to heart. The matter might have been easily settled eye-to-eye and without any outside interference in a secluded corner of the fort. But what could I do? He chose to select a more effective path to justice. Had I not made reference to his mother with a few simple little words, he might not have made such a great fuss over all this. For me, it was the day after the Fair. And probably much worse!

Our Captain, bless his heart, had enough sympathy to want to hear my side of the story in addition to Mortier's statement. I described, in minute detail, the painstaking efforts and exertion involved in preparing for the mission up to the time Mortier informed me that I had to stay home.

"I would think, that put in the same position, others would have lost their temper too. Who knows? Another man might have given over to an even stronger outburst."

I was terribly apologetic over it and swore up and down that given a similar situation, it would never happen again. Furthermore, I would make every effort to retrieve my honor. Why Sergeant Mortier and I had always understood each other so well and I would be very sorry if our amiable relationship could not be restored.

I was under the distinct impression that my speech had made the desired impact because Plessiner's facial features relaxed, and my sentence was a mere five days in jail. He assured me though, that if something like this ever happened again I would not escape the penal colony.

I came out of the office, went to Mercier and extend my hand as a token of peace. He accepted.

"Sergeant, I am truly sorry for my outburst and I promise you, it will never happen again."

With this peace was restored, and I began my five days of life as a convict.

March 12, 1949

I was restored to liberty, and the first thing I noticed was that my monkey had disappeared. Somebody had restored him to liberty as well! I was not all that broken-hearted over it since the beast had taken to falling asleep on guard duty much sooner than I and I had been forced to keep an eye on him as well.

Bep had carved his niche, and had adjusted to the order and discipline of army life so well that we hardly noticed him anymore. Even the number of fathers had dwindled to almost nothing. Now the poor little boy's problem was that virtually no one paid any attention to him. Almost everyone was sick and tired of fatherhood. There was no one around to even put him to bed at night. Only his puppy remained faithful.

Once in a while one of us tried to teach Bep how to write. The lad was not in the least inclined toward learning and made only minimal progress. If we were going on a mission, however, he was always eager to come along. We tried to explain to him many times why he could not come, but he did not understand this either. I worried about the poor little orphan, but all in all, life was still better for him here than to be pushed around and deserted somewhere.

March 16 – 18, 1949

A thick fog and drizzling rain greeted me upon waking. I was in no mood for breakfast and went back to bed. In weather like this even Plessiner had no desire to loaf around the yard bellowing his orders. He called the platoon leaders to assemble in his office and had his say in there. I lay in bed, stared at the ceiling and listened to the rain against the windowpane. My dreams were cut asunder by a brazen voice.

"Prepare for combat!"

Hmm! This was different. To go now, when it was almost noon? Something extraordinary must have happened. Usually they drag us out before the crack of dawn. We stuffed some food down and were rushing toward Dong-Dang just as fast as the chauffeur's nerves would allow. All indications led us to believe that our chauffeur had nerves of steel. He was driving at 120 kilometres per hour, which on this road was attempted suicide.

We were attacked a few kilometres beyond Dong-Dang, and as usual, we had no idea where the fire was coming from. We jumped to take cover where possible and began blindly shooting among the trees and bushes. Our fire must have been effective because within ten minutes the enemy guns were silent. We continued toward Na-Cham, but less than two kilometres later they raked us again. We had a specific target to aim for only when we were lucky enough to spot a spark of gunfire. We infiltrated the entire area from the base of the bushes to the tops of the trees. It was 8:00 p.m. by the time we arrived in Na-Cham, where we spent the night before going on to That-Khe.

The better part of the journey was spent on foot, and we reached the That-Khe bridge by 5:00 p.m. only to find it blown to bits, and the outpost beside the bridge burned to the ground.

Three thousand Vietmins had raided the guard watch in the early morning. The Vietmins had crossed through China and were able to advance upon the outpost camouflaged by the night. They had cut the radio wires leading to the That-Khe garrison and had linked them to their own. Those in That-Khe who heard the shooting wired the garrison to inquire about the commotion, but it was the Vietmins who responded, saying that everything was in order and the Vietmins had attacked some paratroopers heading this way from Lang-Son. The commanding officers of that garrison were satisfied with this explanation and did not lift a finger to ascertain its validity.

Of the fifty-nine legionnaires, there were fourteen casualties, fourteen were taken prisoner and the rest slain. The entire area was scattered with bodies. Dead Vietmins were hanging from the dense barb wire fence that surrounded the outpost, other bodies were piled among the collapsed and burned buildings.

If not for those attacks yesterday, my unit may have arrived before midnight. A unit of over one hundred men would have made an enormous difference. The Vietmin commander had been well-aware of this. And thus, he ordered a separate detachment out on the road before Na-Cham, so they would slow us down with their attacks. The result was, that he had plenty of time to invade, destroy and retreat from the outpost, all without the risk of interference. The Vietmins knew the strength of the defense and the type of weapons they had. They were aware of the most vulnerable points and knew precisely where to concentrate the bulk of their thrust. Their commander, the "One Armed Colonel," had been best friends with the officers of the That-Khe military station for many years. The offensive forces numbered in the thousands so that the raid could be executed as quickly and successfully as possible. In case the tampering with the radio wires backfired and a relief group from That-Khe came after-all, they wanted to see the plan completed before help arrived.

It was late before we were able to stop and rest. We made the injured as comfortable as we possibly could by putting the seriously wounded on the driver's seats and those with minor injuries underneath the cars to sleep. Guards were doubled and rotated frequently.

We woke during the night to violent shelling. A detail of Vietmins had been left behind and were dropping mines on us. Fortunately, the injured were well-protected and out of range. The rest of us stayed out in the open. We should have had the foresight to entrench ourselves in case the enemy risked another go at us, but since nobody had thought of this, we put our trust in good luck instead. It did not desert us. Not a scratch on any of us. After this not only the guards but almost the entire unit stayed awake. After all, we could sustain another heavy attack any second. Who knows, maybe they had tried to distract our attention from the approaching forces by shelling us with mines.

Morning arrived with the garrison in a state of nervous tension. We cared for our injured to the best of our ability, fed them breakfast, then laid them on the seats and floors of the trucks. We crowded into the remaining empty trucks and headed back for Lang-Son. We left Na-Cham behind and were promptly shot at. It was one shot and not worth stopping for. When we arrived at the fort, the tightly packed men, anxious to get off the truck, prepared to disembark. As the row of men slackened, the lad opposite me toppled forward, and if not for those who caught his fall, he would have landed in my lap.

That solitary shot along the road had caught him in the back of the head. He was unable to fall forward or roll sideways because we were sitting so close. I had noticed his head tilt slightly, but the man beside him had pushed it back, off his shoulder, thinking, as we all did. that the guy had fallen asleep.

March 19, 1949

I spent a restless night and woke up feeling very tired. As was usual after any operation we cleaned all morning and put things in proper order. After dinner, I sought out Joe and tried to talk him into paying Chantal and her family a visit. He did not need much persuading, and just as we were starting off, the order came.

"Prepare for combat!"

We were summoned to rescue a caravan that had been stormed somewhere around Na-Cham.

Within ten minutes we were dashing along the road leading to Dong-Dang. We entered the village and found that the road to Na-Cham had been barricaded, and according to all reports, the area was overrun with Vietmins and to continue on was suicide. Our commander had suicidal tendencies and he ordered the barricades removed and on we went to Na-Cham.

The country on either side of the road was flat and overgrown with bushes, a perfect spot for heavy machine guns to hide. We scanned the landscape for any sort of movement. We fired into the bushs on both sides of the truck, but our efforts yielded nothing. Mercier ordered that we continue on foot. If the Vietmins shot at us, it was less dangerous to be scattered about the road then crammed on a truck.

It must have been his sixth sense warned him because hardly one hundred metres down the road we found a mine that would have blown us to bits. We rendered it harmless and continued. We did not see a single Vietmin, nor were we shot at for the rest of the way.

The caravan was waiting for us when we arrived, and we turned back without resting, again on foot with troops covering the road. The caravan crawled behind us. It was quite annoying, to plod along like this in the dark. Our commander agreed, though it took him awhile, and after walking ten kilometres we boarded the trucks and sped home as fast as possible.

March 20, 1949

It was almost noon when I woke up, and the multi-course dinner reminded me that it was Sunday. Again, I tried to persuade Joe to pay Chantal a visit with me, but this time, he could not be swayed. The week of running around had been enough for him and all he wanted to do was rest.

"Let's go listen to some gypsy music in the canteen."

Nothing came of the singing since somebody had ruined the record player. And since we were in no mood to drink in the absence of music, we went back to our rooms.

"Hey Joe! Charlie! Come on over for a game of cards!" I yelled to their rooms.

"Like hell we wanna play cards!" they yelled back. "Leave us alone to rest. If you are itching to play so badly, then why don't you go bother the Vietmins around Na-Long? Last time you were there about the only thing you managed to exterminate were the ants!"

"I don't think you guys would make fun, or be so lippy, if you had been in my shoes."

"We wouldn't be stupid enough to hide in a rotten tree trunk!"

"Not now," I yelled back, "but if you were surrounded by two hundred Vietmins I bet you'd be desperate to hide. It's easy for you to talk. You weren't in the same fix I was!"

"I would not have been fool enough to volunteer!"

"Of course not, that takes guts! Anyone who shits his pants doesn't belong with volunteers. Are you coming over for a game or not?"

"For the last time, no!"

So nobody wanted to do anything. This made Bep happy, because I played hide and seek with him. Every now and then I tried to teach him how to write. I traced the letters in the sand and instructed him to copy me but it soon became clear that the experiment was a flop. Well, I thought, I was not destined to be a teacher.

After supper I did succeed in gathering the members of the *Devil's Bible Society* together and we banged the tables until 3:00 a.m.

March 22, 1949

It was only the third day with nothing to do and nowhere to go but we were getting restless. Continual marching, constant danger and permanent nervous strain had become a way of life and if nothing happened for two or three days then everyone was unsettled. Our blood was becoming moldy and we needed to go somewhere. I disliked these passive days, a man had nothing to do but lie in bed for hours on end and stare at the ceiling.

This pastime resulted in daydreaming. The leading lady of my dreams was always Eva: Always Eva. She was the first and the last. This vision of loveliness, a beauty whose voice was the music of the heavens, who inherited her milky skin from the snow capped mountains, whose tender brown eyes reflected gentleness. But a dream world, as always, was shattered by the rattle of doucettes. It made me aware that Eva was not here, there were no sparkling brown eyes or gently caressing hands. Reality was tropical jungles and Vietmins. It was not a good idea to stray from reality too often because the return journey became even more painful.

My healing process of visiting the bar was interrupted by a call from the Captain to make myself scarce, because a caravan was to be escorted to Cao-Bang in the morning.

March 23, 1949

It seemed that everyone overslept because the roaring did not begin until 6:00. My section would serve as the advance guard for today's convoy. We would suffer the first attack should the Vietmins be waiting somewhere. We travelled by truck until the Na-Long junction and from there we walked down both sides of the road. We surveyed the area with care, but everything was still.

Our path passed alongside a stunted hill. Facing the road, its side ascended steeply to the height of a man from about two hundred metres from the road to the hilltop. The entire hill was densely overgrown with brushwood. A splendid place from which to mount a powerful surprise attack. We detonated a bomb we had found, and the lieutenant ordered me to take five men and comb the entire hill from base to top.

Spread out over a distance of eight to ten metres and by tracing S-shaped curves along the way, we investigated the whole area and left not a bush untouched. It was the same on the way down. Back on the road I reported to Mercier that we had found nothing and seen no one. I hadn't finished my sentence when a gunner or two from this very same hill shot between us. In our surprise, we did not even know where to hide.

They continued firing at us for about ten minutes which resulted, thank goodness, in only one minor leg wound. When the firing ceased our lieutenant gave the order to storm the hill. We scattered about and charged to the top but there was not a soul in sight. God only knows where they had vanished to.

One of the trucks transported the injured man back to Lang-Son while we continued on.

While crossing a bridge I glanced between the slabs of concrete and noticed a bomb underneath my feet.

"Stop! Take cover!"

Our lieutenant, who was the first to cross over, hurried back and asked me why I was screaming my head off. Was I perhaps trying to get the Vietmins' attention? Still standing on, or rather above, the bomb, I pointed down. Mercier saw the bomb, then grabbed my arm and jerked it so hard that I toppled into the ditch.

"Have you gone mad? Standing there like that when it could go off any second?" he asked.

I was too scared to tell him that fear had made me lose my head and forget to jump.

I was surprised that it had not exploded yet. We looked around the bridge but could not see the mechanism which would set off the explosion when contact was made. We took a closer look at the bomb from underneath the bridge and saw that it needed to be manually detonated. We were extremely fortunate in that one of the wires had slipped out of place, and it couldn't be detonated. To save the Vietmins time and trouble, we detonated it ourselves. We turned back after a few kilometres, met the Arab detail, and informed them that the road was safe.

A few minutes after we had parted ways, the Arabs were invaded in the same area we had just retreated from. We did not understand why the Vietmins had chosen to attack the Arabs instead of us. Less than half an hour ago we had stood on the same spot and not a single shot was fired. How lucky we were!

We continued our journey toward Na-Long but with greater awareness. Mercier ordered the troops to rest after the last truck had disappeared around the corner and told us that we would wait here for the trucks to pick us up. They were due to arrive soon and we may as well rest until then. We had hiked more than twenty kilometres and seeing that we were going back to Lang-Son there was not much point in walking any further. A few minutes later the trucks came into sight and the crackling sound of heavy machine guns broke the silence. The third section had been attacked in the same spot where the Arabs had fought back. We quickly sped back to offer assistance but by the time we arrived the fight was over.

March 25, 1949

What rotten weather again today. The fog touched the ground, the mud was up to our ankles and water dripped off everything. The first unit had gone to Dinh-Lap this morning as a caravan escort, the third unit was in Cao-Bang, and the authorities didn't want the second unit to be bored, so they decided the stairs needed to be fixed. This would amount to about as much as the chicken coop had. Not only was the coop not built, but the grass in the cleared area had grown back even taller than before.

Mortier rushed over around five p.m. and told us to get ready fast, the outpost at Loc-Binh had been attacked and we were needed to take out the wounded. If I had been injured as many times as the number of wounded men I'd collected in the area, our cook could use my body as a flour sifter. Within minutes we snapped up our gear and were rolling toward Loc-Binh. Adieu, stair repair! In Loc-Binh it turned out that the injured men were not in the village, but at the outpost itself which was 12 kilometres away. We had rushed like mad to get here only to have to wait three hours for the wounded men to arrive. It was still better than hauling bricks!

It was past midnight by the time we got back to the fort. Much to the unit's surprise, our captain was waiting up for us with hot coffee and rum. He knew that when we returned we would be cold, wet and grumpy, and was gracious enough to stay up to demonstrate his goodwill.

March 26, 1949

The weather was even more dreadful than yesterday. During supper we were informed that the next few days would be occupied with yet another mission. The Vietmins owned a fort, large enough to warrant serious business and it was our task to secure it on loan.

March 27, 1949

Reveille at 5:00 a.m. As always, everyone was in a sour mood when forced out of bed at this ungodly hour. The reinforcement unit arrived around six and we started for Ban-Xam: the fort we were sent to capture. We covered the final nine kilometres to the fort on foot. Two 105 mm cannon were already firing at the fort from the village to ease our way. The road was unbelievably bad, and I could not believe how quickly I tried. I hoped that there was nothing wrong with me. I had no fever, no feeling of sickness and yet I could hardly take a few steps without having to stop and rest. If this continued I would be hard pressed to drag myself to the fort. I made it even though it was half an hour later than everyone else.

The fort, strengthened by stone walls, was on top of a large hill. From our vantage point it looked like the cannon had not done much damage. After a short conference the Great Chiefs decided that the Arab unit should make the first move against the enemy. The Unit gathered at the foot of the hill to begin their thrust. At about the halfway point, the charge slowed dramatically, one by one they came to a halt and looked at each other. Not a single shot had been fired at them from the fort. The Arabs sauntered through the gates of the fort undisturbed and as soon as they gave the go ahead from the walls, we followed.

For the Vietmins to have surrendered this important fort without putting up a fight was unbelievable, especially when it was stocked with machine guns, small cannons, pistols, automatics, and loads of ammunition.

The Arabs took up position in the fort while we dug foxholes outside the walls. The axe fell. The Vietmins began flinging mines from all sides.

They had walked out and let us walk into a mousetrap where they could make a clean sweep of us. The Vietmin's aim was poor and we were able to finish digging our foxholes. We waited for darkness, built a number of campfires as decoys, and escaped by creeping down the hill on our bellies, leaving the campfire to give the Vietmins something to shoot at. And shoot they did!

March 28, 1949

We waited for the trucks which were due to arrive around noon. When we got home Julius told us that our unit, who else but our unit, would escort a caravan to Cao-Bang in the morning. We had barely arrived home with one and we were off with another! At least we were not bored.

Julius had other news to relay that was far worse. We were not to return to the fort but were to stay in That-Khe where the rest of the squadron would join us later. He could not have greeted us with worse news. That-Khe was the most dangerous place in all of Indochina. Ho-Chi-Minh and General Giap concentrated their most qualified and thoroughly trained, forces in this area. We will be up to our necks in hot water there. All the troubles of the past would be lukewarm in comparison.

March 29, 1949

I managed to weasel my way out of joining the caravan escort by explaining my unusual state of exhaustion near Ban-Xam to the Lieutenant. I requested a visit to the doctor for a checkup. The Lieutenant consented saying that in a few days the entire squadron was going to That-Khe and a few men had to stay behind to pack. The second and third sections were ordered to strengthen the escort. And so, both sections were off to Cao-Bang while I was off to see the doctor.

The doctor did a very thorough examination, and ordered five days of complete bed rest. There was something wrong after all! Doctors were not in the habit of confining legionnaires to their beds for no reason at all. His prescription meant that I was not to get out of bed under any circumstances unless it was absolutely necessary. Hah! Who was he kidding? Right before moving?

March 30, 1949

The customary cool and cloudy weather that never failed to dampen our spirits was the order of the day. The first section departed for That-Khe around noon, barely twenty-five men remained at the fort; I was alone, the only Hungarian. Even Julius had gone. For once I was glad to be on guard duty, it would spare me from gazing into the darkness while lying in bed and waiting for sleep that tonight would no doubt elude me.

March 31, 1949

The first unit returned, bringing with them two wounded men. One shot in the stomach, the other in the thigh. If anyone ever had a run of bad luck, it was these two. Somewhere around Dong-Khe their truck had hit a bump, sent a gun flying from one of the lad's hands, and as he grabbed it, it accidentally discharged and both boys were hit by the one bullet.

April 3, 1949

Confusion and disorder dominated our packing. Everyone rushed from one place to the next accomplishing nothing. Little Bep was packing too, trying to stuff his puppy into a box. The dog, however, was reluctant to take up residence.

April 4, 1949

If anything, the confusion was even greater than yesterday. Everyone was yelling and lugging their loads. The chauffeurs sat idle and bored, and contemplating the panic-stricken and crazed mob before them. Despite the general pandemonium, we were on our way toward That-Khe by 1:00 p.m. Bep was overjoyed. Finally, he was allowed to come with us.

The weather was beautiful. The road was peaceful and calm the entire way, with the exception of one petty attack shortly before That-Khe, but we silenced the Vietmins within half an hour and continued on. The only casulaties were a few of our mattresses.

In That-Khe we were greeted with the comforting news that accommodations were temporarily nonexistent and everyone was to set up their *bedrooms* wherever they pleased. Though half-riddled with bullets I took down my mattress anyway, wanting to furnish my *bedroom* underneath one of the trucks. The rooms, however, were filled to capacity. The most shrewd and practical had hastened under the trucks immediately because each night the Vietmins sounded reveille, and in lieu of alarm clocks, they had a tendency to use large mines.

What a good feeling it was to be greeted with such cheerful news.

To protect myself from the potential shelling, I settled in a depression beside one of the trees that bordered the entrance of our prospective lodgings. The branches, I thought, would cushion the blow of the explosion, should a mine or two drop in, while the depression would do the same with any low flying splinters.

Satisfied with coming up with such a brilliant idea, I slept.

Chapter Ten
That-Khe

April 5, 1949

The promised reveille came as expected. The explosion of the mines woke me from the sweetest of dreams. That-Khe was certainly starting out well. I had no idea what to do. I suppose I should shoot, but which way? No one else had moved so I just laid in my ditch, did nothing and waited for good luck. The three machine guns from the military station nearby started firing. After about ten minutes the fuss was over and we went back to sleep.

It was still dark when the second reveille came. This time, it was not brought on by the Vietmins but by rain and I woke up to the sound of my teeth chattering. The hollow I was lying in had filled with water, my mattress had absorbed it, and as a result, I was soaked from below as well as from above. I crawled out of my "bathtub" and tried to warm up by running in circles. My example was followed by all those who were not lucky enough to find shelter underneath a truck. Thank goodness the trucks had been protected by a canvas covering. We took our baggage down from the truck and changed clothes.

During breakfast we heard the good news from Mortier. This time it really was good news. We had to stay here for three weeks and after that on to Hanoi. Finally, something nice to look forward to: Hanoi! What a promised land it was compared to where we were now. It had been so long that I found it hard to imagine what a large city looked like. We had to get there first, which meant pulling through the next three weeks in order to stay alive. How many of us would be successful?

We moved into our residence after breakfast. The rooms were spacious but with so many men the crowdedness was still too much to bear. Keeping things in order was out of the question. It was a relief to know that we were only staying for three weeks. Under the prevailing conditions we could not possibly stick it out any longer than that.

April 6 – 14, 1949

We walked to the neighboring hills and forests each day so that the Vietmins could not concentrate a strong force on any one place. Seldom did we clash. It was almost as though the enemy were deliberately trying to avoid us; as if some great plot were in the hatching and insignificant collisions were considered a useless waste of time and energy. However, for all their seeming passivity during the day, they more than made up for it at night. In countless places they tore up the roadway and every morning we gathered coolies to repair the damage. This usually took an entire day. Evenings were spent in driving back the Vietmin attacks which consisted of mines thrown from the opposite side of the river.

The goal of the Vietmin's night attacks were not so much to cause physical destruction as to sabotage moral and nerves. We usually arrived back at camp exhausted after a whole day on patrol, wanting to do nothing but rest and gather our strength for the next day. The enemy waited until two or three in the morning, waited until we were in our deepest slumber before shooting and exploding their mines. The attacks never lasted longer than fifteen minutes but this was just long enough to upset our sleep.

April 15, 1949

We received notification of a motorcade leaving Lang-Son, and were detached to safeguard the road. The rain was pouring and we bundled ourselves in tent flaps and paced the road. We found a small bridge that was blown up and a few kilometres later came across a section of road stretching about one hundred metres that was stolen. Literally stolen! The usual practice when ripping apart a road was to cast the excavated asphalt and dirt aside. But this time they had taken it with them. They had cracked the pavement, dug it to the depth of half a metre and had carted it away. This enormous hole had to be closed so the caravan could cross over it. We recruited as many coolies as we could find to haul the dirt from as much as half a kilometre away. They weren't getting very far though because the buckets

*The entrance to our home
in That-Khe*

Main street in the city

Fishing

On road patrol

Our platoon's adopted son, Bep

of rain washed the soil away as soon as they dumped it into the hole. To help overcome this problem we uprooted a bunch of trees, filled the ditch with the tree trunks and branches and scattered the soil on top of that. We toiled, strained and sweated just as hard as the coolies.

There is doubt in my mind that at least 75 percent of these coolies served double time on this ditch. By day they were Vietnamese, but at night they were Vietmins. They dug up the road by night and helped fill it back in by day. In the midst of such hard labor we failed to notice that it had stopped raining. It was thanks to this that the job proceeded much more quickly but quite apart from this, night came and we were still not finished. It was dark already but no excuse to stop working because the caravan could pull in at any time and find itself stuck in mud. The job was done by midnight and the caravan could cross provided that the Vietmins would not steal the road again. We let the coolies go home and hurried to do the same. I dropped into bed fully clothed and was asleep in seconds. Charlie shook me awake a little while later.

"Hey Scout! Your bed is gonna be completely soaked! Here, drink this tin of soup. It will perk you up and give you strength to undress."

I struggled to my feet, thanked Charlie for the soup and drank it. It did not really give me much energy but I painfully peeled the wet clothes off my body anyway and then tipped over into bed. By this time, Charlie had collapsed into bed with his wet clothes on, ignoring his own advice. The mines dropped around two-thirty a.m., but I paid no attention, the machine guns of the garrison took care of silencing the mine throwers.

April 17, 1949: Easter Sunday

Yesterday, Holy Saturday, we mended the blown up bridge and the caravan had yet to arrive. They must be encountering attacks every kilometre along the way.

By some miracle the mining was dispensed with tonight and we were able to sleep through the night. I woke up feeling rested and refreshed. Everyone else was still sleeping. If we were going anywhere today, everyone would have been roused a long time ago. It was a glorious day.

Leaning against a railing in the hallway, I watched the river surge by, and thought of my comrades in Hungary. I wondered if they too would be going to church in their Sunday best or if the Russians had taken these clothes. This of course was assuming that the Russians had been generous enough to spare my comrades. This murdering gang of robbers had promised to endow Hungary with culture and refinement, but they gave only naked lives.

I, however, didn't spare England and the United States my wrath. As far as I was concerned they shared a large part of the blame: "You will pay for this! In time you will be sorry for sacrificing us as prey. For throwing millions of Hungarian men to the Communist bandits. A time will come when you will regret your actions. You will recite words of forgiveness, but it will be too late. You have opened the way for Communism to flourish and sooner or later it will swallow you up. The Good Lord will decide when. It may be ten years, or it may be fifty years, but you will have to face the consequences of your actions and pay a dear price."

April 18, 1949

One year ago today! One year since I met my lover. What a long time, and yet, it feels like only a few days have passed. Does she ever think about that "ugly man"? Does she even vaguely remember the happiness which surrounded our last Easter Monday?

As happy as that was, today was all the more sad. The sun shone warmly, just as it had then. Memories were all that remained of that Easter. The quiet, intimate room, the soothing music, the subtle lighting, the enchanting tango and her sparkling eyes were all remnants of the past.

It was best not to think of what there was instead. The sun set slowly, it was on its way home to Hungary, taking to Her my Easter message of peace and love.

April 19, 1949

Reveille at 5:30, time to go on patrol. We rounded up two dozen coolies to help with road repair. The number of repairs which were needed slowed our progress. We let the coolies go home when we reached That-Khe. We climbed the hill to keep an eye on the road. We spent the entire day perched up there while the caravan, at intervals of a few hours, drove by. Night was approaching, but rather than go back, supper was brought out to us. A section of the caravan lagged behind, and because of them, we were forced to spend the night on the hill. The last section finally sauntered past at 3:00 a.m. and we got to bed by 4:00.

April 25, 1949

The last six days passed in almost the same manner as those before. The difference was that instead of one wake-up call, the Vietmins were sounding reveille two or three times a night. It is useless for me to describe how peaceful our nights were as a result. Rumor has it that we would not go back to Hanoi after all. The commander of the local garrison did not want to let us go because the attacks had all but ceased since our arrival. Good heavens! If what he said were true, what were conditions like before we came? Those who were here before confirmed that only since our arrival have they been able to enjoy a peaceful night's rest.

Today was our turn to repair the road. We gathered the coolies and roamed the long kilometres of the highway only to discover a miracle.

Nowhere was the road torn. We sent the coolies packing and climbed up the hill to secure a vantage point from where we could scan the road. The advance guard appeared around noon, and the caravan was almost past us when all hell broke loose. The Vietmins, hiding in the hills facing Dong-Khe, had waited until most of the caravan had shifted into firing range, and then they had opened fire from all sides. We hastened to assist the others just as fast as we could. We succeeded in running perhaps one kilometre before their shots bogged us down. It was possible to make headway only by creeping and crawling, darting about, and taking cover if we could find it behind trees and bushes. By this time we could see the enemy clearly. There were so many of them!

There was no time to take aim. All we could do was shoot in their general direction. Doucettes, mine throwers and small cannon spread death everywhere. The cars in the caravan ignited one after the other. We tried to force our way through to reach the central point of the attack. The number of defenders had already diminished to half the original number and the cry for assistance was great. The rattle of firearms was deafening. Each section tried to provoke a charge against the enemy but movement of any sort was treacherously difficult on the steep mountainside. We tried to carve a path upwards, while our opponents were shielded and fired at us from the comfort of their trenches. It was thanks to our doucettes and the small cannon on our tanks that we gained ground step-by-step and eventually were able to send the enemy flying.

Every now and then a man senses that the end is near. Never in my life had the wings of death loomed so close.

We collected our dead and wounded. My unit was again the most fortunate with only two minor injuries. The Vietmins had successfully reduced the fifteen cars in the caravan to nothing. I don't know who was responsible for taking the census, but apparently there were two thousand Vietmins in the attack force. I found this hard to believe. Our losses should have been much greater if this were true, but who knows? I had not bothered to count.

Mopping up after the battle was an unpleasant experience. My unit stalked the hillside collecting discarded weapons and injured Vietmins, while the others attended to the needs of our own injured. Drawing upon my limited knowledge in these matters, I attempted to bandage two of them, but by the time I finished with the second I was covered in more blood than they were. When Charlie saw me in this condition he set down to bandage me. It took a lot of convincing to make him believe that I had merely been administering my own version of first aid.

The remainder of the day was taken up with funerals. It was midnight before we got to bed, and in keeping with the norm, two mines were dropped during the night. Heaven forbid that we should spend a night undisturbed!

April 26, 1949

A day of rest.

April 27, 1949

The Vietmins troubled us three times last night and we could not call ourselves particularly well-rested. We had to secure the road Dong-Khe because an Arab contingent was coming up to Cao-Bang. We found the roads in one piece and we reached Dong-Khe without any difficulty. There were no problems on the return trip either. The detachment passed us and shortly after we heard the crackling sound of rifles. By the time we reached the battlefield all was quiet. The outcome was six dead and several injured. We loaded the corpses in our trucks and took them back to That-Khe while the others continued on their way to Cao-Bang.

The remainder of the day was again occupied with burials.

April 28, 1949

The wake-up call came at 5:30. I somehow managed to be excluded from today's road patrol. The Vietmins mined us three times last night and I had hardly slept at all. It was a veritable holiday to be left behind as an observer, and to make the heat more tolerable, I went swimming every hour. According to the thermometer it was thirty-eight degrees in the shade. Now and again the Vietmins saw fit to drop mines, almost all of which landed in the river. The local garrison did not even bother shooting back.

It was late in the afternoon by the time the boys returned. They had not been fired at once all day.

The order during supper was that we were on to Hanoi tomorrow! At long last, a little vacation after five months of harassment. Too impatient to wait until the next day, we spent half the night packing. The Vietmins must have been happy over our impending departure because they called a cease fire and permitted us the luxury of sleeping through the remainder of the night. What the hell was this? Didn't they even want to say good-bye?

April 29, 1949

One would have thought that we had been granted the freedom to return to Europe. Deliverance from this place meant that a great burden was lifted from our hearts and souls. Little Bep, however, stayed behind in the care of the priest. It was best that he stay here in the company of so many children.

We would spend the night in Na-Cham, then on to Lang-Son tomorrow. The Vietmins said their goodbyes here instead of in That-Khe. They threw the odd grenade and shot at us a couple times, but we paid no heed and went all the way to Na-Cham without stopping.

April 30, 1949

The night was very pleasant but it was the elements and not the Vietmins who behaved in a nasty manner. All night we had to contend with pouring rain, windstorms and lightening. In the absence of a military station we were forced to sleep outdoors. The storm subsided by the morning and when we wriggled out from beneath the cars and tent flaps around eight, the sun was shining. It was welcoming the most important feast day for the Legion: Camerone!

To legionnaires, Camerone means what Alamo does to Americans. It was an unforgettable event in the history of the Legion. The French government held a deep interest in the internal affairs of Mexico at the beginning of the nineteenth century. To further French interest, Napolean the Third wanted to institute a Latin empire with Mexico at its centre and weaken the hegemony of the United States. He selected Archduke Maximilian for this purpose, the younger brother of Austrian emperor Franz Joseph. The number of French military forces in Mexico swelled to about 30 000 by 1863. The legionnaire's primary objective was to guard and protect the narrow zone that stretched between Vera Cruz and Puebla. Only by passing through this zone could the reinforcements join the French troops in their assault against Puebla.

The legionnaires were assigned to accompany a caravan, commanded by Captain Saussier, that was transferring a large amount of gold to Puebla. On the afternoon of April 29, an Indian spy in the service of the French, reported to Colonel Pierre Jenningros that a strong Mexican column, led by Colonel Paula Milan, was to attack the convoy somewhere around Soledad and seize the gold. Colonel Jenningros knew that Captain Saussier, with his few troops, was not strong enough to mount a battle, and dispatched the only men he could afford to part with. He sent the Third Company of the First Regiment; half of whom were in the hospital with malaria or yellow fever. Colonel Jenningros' adjutant, Captain Jean Danjou, volunteered to lead the company.

Captain Danjou had a radiant military career. At the battle of Crimea, he lost his left hand while firing a signal pistol which burst. An artificial limb was constructed and he was assigned a desk job. Lieutenant Villain and Lieutenant Maudet volunteered also to serve in the newly appointed officers positions.

Captain Danjou's company, sixty-two men and three officers, began their march on April 30. Captain Saussier greeted Danjou's company when they reached the Paso del Macho (Mule Pass) at 2:00 a.m. Captain Danjou's company marched on from here to safeguard the road for the gold. Around nine a.m. Captain Danjou's company reached the uninhabited settlement of Camerone. The legionnaires plodded on to Palo Verde without stopping.

The terrain around Palo Verde was level and offered no natural shelter. A small group of guerillas would be ample to finish the company. Despite this, Captain Danjou ordered a rest and coffee. Minutes later, a lookout signalled the approach of a score of Mexican cavalry. Captain Danjou glanced toward the skyline and yelled, "Aux Arms!"

The company doubled back toward Camerone, wanting to counter the attack from the hacienda buildings. There was no time for the legionnaires to split among the buildings, instead they formed a square and waited for the attack. The Mexican cavalry's first charge was defeated.

The mules became frightened during the attack and fled, thus leaving the legionnaires without food or water.

Danjou's company hurried to disperse among the buildings, intent upon holding back further attacks until Captain Saussier and his relief troops arrived. The Mexicans, however, had beaten them to the hacienda and occupied the main building. All that remained for the legionnaires were half-collapsed buildings and a yard enclosed by a hole-poked wall of stone. The group sergeant, from his perch on an intact section of roof, informed Captain Danjou that the Mexican calvary was standing ready to attack from all sides.

It was 9:30 a.m.

One of the Mexicans separated from the calvary line and waved a white truce flag. He called to the Sergeant on the roof, and relayed Colonel Milan's appeal to surrender. The legionnaires were greatly outnumbered and Colonel Milan wanted to avoid needless bloodshed, "If you surrender, Colonel Milan promises to spare your lives."

The Sergeant passed on the message to Captain Danjou, "We'll die before surrendering!"

The Mexican captain dropped the truce flag – a signal to start the attack. The cavalry stormed, but the legionnaires picked them off by the dozens.

In the blistering heat, thirst was beginning to take its toll. The mules had fled during the first attack, thus leaving the legionnaires without food and water. Danjou asked for his wine and gave each man a sip while making them swear an oath to die rather than surrender.

Captain Danjou died at 11:00 a.m. He had tried to cross the yard and in his attempt to reach the barricade he was gunned down by the Mexicans. One of the lieutenants rushed to his assistance but it was too late. Out of sixty-five men, there were only forty left.

For the second time Colonel Milan offered terms of surrender. For the second time he was refused.

At midday a long bugle call and drums sounded.

"It's Saussier!" yelled the lieutenant who had taken over command. "Finally! Help is on its way!"

"That's not Saussier," replied the company's drummer. "They're Mexican drums."

The Sergeant from his place on the roof confirmed this, and informed his commander that he saw more than one thousand Mexican infantrymen lined up behind the cavalry.

For the third time Colonel Milan offered surrender terms and again they were refused.

The infantrymen attacked and within the hour, a dozen more legionnaires lay dead or wounded.

The heat suffocated the legionnaires to the point of madness. The sun reflected off the white walls of the courtyard seared their eyes, while their tongues were swollen from thirst. When they opened their mouths to breathe they seemed to inhale fire. They watched as the bodies of the men who had fallen decomposed before them. The Mexican wounded cursed and pleaded for water, but the wounded legionnaires lay silent, not wanting to betray the number of losses. They licked each other's blood or sucked it from their own wounds to blunt their thirst.

Captain Danjou's replacement was killed. The lieutenant in command reminded the handful of able men of their oath to Captain Danjou. Yes, they remembered, but how much longer could they stand it? One of the corporals was holding the northern gate alone. His face, black from gunpowder, his eyes, bloodshot. He and the others counted their last cartridges.

Another Mexican charge carried away most of the last defenders. Corporal Maine lay under the sergeant who had been on the roof.

"The Sergeant is dead," he croaked to his commander.

"Soon it'll be our turn," was the reply.

There were five men left of the company against almost seventeen hundred.

Corporal Maine searched the sergeant's pockets for ammunition. He found two.

Another rush forced the five able legionnaires to retreat behind the stable doors. Mexican infantrymen by the hundreds stood a few steps away.

"Charge your rifles," ordered the commander. "Fire on my command, then we will charge."

He gave the command. A burst of Mexican fire, and at that moment one of the legionnaires threw himself in front of his commander, but the sacrifice was in vain for seconds later he too was riddled with bullets.

By some miracle Corporal Maine, Legionnaire Constantin and Legionnaire Wenzel were still standing with bayonets levelled at the enemy. It would have been a mere formality on the part of the enemy to dispense with them on the spot, but the expected fire did not come. The line opened, and a Mexican officer of French origin stepped forward.

"Gentlemen, I trust you will surrender now."

"Only," replied Corporal Maine in Spanish, "if you leave us our arms and allow us to look after our wounded."

"Speak French," warned the officer. "If my men hear you speaking Spanish, they will think you're Spanish and kill you."

He led the three legionnaires to Colonel Milan who, when he saw them, was astonished.

"Where are the rest?"

"There aren't any more!"

"This is it? This is what we fought against? They're devils!" yelled the angry Colonel Milan.

The battle had lasted nine hours. Nine hours, with sixty-five men against two thousand.

Thirty-one men died in the hacienda. The last lieutenant in command died from his injuries in a military hospital several days later. Even though Colonel Milan treated the wounded legionnaires like heros, few survived their exposure to the grilling sun. Through the self-sacrificing heroism of these sixty-five men, the gold carrying convoy reached Puebla safely.

When the dead were being gathered, Captain Danjou's wooden hand was found. It has become a symbol of devotion, dedication, honor and heroism. It is the most precious relic of the French Foreign Legion and is guarded in the Legion museum. These sixty-five men, obscure to most, remain alive in the hearts of legionnaires.

My company paid homage to this historic event after our arrival in Lang-Son. While the company drank, I paid homage to my deceased grandmother. When I arrived at camp a letter from home told of this sad news. The company enjoyed a twelve-course dinner followed by wine, and its effects apparent within a matters of hours. The carousing finished late at night and all was quiet. I was on guard duty, for hardly a man besides myself was able to stand. I was patrolling the area when the light filtering from a window illuminated an object on the ground. I picked it up and discovered it was a weighty gold bracelet. I wondered which prostitute had lost it.

If the Vietmins chose to attack now, half a unit could easily liquidate our entire company without sustaining serious losses themselves. That unseen power stretched a protective hand over us.

May 1, 1949

The company was not quite cured of the ill-effects from yesterday's partying. The men were slow and hung over. Served them right, and no matter how hard it was for them now, they should have put more effort into being up and about sooner. The authorities beat some life into the still bodies in no time and soon after breakfast we departed for Tien-Yen. From there a ship would take us to Haiphong, then a train to Hanoi.

Lang-Son, then Loc-Binh, Na-Ba and Dinh-Lap, were all names I hoped I was seeing for the last time. I remembered the many missions I took part in along here, the week long roving through the jungle, the gathering of wounded or dead bodies. Here I was, in good health and sound mind having lived through it all. It was a good feeling.

The rain had damaged the road, and we could advance only at a snail's pace for kilometres on end. All eyes watched the forest alert for any suspicious movement that would force us from the trucks with lightening speed. We pulled into Tien-Yen at 5:00 p.m. We did not spend time in the city but headed straight for the harbor, where we would await the ship's arrival.

The gulf was beautiful, but the harbor itself was wretched. A makeshift wooden pier, a tall house made of adobe and the few bamboo huts were a stark contrast to the surrounding scenic beauty. Further down the road were two brick buildings – our accommodations. What a beautiful place this could be if somebody cared. The billions of mosquitos posed the only problem. We were given some oily concoction blended with alcohol to use as a repellent. It worked. Even the flies took the long way around.

May 6, 1949

The ship finally arrived today. We had been here for five days, five very boring days. Nothing to do but swim or play cards, and I had to stop the cards after three days and half my monthly salary. I wanted to round up some fishing equipment but the native population, all of ten people, were so unfriendly that I surrendered all hopes of fishing.

Our ship left the harbor early this morning. I could hardly wait to reach an open sea that would spell freedom from the swarms of mosquitoes.

A considerable storm hit us just as we left the Gulf of Tonkin. Our fragile ship was bounced in the enormous waves. It was the first time I was in a storm at sea and it had to be on a light boat. Men by the dozen fell prey to seasickness. It was not so much the surge of the sea that turned my stomach as the green and yellow faces leaning over the railing. I fought my way through several dozen retching passengers and found a place of refuge in the bow of the ship. Here, I was more conscious of the dancing than anywhere else on board, but it was still better to watch the combing waves, once high above and in an instant fat below, than a sick assembly.

We dropped anchor by a summer resort in the late afternoon. We would spend the night on land while the natives would spend theirs on the ship. The moon was rising, tracing a thin silvery bridge on the softly rippling deep blue sea.

Charlie's voice startled me from my daydream,

"Hey Scout! Let's go eat some oysters."

"Oysters? Here? Where the hell do you intend to buy oysters? There's not a store in sight."

"Oh come on, who needs a store? We'll hire a couple of kids and they'll bring some up from the ocean floor."

"How the hell would you know if they are there or not?"

"Don't bother yourself over it. Come on! Let's see who can eat the most. Here, I brought a couple of lemons from the canteen. Fresh oysters with lemon! You've never tasted anything more delicious."

We hired a couple of kids to bring up the shells for one piaster – two cents, per dive. I decided after one taste that plum dumplings and cream cheese crepes were ever so much better, but I bravely swallowed the slimy little monsters because my pride would not allow Charlie to get the better of me. Charlie did not get the better of me, but the oysters did. I think I was on my twentieth oyster when my stomach gave out. I had ridden out the storm on the boat without encountering difficulties, and here I was, done in by a bunch of oysters. To this day I have not reconciled with seafood of any sort, even the smell of it runs my stomach.

May 7, 1949

It was a beautiful, mild and refreshing sun drenched morning. It was still early and everyone was still sound asleep. In the two hours until departure I could swim to my heart's content. The cool and crisp water revived me and by the time the breakfast gong sounded I felt like a new man.

A quick breakfast, departure at 6:30 and arrival in Haiphong by 3:30 p.m. I could hardly wait to settle into our accommodations so I could do the town. I wanted to squeeze all the sights, sounds and social activities a big city had to offer, all the things I had sorely missed over the long dreary months into the few hours we had.

Haiphong was huge after the isolated fort in Lang-Son. I wandered aimlessly for quite some time, lost among scores of buildings. After the marshes, the rice paddies, the wild jungles and towering mountains, I was at long last surrounded by life. The first bistro I strayed into proved to be an ideal pick-up joint. My head was swimming from all the whirling commotion of life in the big city, not to mention the eyes of my companion.

May 8, 1949

I was barely rested after last night's sporting, but we had to be up and about by six to prepare for the trip to Hanoi. The train departed at 11:00, and made its way along the same track where last November a bomb had terrorized us. The ancient locomotive limped along as if afraid that this journey might be its last. The houses of Haiphong fell behind and rice paddies took their place.

I went out on the platform and before my eyes the tragedy of last November 15 was re-lived. I stood there, holding my breath, would it happen again? As we left the tragic site behind, unharmed, tension dissolved and I sighed a giant breath of relief.

Cao Bang
That-Khe • Dong-Khe
Dong Dang • •Na-Sam
Lang-Son •

HANOI
Gia-Lam • Haiphong
Do-Son

NORTH
VIETNAM

Tourane

SOUTH
VIETNAM

Dalat •

SAIGON

Chapter Eleven
Hanoi

May 8, 1949

The journey ended in the late afternoon, and it was midnight before everyone had finished unloading, unpacking and putting things in order.

Sleep was impossible, as it was hotter here than up north. I lay in bed motionless, yet drenched in sweat. Fortunately, there was a large lake behind the garrison, a sanctuary that promised solace from the heat.

May 10, 1949

Yesterday, I sought out my friends who I had parted from last December and not heard of since. Leo, alias Fetus, was working in a clinic, and had been awarded the rank of corporal. Walter was doing his bit in the company. Both were in good spirits, not something one would expect from someone in the Legion. What they knew of the north was hearsay. Lang-Son, That-Khe and Cao-Bang were names to them, nothing more. They hardly ever went on an operation. We talked for hours and the stories they told of Hanoi were dazzling. Excellent bistros, elegant dancing saloons and women who did not close their eyes. Another Hungarian, Steve Bidon, joined the fun. He was powerfully built with curly black hair and brown eyes, a lieutenant who had graduated from the Ludovika Hungarian Military Academy prior to 1945. He too donated his bit in depicting the trappings and glitter of Hanoi.

A theatre in Hanoi

A nightclub on the lake

A view of the city

The Hanoi Cathedral

Walkway on the lakeshore

A fisherman's boat is moored on the Red River. The bridge linking Gia-lam and Hanoi can be seen in the background.

May 11, 1949

Each day started with morning exercise.

The days were incredibly boring. We worked for five hours, meaning those who were assigned duties, slept through ten and with the remaining nine we didn't know what to do. This latter applied especially to me because I did not have a blessed piaster to my name and payday was a long way away still. The lovely bistros and elegant dance halls and what was most painful, the ladies all meandered in the nebulous future.

We were given two new suits of clothing. What the hell for? We had more clothes than we knew what to do with. I wish they would at least take back a few of the old ones.

May 12, 1949

The silly morning exercise, breakfast then two hours on watch. By 10:00 a.m. the heat was so intense that sweat streamed down my body. Standing idle was no avail and the guardhouse was not shaded. My clothes could stand wringing out from the moisture after ten minutes of just standing. How long will it take me to get used to this heat? The climate up north was downright pleasant compared to this. Maybe we should go back!?

Change of guard at 10:00, and at half-hour intervals from then on. I went up to my room to change clothes, put on a pair of sweat pants, then fell into bed and a deep sleep. I woke in the late afternoon, or rather, was woken by Alex who wanted to go fishing.

"Are you crazy? Beating me out of bed like this for such nonsense? Where on earth do you expect to go fishing and where did you buy fishing gear from?"

"Who the hell needs gear? We'll adopt the Legion's way of fishing. I have two hand grenades, and the lake behind the garrison is teeming with fish."

"But you know I detest water creatures of any kind. I'm not going to fish and I most certainly won't eat fish."

"Who the hell wants to eat that smelly stuff? I'm not that stupid."

"For Christ's sakes then, what's the point of going fishing?"

"Just for something to do. I'm turning green from all this vegetating."

"Come to think of it, you do look a bit like bald parsley!"

We went fishing with hand grenades. Dead fish by the dozen rose to the surface and that's exactly where they stayed. We had no intention of picking them up. What the hell could we do with all those fish? If we carted them to the kitchen the cook would boot us out so that we would land in Saigon.

May 14, 1949

In my attempt to relieve the monotony of the idle afternoon, I sat down to write letters. I was stuck and having a tough time putting together a complete sentence, when Alex charged into the room wanting to disclose some sensational news of supposedly worldwide interest.

"You don't have to break out in such a fit over a news release! Can't you see that I'm trying to write? I can hardly string a sentence together as it is, without you breaking in on me like this."

"But Scout, this is truly sensational! You've never heard anything like it before."

"Probably not, if it's some piece of rank stupidity that you cooked up."

"But listen! This is so incredible, it can't be true!"

"If it's not true, then I don't want to hear about it. Go away and let me finish this letter."

"Can't you hear what I'm saying? You're always interrupting. I told you, I heard something that will bowl you over!"

"Alex! I have no intention of bowling over. Either tell me this sensational bit of news or go to hell."

"There you go interrupting again! At least let me try."

"Okay, okay, I'm listening, just tell me! I can't get rid of you until you do anyway."

"There's a bistro not too far from here where only legionnaire's are allowed in. What a bistro! And do you believe this? Apparently, you don't have to pay a cent for anything. I heard that you only have to pay the first time you go and after that, they will take your credit and you can eat and drink to your heart's content and pay later when you have the money."

"Alex, have you gone completely mad? Can you imagine any manager fool enough to make an offer like that? To feed just anybody and give drinks out for free? Who fed you this nonsense?"

"My friend, that's not all! The best part is yet to come. Are you ready for this?"

"I'm ready, I'm hanging on to my chair, just say it!"

"The waitresses, my friend! They wear see through silk kimonos with nothing underneath! Do you get the idea? Nothing!"

"I understand, Alex. Now you just trot yourself down to the infirmary, ask the doctor for a strong sedative and tell him to examine your head. I think you're suffering from sunstroke."

"You doubting Thomas you! I swear what I've said is true. This is the way it really is. We're gonna go there tonight. I've talked to Julius and Joe, and they're coming too."

"Okay Alex, I'll join you. But be forewarned, if you let me down, if all this turns out to be nothing but a bunch of baloney, then so help me God, I will beat the living daylights out of you. And by the way, I can only go if you guys pay my share. Sorry, but I'm flat broke."

"We have one hundred piasters between the three of us. More than enough. My friend, they're not wearing a stitch! It's driving me wild just thinking about it."

"You can rave as much as you want to Alex, but do me a favor and trot your ecstatic ass out of here and into the yard so I can finish my stupid letter."

We skipped supper in the mess hall so we could eat in this legionnaire's paradise. I conjured up a bistro as portrayed by Leo and Walter, with a plush interior and many other allurements. Mirrors all over the place, couches you could sink into, wall to wall carpeting, and of course, the charmingly naked waitresses. Needless to say, I was itching to get there as fast as possible.

It was obvious that Alex had made certain of getting very specific directions because in less than ten minutes there we were, standing outside the door. Its exterior appearance was shabby enough, but inside? Mirrors? Carpets? Couches? No. We found a tiny hole-in-the-wall that had not been cleaned for God only knows how long. And the plush furnishings? Three coarse plank tables, wobbly chairs that looked like they would fall apart any minute, and an improvised bar.

I turned to Alex, "What kind of place is this? Is this what you were referring to when you said 'What a bistro'?"

"Hey Alex, has your face ever been smashed in before?" Julius inquired.

Joe's voice was stone cold, yet quietly threatening. "Wait 'till I get my hands on you. You'll be a dead man before I'm through," he promised.

At this we turned away, wanting to desert this legionnaire's paradise, but then out stepped the waitress and we changed our minds. We stood on the rough plank floor as though our feet had suddenly sprouted roots, and stared at the presence of this miracle standing in the semi-darkness of the open doorway. Under the subdued lighting, her snow white kimono was inticing, and under the transparent silks, nothing. I'm sure that the expression on our faces must have been idiotic because she started to laugh. This brought us to our senses and with the greatest of joy we ascertained that this white kimono clad figure was not illusion.

"Come! I'll bring you a bottle of wine and while you're sipping it, I'll fix your supper."

She put her arms around Joe and Julius and led them to a table. Alex and I stood-by in a fit of jealousy because it was they and not us she was embracing. The bistro looked a lot prettier now, and by the time we were seated, wild horses couldn't have dragged us away.

Alex could not stand it any longer and his hand started for the girl's chest. However, before his hand had a chance to reach its intended target, Julius gave him a generous kick. It's not as if Julius was objecting to Alex's not so innocent advances on the grounds of his own pure and holy moral principles, it's just that he had already singled out those particular specimens for himself and was not about to relinquish them to anyone.

"Keep your hands to yourself, Alex," he warned, "or with one kick, I'll send you flying right back to the garrison."

"To hell with you! I don't believe it. Don't forget that it's thanks to me you're here in the first place! You see, Scout? Welcome the Slovak into your house, and he'll forget your kindness and drive you from your home! I pick the chestnuts and he wants to eat them!"

Alex was absolutely right, but principles of fairness did not matter here. The shrewd took what they could get while arrogant bastards were booted in the shins.

The waitress had extracted herself from the grip of Alex's hands which adhered to her like those of an octopus, and disappeared through the door. She reappeared in less than a minute with our bottles of wine, then disappeared again. Our throats were parched after the flurry of excitement and we gulped the wine.

"You guys realize of course," I said, "that we have a serious problem on our hands – four of us and only one of her. We're gonna have to come up with some kind of solution. After all, no use killing each other over a woman. I think Alex should have more rights to her than the rest of us. After all, he discovered this place. He is the captain and we are only the crew. So tonight, I propose that she be his and tomorrow we will draw lots. It goes without saying that we will frequent this place from now on. Especially since we don't even have to pay the second time around."

"There you go! Scout is the only one thinking fairly," replied Alex, bubbling with enthusiasm. "He is a gentleman. He has some sense of decency, not like the rest of you!"

"Let's drink to it, Scout!"

Julius swelled with anger. "Not so fast. I have just as much right to that woman as Alex does."

"Settle down!" yelled Alex. "Scout had the final say, so let's just leave it at that."

Not to be left out, Joe barked. "What about me? What do I get out of this? You guys are acting as if I'm not even here. You're making all the decisions just between the two of you. I'll have you know that I have just as much right to her as the rest of you!"

I slammed my fist down on the table and said, "You don't have to scream like that. You're gonna scare her away and then none of us will have her today or the next day."

At this they calmed down a bit, but the arguing persisted. It was finally decided that Alex had priority after all. Just then the waitress appeared balancing our dinner trays on her hands. We just about fell off our chairs because behind her was another who, like the first, was almost naked.

We had not counted on this. Now we were really in a bind. How was a man expected to share one woman with three others? It had taken all that bickering just to arrive at a compromise and now here we were facing another dilemma. How were four men supposed to share two women? For starters, by going right back to the drawing board to try and settle the dispute all over again.

The waitresses placed the dishes on the table and served the food, none too anxious to keep a respectable distance from us while doing so. On the contrary, they desired, and inspired, physical contact. No man in his right mind could rebuff such an overt come-on, not even a tough and hardened legionnaire. Strength and resolve melted, and nothing that was pure or virtuous mattered any longer. We were about to stray and willingly, even if our corrupt deeds gave rise to the fall of Hanoi.

Hands went into action. That they were met with no resistance came as little surprise. One of the girls settled into my lap. How stupid of me not to raise any objections in the face of such blatant indiscretion, but what the hell, I forgot. The delicate scent of her hair acted like an aphrodisiac that gave birth to amnesia. Supper too, was the last thing on my mind. Her full breasts were like golden apples that crushed against her blouse in a manner that was undeniably provocative. It was impossible to pass up a thorough investigation of their firmness, especially when they were damn near being served on a silver platter. Under these circumstances, not to have done so would have qualified me as the world's greatest Ass.

This pleasant state of affairs did not last long. With a friendly smile the girls got up and left saying, that if they lingered over us we would never get around to eating our supper. I tried to convince them to stay by saying we were very clever legionnaires who could eat with only one hand. They, however, were not inclined to concur and disappeared through the doorway.

Supper was cold by now but we ate it anyway. I was the first to sample a large mouthful of the salad and found that the cook had killed it with an atrocious vinegar dressing. Alex had a nibble of it too, despite my warning to stay away. We ordered two more bottles of wine, which were brought in a hurry and just as quickly, the waitress made a race for the door.

We frequently glanced in the direction of the door, wondering when those white kimonos would reappear, but it was all for nothing. My patience spent, I went in hot pursuit but found a Methuselah instead. She informed us that the girls had been suddenly called away.

We were dumbfounded. Our brilliant plans for a jolly evening went up in a puff of smoke. We broke into a torrent of abuse and showered the sneaky waitresses with every imaginable profanity. Furious, we drained the leftover wine and made a hasty exit while the crone sneered with malicious joy over our misfortune. In our rage we forgot to pay the bill, but who cares? Served them right, firing up a man like that and then pulling the rug from under his feet. The nerve!

It was 9:00 by the time we got back to the garrison and 10:00 before we got to bed, still rabid over the ruined evening. I fell asleep determined that tomorrow I would not let the woman out of my clutches or out of my sight. They would not make fools out of us again, that's for sure!

During the night I was woken by an excruciating pain. I was crawling the walls in agony. The sensation was as though several dozen starved cats were slashing at the lining of my stomach.

That's the last thing I remember before I dropped into a coma.

When I came to, I vaguely recall squid-like tentacles pointed my way. As my vision sharpened the tentacles became a nurse straining to change me into a pair of dry pyjamas.

"How do you feel, Scout?" asked the nurse after she saw that I had revived. "Does your stomach still hurt?"

"My stomach? Why would it hurt? Oh yeah, now I remember, yesterday I woke up with horrible stomach cramps."

"I hate to tell you this, but that yesterday was eight days ago."

"What do you mean, eight days ago?"

"You've been in the hospital for eight days."

"I've been here for eight days? You're kidding! What happened?"

"You were poisoned. Do you remember having supper in a Chinese bistro?"

"Sure! With Julius, Alex and Joe."

And then it all started coming back. The bistro, the two women and that awful salad. So that's why it tasted so bad. There was poison mixed in with the vinegar. But Alex ate some of it too. He should be in here with me.

"But Alex Bofort also ate some of that salad. Can you tell me where he is?"

"He went back to the garrison four days ago. He was luckier than you because he only had a small taste. And lucky for you that you didn't eat more. As it is, we didn't think you'd pull through. Thank goodness your stomach was pumped at the garrison. I think that's what saved you. You must feel very tired. You were just about a goner. On top of everything else, you suffered bouts of fever that are symptomatic of malaria. But don't worry. The worst is over and in a few days you can go back to the garrison."

The fever was burning and I felt completely exhausted. I could hardly move, and the way I felt, it would be more like a few months before I returned to the garrison.

May 24 - 26, 1949

I woke up much more refreshed and alive than yesterday. Outside the sun was shining and if my condition would have permitted it I would have been out there walking. I just had to get myself together that's all. The nurses were certainly making sure of that. They wanted to see me whole again as soon as possible, and to that end were stuffing me with food and pills. Every night they gave me injections that ensured a deep peaceful sleep.

May 27, 1949

I was gaining strength by the hour and the doctor gave me the good news, I would be free to go back to my unit the following day. It was a beautiful morning. Outside the hallway window the palms were gently swaying, bird song and the sweet fragrance of flowers filled the air, and I had come within a hair of leaving it all behind.

Those two waitresses had tricked us but good. Who is to know how many naive legionnaires they have sacrificed already? Those two sluts selected the deadliest and most persuasive bait possible: themselves. Receive the victim half-naked, sit in his lap, let his hand wander freely and while he is eating poison laced food, slip out the back door.

I wonder what happened to them? Were they caught? If so, I sincerely hope that they are fed a few spoonfuls of their own poison.

May 28, 1949

One last physical examination this morning, and the doctor concluded that further treatment was not necessary. The sentence was declared, but there was one problem. He had not consulted with me. Obviously, how I was feeling did not carry any weight. If the decision had been left up to me, I would have gladly stayed on as a guest to be entertained by the nurses for another month. My word did not count and after dinner the hospital gates closed behind me. The garrison was quite a ways from Lanessan Hospital, and I had no idea how I would make it on foot. By the time I reached Rue Paul Bert, a main street in Hanoi, I had to stop and rest. A coffee house terrace would be ideally suited for this purpose, a place where I could sip iced tea and watch the early afternoon traffic.

With the help of frequent stops for iced tea I made it back to the garrison, only to find that everyone was in a terrible mood. They were packing up for our move to Gia-Lam. Just what I needed in my present condition. I had a slight fever and it was very hot, at least the trees offered some shelter from the scorching rays of the sun. There were practically no trees at all in Gia-Lam, and the lakes were hotter than hell. But no matter how unpleasant the climate, anything was better than That-Khe.

During our miserable existence up north our dream of dreams was to go to Hanoi, and now everybody was upset because we had to go to Gia-Lam – only a skip across the river. We should thank our lucky stars instead of bitching and complaining. Crawling through jungles and over mountains day after day, worrying over potential enemy attacks around every corner, the thought of a nice and relaxing summer holiday in Gia-Lam was heaven by comparison. By the time I reported my arrival at the office, Gia-Lam seemed so promising that I was in good-spirits. I reported to Mercier, went to my room and found the Hungarians gathered there. They were lashing out at the higher authorities for forcing them to move again, and were not being particularly selective in their language.

"Scout is here!" shouted Joe upon seeing me. "Nice to see you alive. We thought you were going to kick the bucket for sure."

"You're just in time!" shouted Charlie. "Start packing. We're moving to Gia-Lam."

"So I hear. But what's with you guys? There's lots of time to pack, we're not going for another three or four days. And what the hell are you doing in my room? Can't you hold a meeting in your own? All right you bums, get the hell out of here. I'm really tired and I'd like to lie down."

"Get yourself together, old chap. It's not quite that simple. We're going jumping before moving on to Gia-Lam."

"Well you guys go right ahead. There's no way they can make me go. I'm so weak that I can hardly crawl out of bed. Jumping? Hah! Hey Alex, we were hard done by those two women, eh? I even caught malaria."

"They dealt you guys a low hand, that's for sure. If it's any consulation they'll never poison anyone again. You can bet your bottom dollar on it."

"Charlie, if you mention poison one more time, I'll kick you all the way to the moon."

"I suggest you gather strength to stand up straight before you try kicking anyone around."

"So what happened to those two sluts anyway? Were they caught?"

"You bet. That night when you and Alex were howling like jackals, I told the doctor where you had been that evening. A whole squad went over there and settled them for good. All three of them. I was there, and we made mincemeat of the place. Then we threw all their crap into the yard and burned it. So long as I live, that'll never be a bistro again."

"Yeah, maybe not there, but some place else. You really think the Vietmins will give up their battle against us? No way. They'll think of something else to use, some other way besides poisoning."

"Alex, who suggested that place to you?"

"One of the partisans. May he rot in hell where ever he is. I've been looking for him ever since I got out of the hospital, but I haven't been able to track him down."

"Of course not, what do you expect? You don't really think he's hanging around waiting for us to grab him by the collar, now do you? And I just can't understand the stupidity of those women, for sleeping at the bistro. Didn't it occur to them that they might be found out?"

"Remember the old saying, 'the pitcher goes so often to the well that at last it breaks.' A thief will be a thief until caught. So will a murderer."

"It broke a little too late, don't you think? They must have poisoned a good many legionnaires before their 'pitcher broke'."

"All right you guys, enough. No use talking about it any more. Go away and leave me alone now. I'm really tired and I have to get some rest."

"Alex!" I called after them. "Would you do me a favor and bring me up my supper?"

"Sure. Just get some sleep and don't worry, I'll wake you up," answered Charlie.

"Why you? Scout asked me to do it, not you," said Alex.

"So both of you can bring it up," I retorted as exhaustion forced me to sleep.

I slept until an unshaven character poked his head through the doorway the next morning to say I had ten minutes to boot myself out of bed and hurry down to the yard for morning exercise.

By now I was conscious of where I was. I crawled out of bed while using a couple of expletives, and pulled on some sweat pants. When a man was granted a few days rest here, he is also excused from physical activity. I thought it habit forming. No, I dressed in order to find Charlie and Alex to offer my profound thanks for their most charitable kindness of forgetting my supper tray. I found Charlie racing down the hallway, eager to get to exercise hour.

"Thanks a lot, Charlie. I can really count on you. If you can't trust your friends, who can you trust?"

"But I swear upon your dear mother's health that we brought you the tray! Just ask Alex. My dear chap, you were sleeping so deeply that we didn't have the heart to wake you up. We were acting in you best interest. You didn't get any supper because of our kindness, not in spite of it. Besides, you wouldn't have wanted it anyway. It was just some measly old roast chicken with roast potatoes and cucumber salad."

"I wish you would have choked on it! I have no doubt that you guys ate my share. And then, you can try swearing upon your own mother's health, then maybe I'll believe half of that ridiculous story you hatched."

"My friend, don't you believe me? You must! You know me better than that."

"That's exactly why I don't believe a word you say, 'friend'!"

"Well friend, must run now. Mortier will skin me alive if I'm late for exercise. That the devil may take that idiot who thought of this idea!" he yelled back.

I think I'll go down to the kitchen for a little private breakfast while those fools are breaking their backs. Maybe the cook is in a good mood and won't boot me out. I'm famished. I haven't eaten anything since noon yesterday, thanks to Charlie and Alex. My fever is making me feel dizzy and my hunger is making me feel giddy. I was out of luck. The cook must have gotten up on the wrong side of the bed this morning because I hardly stepped inside and I was out the door.

The office messenger called me in the afternoon and said that I was to go to the office right away. Plessiner wanted to see me.

I wonder what he wants? Oh yes. It was logical. The man no doubt had taken notice of my still wobbly legs and was moved to pity. He felt sorry for me and wanted to send me back to the hospital for more rest. I couldn't think of any other reason for his summons. The prospect was enticing. I pictured myself as the needy patient under the tender care of nurses. My head was still swimming in this dazzling scheme of things when I stepped into Plessiner's office. Plessiner greeted me with a smile. That was enough for me. It proved that I was right. Now all I needed was his verbal approval. However, our smiling captain declared that starting tomorrow morning my summer vacation was over and I would have to return to my duties. Still smiling and with a pat on the back he pushed me out the door. He called after me to say that I needed a little exercise if I was to get any stronger. The early morning exercise would do me some good.

"Early morning dust swallowing was more like it," I wanted to yell back, but thought I had better keep my mouth shut.

May 30, 1949

The first thing our drill sergeant did was send me on sentry duty from seven until nine in the morning. Between the two evils, I should fancy half an hour of push-ups in the dirt to standing in the guardhouse streaming with perspiration for two solid hours. When I was relieved of my post I went back to my room, fell into bed, clothes and all, and woke up only when the dinner gong sounded. Practice jumping in the morning, packing for the move in the afternoon.

True, the jumping was only a drill, but safety in these parts was not guaranteed, and a man could meet his doom just as easily during training as in actual combat.

This would be my first jump since leaving Philippeville, and I gladly would stay out of it now if there was some way. For ten days already the rest of the company had prepared for the occasion, but with my luck they had to wait until my release from the hospital before taking a practice jump. The Commander just had to pick now of all times to discontinue my time off. I showered him with all the compliments of the Legion that came to mind. It was a fruitless effort on my part, for he continued his peaceful stroll around the yard, a smile pasted on his face as he greeted all who crossed his path.

To the casual observer, the Hungarian colony did not seem overtly bothered by the matter. What's the point of worrying? It was party time! We were a noisy bunch who guzzled many bottles of wine and kicked up a terrific racket. My mind was feeling ill-at-ease over tomorrow's jump. I needed something to relieve the burden and thought it best to join the card game. I did just that, hoping that a bit of escapism would take my mind off my worries. It worked. Just a few glasses of wine, and all my cares were forgotten.

May 31, 1949

After the inevitable exercise and hearty breakfast, we moved to the airport. Parachutes were distributed, and we hitched them on only after the most detailed scrutiny possible.

Irrational as it may seem, the employees of the warehouse were natives. And it was these natives who would cut the durable threads of the parachute reserve lines, the plot was often successful. Their strategic expertise was executed with such proficiency that no matter how well a man inspected his parachute, the sabotage went undetected. He noticed it only after taking the leap. Provided he didn't lose his composure, the paratrooper could still save his life by yanking the line connected to his secondary chute.

"Hey Scout!" shouted Joe. "Have you written your will yet? I can see from here that the wires are missing from your umbrella."

"Don't be so cocky! What makes you think your so special? Your wires might be severed too."

"Mine? Out of the question! I spoke to the Vietmins personally and asked them to please leave mine just the way they are."

"Oh yeah, as if they would pick a freak of nature like you to spare!" hollered Charlie from the front of the line.

"A pack of wretches all of you, may you rot in hell!" cut in a highly incensed Gypsy. "I'm trying not to think of it and you guys are shooting off your traps, sayin' them wires are cut. A man loses his last bit of guts, he does."

"Gypsy, your last bit of guts went down you pants a long time ago."

"Yeah, well that's just where it'll end up if you keep talkin' 'bout this. If only those..."

The rest was swallowed by the clatter of airplane engines starting up.

We were airborne and the airport lay far below us. "Judy" traced a few curves in the air, then pulled into position. I don't know about anybody else, but I stared at the open door with more than some mental anguish. A few minutes later the red indicator light blinked on and we stood, fastening our padlocks of the self-engaging straps onto the taut wires. The lieutenant jumped first, then Mortier, then one-by-one the crouching figures. I heaved a sigh, felt a brief rush, a tear and then peace as my parachute jerked open.

Back at the garrison, packing started after dinner. The men were beside themselves with joy. My things were thrown all over the place. I was up to my neck in the litter when the office messenger popped in to tell me Plessiner wanted to see me. Good Lord, what did I do now? Nothing as far as I know. I didn't beat anybody – hell, I didn't have the strength for it. I didn't curse the sergeant's mother, at least not out loud or in front of him.

Just like the other day, Plessiner was beaming when I reported to his office. This time, I took it to be a bad omen. Thousands of papers were scattered all over the desk in front of him and on one, I caught a glimpse of my name. Plessiner was scanning the documents as I stood there, and I thought: Penal colony? Discharge? Nothing I could think of had a logical reason behind it.

"How are you Scout? How are you feeling?"

"Oh, so-so. Not bad, but not great either." I began cautiously because I had no idea what he was fishing for.

He pointed to the mess of papers in front of him. "I've got the hospital reports here, and the doctor's recommendation. Looks like he's suggesting a short rest, so I think I'll send you down to Do-Son for fifteen days."

"Wh-wh-where?" thinking I didn't hear him correctly.

"Do-Son is a military summer resort, south of Haiphong on the shores of the Gulf of Tonkin. A narrow strip of land surrounded with tiny islands extend into the gulf. The climate is terrific. It's an ideal place to vacation. Only place I can think of that's better is Da-Lat, but that's a dream away."

I must have made a fool of myself with a ridiculous expression on my face when I struttered because Plessiner broke in laughter, and he assured me that my ears had not deceived me. He was sending me away, on the condition that Duvallieux gave his consent.

"Now hurry back and finish packing. Our departure for Gia-Lam is pretty early tomorrow morning."

Nothing will come of it, I mumbled to myself. He's just trying to make me look like a fool. I'll bet anything he only wanted to watch my reaction to his proposal, so he can pull the wool over my eyes and have the last laugh.

I bumped into Charlie just as I entered the hallway.

"And just where the hell have you been loitering about?" he screamed. "Everyone else is just about finished packing, and your stuff is still all over creation."

"Quit yelling like a hyena! It's none of your business where I was. But if you really wannna know, I was down at the office, because Plessiner wanted to see me. And do you know why he wanted to see me? He wants to send me to Do-Son for a fifteen day vacation. What do you think of that, old friend?"

"Where does he want to send you? To Do-Son? Maybe to hell, but not to Do-Son. Just because of a little poisoning?"

"What the hell are you yelling so loud for? Are you nuts? If you don't believe me, trot yourself down to the office and ask Plessiner yourself. Then *you* can trot to hell."

"You'll end up in hell before me if you don't shut your trap. Do-Son? I'll beat the living daylights out of you before that."

"You're still a small boy to be talking like that! At least wait 'till you're a sergeant, but only with Plessiner's approval of course."

"Oh, shut your face. Go and pack."

He was in one of his moods I could tell, so following the 'better to bend than break' motto I left him and did what I was told.

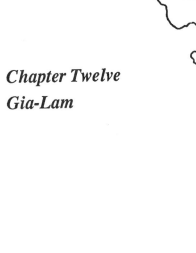

Chapter Twelve
Gia-Lam

Our supervisors had not taken kindly to the easy going and stable nature of our existence in Hanoi. So, they deposited us in Gia-Lam to relieve the monotony.

The sun had barely peeped over the horizon when the trucks came charging into the garrison yard. We ran back and forth in a last minute rush, flinging everything on the trucks that happened our way. One could always find some use for a couple of extra chairs or tables, or find an empty spot on the wall to hang a picture. As it turned out, our claim to ownership was short-lived because even two weeks later the rightful owners hounded us and tried to steal back all that we had stolen from them.

It came as quite a surprise that we were housed in the service warehouse three hundred metres from the station. We made ourselves comfortable after several hours of running around in search of our own things. We divided the borrowed furniture and other odds and ends in a brotherly fashion, with a profusion of slaps and kicks, as loving siblings in a warm family circle usually do. The Hungarians assembled after dinner to take stock of the area around the warehouse. After a few minutes of sight-seeing it was unanimously decided that our unit had been set-up. These old buildings were sitting ducks. The terrain was flat except for one giant tree behind the station. The enemy could creep down to within twenty or thirty metres and riddle those on guard duty with bullets. For those who happened to be on duty, such minor incidents were no cause for a headache.

"Well Charlie," I said. "We can consider ourselves incredibly lucky if the Vietmins don't shoot us to pieces in a few days."

"My friend, we have about as much of a chance of staying alive here as a cow in a slaughterhouse."

"May the devil rot the nitwit who sent us here! He's likely sittin' on his behind while our's are shot to pieces. I'd like to see that big-wig prowl on guard beside them tracks and settled for good. I'd like to see that whole lot croak!"

"Hey look, you know those guys have no guts to show their faces around here. You ain't gonna see a one of them."

"What difference does it make?" mumbled Alex. "Sooner or later we'll all be dead."

"What's it matter? I'd wanna pick later, and the later the better. If it don't matter none to you, then yuz can always go on guard in my place. I'd even give ya a bottle of wine for it."

To top off our expectations of a hopeless future, Plessiner assured the company that our posting was permanent.

"Throw 'em to the dogs, all o' 'em!" shouted Gypsy.

"Oh Gypsy, shut up. There's nothing you can do about it anyway."

"No? How about if I change sides an' join them Vietmins?"

"Just try it! I'll skin you alive if I catch you."

"Hey, just kiddin'! Gypsys have some sense of honor too, ya know."

"Just be careful not to joke like that in front of others, 'cause you'll find yourself in front of a firing squad!"

June 2, 1949

When I woke up my fever had returned and the Sergeant took me to the infirmary where Leo forced a handful of Quinine into me. It was late in the afternoon before I could gather enough strength to return to my room. Mortier stuffed more Quinine into me for supper. I swallowed but only because he was standing next to me holding a bludgeon and assuring me that he was not at all reluctant to clobber me with it.

June 3, 1949

I woke feeling tired and wet after a night of feverish dreams. Gypsy brought my breakfast as I was helpless to go as far as the kitchen, then more Quinine. I woke in the early afternoon somewhat surprised and wondering why in the blazes I was in bed. No fever, no feeling of sickness at all. I was getting out of bed when Leo appeared in the doorway and ordered me back to bed.

"But Fetus, I'm perfectly all right! Just awfully hungry, and don't you dare try shoving any more of that Quinine into me."

"Not a bunch, but a couple, yes. You've got to stay in bed until the morning, then come to the doctor's office after breakfast."

Gypsy was kind enough to bring my supper again, along with a couple of large glasses of wine, which served as a terrific sleeping inducement.

June 4, 1989

I woke up feeling completely refreshed. After breakfast I went to see the doctor who, after stuffing three more Quinine down my throat, booted me out.

On my way back I met Charlie and we continued to the residence. In the shadows of the station buildings the guards were drawn and sleeping, while four partisans had taken their place. Charlie and I, listened to their loud talk and brazen laughter. An explosion, however, changed their laughter to wailing.

Charlie and I ran over and saw that one of the partisans trouser legs was hanging in shreds and blood was gushing from both his limbs. We pulled out handkerchiefs and tied each leg above the knee. By the time the guards arrived, Charlie had already picked up the injured man and was rushing him to the infirmary. Half the company had assembled by now, Plessiner and Mercier at the forefront. Little investigation was needed to see that the Vietmins had mined the tracks during the night and the partisan had tripped over one of their trigger wires.

"How is it possible," asked the Captain, "that the Vietmins simply strolled in here to mine the trucks?"

"Where on earth was the guard?"

"How was it, that he didn't see the Vietmins?"

"Why wasn't he working his designated line?"

"Why wasn't he being supervised?"

"It is the job of the commander of the guard to periodically monitor the guards on duty, not to sleep in the guard room!"

As Plessiner's composed voice grew more intense as the questioning wore on, so the commander's face paled. Plessiner relieved him of his duties and sent him to headquarters for a hearing.

Well, I thought, I certainly wouldn't want to be in his shoes. Duvallieux was not known to pardon men who had failed in the line of duty.

Thanks to this little incident, the guards on night duty were doubled and inspected every quarter hour, while the morning shift was forced to carry out a step-by-step investigation of the tracks. Despite all precautions the Vietmins managed to keep busy, and every three or four days we found one or two of their handiwork.

June 5, 1949: Pentecost Sunday

I remember bells sounding from the church calling the people of Hungary to gather and commemorate the holy day with Mass. Dressed in their holiday best, they hurried to the churches where the fragrance of flowers which draped the alters filled the church. Pentecost was not a holiday here and this Sunday was like any other. The days were unvaried, and if not for keeping a diary, I like most of the others would know it was Sunday only because of the extra courses at dinner.

June 6, 1949

Just to lend a little variety to our existence, this morning we were shaken out of bed one hour earlier than usual. Some idiot of a big shot, a minister of sorts attended by several generals, was arriving at the airport and we had to be present to accord him the usual banal military honors. It is thirty-nine degrees in the shade and I'm sure we will broil nicely under the blazing sun while lingering around for hours, dressed in thick broadcloth suits with two belts and a tie.

June 12, 1949

Giovanni and I were on night guard duty. Great, another chance for the Vietmins to rip us to shreds. If a twig so much as stirred, we took it to mean that the enemy was lurking behind. We froze at the tiniest noise and waited for something to happen. This went on hour after hour until our relief arrived, and then it took us several hours to calm down to go to sleep.

At one point during our watch Giovanni and I drew closer together and he pointed to a suspicious bush on the other side of the railway tracks. We flung ourselves to the ground and while eyeing the bush we saw two shadows. I motioned to Giovanni, and inch by inch we wormed our way forward. After fifteen metres we stopped to listen but heard nothing. Just as we began to think that the shadows must have been our imaginations, the bush moved slightly and we saw them – their conical caps appeared above the tracks and gave them away. They operated in silence. Not a rustle, though they were only twenty metres away.

Giovanni and I watched them for another few minutes and then leaped up and began firing. We were slightly off target and our shots produced only wild screams and mad efforts to flee. In hot pursuit, we released a couple of rounds into the bushes, but no luck, the echo of running feet continued. All our guards were out and running, but by the time they reached us not a leaf was stirring. We searched the area and found wires, mines, tools and some blood.

Enemy or not, hats down for their nerve. More than a small dose of courage was needed to saunter into the enemy camp without any back up.

June 13, 1949

The Master of our company told me I would be leaving tomorrow for Do-Son and my promised holiday. I had given up all hope of going, especially after I had been booted out of the infirmary with a clean bill of health. I broke the good news to Charlie: "You see, you idiot. I'm going to Do-Son after all! Plessiner just finished telling me I'm to leave tomorrow morning."

" I'll believe it when I see it, my friend!"

"You're nuts! Why would I lie? Wanna bet a hundred piasters? How about five hundred? Sure would come in handy right before a holiday."

"Don't talk nonsense Scout. Seriously? You're really going away?"

"Yep, I'm gone. Just ask Plessiner!"

"What a lucky beggar you are! Not a thing wrong with you and they send you on a vacation. Look at poor Nick over there. They didn't send him no place with his nervous breakdown and here you are, perfectly okay, and they send you away. You were born under a lucky star, my friend. With your good fortune, you'll be one of the few to make it home."

"Is that the prophet in you crying out the truth? Wonderful so long as it's not like Little Angel the prophet who predicted my dislocated arm would save me from the Legion. If your prophesy is like his was, then I worry that you will be the one to bury me. Do you remember last year when they blew up our train? I'll be going through that same place again. Maybe in a few days you'll hear my name as the victim of another explosion and you can scribble it on the wall beside Steve's."

June 14, 1949

I've always liked to travel. Didn't matter whether it was to a neighboring city or a neighboring country, so long as I was going some place. A childlike happiness takes hold of me on every such occasion, like it does a young student who is on his way to summer camp after the school term has expired. My mood was no different as I prepared to go to Do-Son. No night guard, nervous tension or conforming to strict regulations for fifteen glorious days. I will remove myself from it all and shake off the iron shackles of discipline. Amid the jealous glances and smart remarks of the others, I made my way to the station where the train was standing-by.

Once in Haiphong I hastened to settle my affairs as quickly as possible, put my bags in a secure place and set out to do the town. I had the rest of the day and all of that night in Haiphong before my ship left for Do-Son. I looked at all the bistros before deciding to enter. They wouldn't poison anybody in a nice place like this or would they? I entered one that looked respectable, and heard someone speaking Hungarian. I went over to their table.

"Excuse my disturbing you, but would it be okay if I joined you? I've just come from Hanoi, and I leave for Do-Son in the morning."

"Of course, brother! Sit down! See, there's still half a bottle to go."

I ordered another bottle, but half of it went when three ladies appeared. They dispensed with formalities and perched themselves between us without a word.

I received this spontaneous intimacy with some distress. My two companions, on the other hand, called them by name and gave the women a tremendous reception. Well, I thought, if they know each other, they can't be bad. The hours flew by as we wandered from one bistro to the next. The girls invited us to their home for coffee, cognac and conversation. It was thanks to this conversation that I did not look in my wallet until morning and discovered my piasters had taken a dive. By the time our little talk was over there was no time to do anything but race to my hotel, collect my stuff and race to the harbor to catch my ship.

Chapter Thirteen
Do-Son

June 15, 1949

I boarded the ship at 7:00 a.m. with the repercussions of a sleepless night dragging me down. More than anything else, I wanted to find a quiet and secluded corner where I could lie down and sleep all the way to Do-Son. I found a corner well-sheltered from the storm which raged outside and fell asleep.

June 16, 1949

The sun was high above when I woke. All signs of the storm had vanished. The ship was drifting through a cramped and narrow canal. The tapering strait and islands on which Do-Son was built soon rose in the distance.

The whitewall houses peeped out from between the trees and bushes. The resort buildings, most of which served military purposes, were sparsely scattered. The residential quarters of the natives were likely further away, because the bamboo huts that were without question permanent fixtures of all such villages, were nowhere to be seen.

We disembarked and as newcomers we were welcomed by officers and junior officers alike, who summoned us by name and directed us to the residences not too far from the sandy beaches. I cannot say that the accommodations were of the calibre of a first class hotel, but with respect to the lowly needs of a solider, they exceeded all expectations. After officially registering, I had enough time to nose around before supper.

Wherever I looked there was only ocean and islands. The cool, fresh air was something that I had been sorely missing, and I hoped that in the next fifteen days I could pull myself together. The sweet green flora and softly undulating sea made for a most idyllic setting, that was made even more romantic by the blooming trees and shrubs which surrounded the dwellings. I quickly realized that boredom was not possible.

Yes. This was what I called a holiday.

Only that special someone was missing. What a holiday these fifteen days would be then. However, since that someone was 15 000 kilometres away I would have to be satisfied with the local editions.

The supper bell sounded and put an end to my appraisal. The sunbathers, swimmers and fishermen vanished in moments so they could change, and be ready to go to the dining barracks fully clothed by the time the second call sounded. (It was prohibited to appear at the meal in a swimming suit.) The quality of food was faultless and the amount of it far surpassed the capacity of the recipients.

The generous supper and fresh evening air left me feeling languid and so I postponed my hunting the local editions and recruiting until the next day. I sauntered down to the shore sat on a cliff and watched the moon slowly rise between the islands, as it carved the silvery bridge on the gently rippling water. Stars by the million sparkled and from the depths of the jungle, bird shrieks penetrated the night.

June 19, 1949

My days passed gloriously. We could sleep in as late as we wanted and breakfast was available until 10:00. Terrific meals were literally crammed down our throats and when not eating, activities like swimming, tanning, bathing, chess, reading, fishing, movies and ping-pong made the hours and days simply soar by. These last three days seemed no longer than a passing thought. I was so busy that I had found no time to go hunting for that stuffed kimono which I had in mind from the beginning. No matter, there was plenty of time.

Early in the morning I set out for the battlefield. Armed with a heap of hooks and spider crabs, I selected a large and comfortable cliff to sit on, because in its centre was a water hole large enough to put my catch into. I cast my four lines out as far as possible, and as hour after hour passed not a single bite.

It was 9:30 when I decided that if I wanted breakfast I had better go, but just then I felt a strong tug on one of my lines.

I can't go for breakfast, they're just starting to bite! Rotten swines! Why couldn't you have started to bite earlier!?

Another bite. I yanked the line really hard and thought, boy oh boy, this must be a big one.

I was straining to pull in the sucker when I noticed the critter was not dragging the line to the right or to the left. My line was taut and drawn straight into the water. A good catch for sure, I reassured myself.

Other fishermen parked themselves in the vicinity during the morning. My antics attracted their attention, and with great enthusiasm, they followed my progress as I toiled and labored under the strain. Suggestions flew from all sides. "Don't draw so hard, the line will snap! Give it to me you stupid idiot, you don't know what you're doing," and then some. Inspite of their friendly words of wisdom, I dragged in the lines until the hook appeared. Empty!

No fish, no bait.

Second hook, empty again.

Third hook, a cute little two ounce darling wriggled at the end.

Fourth hook, a good-sized log! It had burrowed its nose into the ocean bed and thus made it difficult to pull out.

For this, I passed up a great breakfast?

By now it was almost time for lunch. No way I was gonna miss that? I left the equipment behind, bait and all and went to eat. After lunch I strung the bait on the hooks, cast the lines as far as possible and began to wait. Less than five minutes later, a strong tug and I quickly drew in the line. No fish, no spider. They had nibbed it off, the hogs!

More bait, another bite, but this time, much stronger than before. I drew it in, pulled it out and saw a large red and black fish dangling from the hook. With great triumph I took it off the hook, but my grip was not secure and the fish took a bite of my finger. Never mind. The important thing was that it was my second catch of the day while those around had not even a block of timber to show for their efforts. One more time. Bait, cast, bites, but nothing on the other end. The little monsters had nibbled it off again!

Again, spider. Again, bites. Again, nothing.

This went on hour after hour. In my excitement, I failed to notice that the end was near. The tide had inched its way in and by the time I was aware of it, it had overrun the cliff I was on and my fish escaped. I thought I was going to suffer a seizure on the spot.

My fellow fishermen roared with laughter, and I, feeling the crush of defeat, fled the battlefield. Just wait, I thought. I'll show them all tomorrow!

"What are you smirking about, you hopeless twit?" I shouted as an Arab Regular went by me with a malicious grin. "I don't remember seeing you haul up a worthless twig all day. And a fish? Hah! Come out tomorrow and I'll teach you how to fish! You just wait. I'll have the last laugh yet!" I thought about beating up the offender, but I noticed two of his friends close by and quickly put a lid on that idea.

Once inside the dormitory I grabbed my chess partner and reduced him to a rag. After my fool's mate, he overturned the table in rage and stormed out of the room. Well, this gave me more than a little satisfaction.

June 30, 1949

After a quick breakfast, and with the greatest of expectations for a profitable day, I laced massive spiders to my fish hooks and headed for the battle ground. I hurried so that no one would beat me to my place. I was willing to lay my neck on the line and swear that today, my fish would not make a clean getaway. There was no doubt about it that I would make a good catch or two. This cliff had to be the best spot in the whole area. A catch was undeniable because somewhere ahead, I was sure that there was a depression where the fish flocked.

I cast the line out as far as I could, and with a loose grip on the rod, I waited for the inevitable bite. In less than five minutes something dragged on the line with such force that the rod almost flew out of my hand.

Ah yes, this was more like it.

I yelled to those who had jeered me yesterday, "Look at what I'm about to haul in. Look you fools! You've never seen a fish like this in your life! Now try laughing."

By now I had pulled my fish close enough to see it through the transparent water and it looked to be about a pound. I pulled it out of the water to show my tormentors.

"So scab face, are you green with envy yet?"

"It will escape too, just like yesterday's did!" they yelled back and they rolled with laughter.

I took it off the hook very carefully, and to omit any possibility of attempted escape, I pulled it onto a rope and tied that around my waist. I was satisfied with myself and thoroughly convinced that there would be no escaping today. Less than fifteen minutes later I was in luck again, but this time the catch was considerably smaller.

"See this?" I yelled. "How come you're not laughing now? You haven't had a single bite yet. Ha ha ha!"

I tied more bait on and threw the line in the water, but rain started pouring within minutes and I was in no mood to fish in the rain. I went up to the dormitory and found a pickle jar, put the jar on top of the bureau beside my bed and in it went the fish. I sat back and through the glass I was able to admire the colorful hues of the fish. The view lasted all of a few minutes because after that, my beautiful fish simply died.

Well that was really brilliant of me! I didn't stop to think that fish from the salt water of the ocean could not survive in fresh water. Fortunately I was alone in the dorms at the time and no one else witnessed the passing. Out of fish again. No matter, there's always tomorrow. Confounded anyway, I'll show them. But nothing came of it, because all the next day the rain poured and fishing was the last thing on my mind.

June 22, 1949

It was a year ago today that I crossed the border from Hungary. The last time that I heard my parent's voices bidding me goodbye and saw their hands waving a fond farewell. The last time that my faithful dog Aigo followed me out to the gate with his tail wagging. It was the last time that he gave me a goodbye bark as if sensing that never again would I stroke his head. These flashes of memory came rushing back as I sat on the fishing cliff.

It was one year ago today that my lover waved her last goodbye with teary eyes, as if knowing that fate would never again bring us together. All that I held dear from days gone by was too long to list but very much with me now. The promenade along the Danube, the weeping willows by the lake shores, the streams and forests of the countryside, the enchanting evenings in the city were but a few of the memories shoved aside by jungles, chest deep rancid marshes, the rattle of machine guns and the imperceptible blood thirsty enemy.

It was one year ago today, a handful of politicians surfaced who acted only in their own selfish interest with no regard for the fate of millions of innocent people. Their turbulent decisions rocked the country, stirred a storm, crushed the people and drove thousands of people out of their homes and into the unknown.

While gazing at the scattered islands I saw a small black fishing boat. A platform rose from the centre of the vessel and on it lay a coffin. The deceased was a memory now, just as I was perhaps to remain but a memory to all those I left behind. The furneral procession duly reminded me of my own mortality. Just as his life came to a pass, so did one year of mine. And I wonder, how many more anniversaries will be granted me?

Hard as I tried to banish the memories, the faces, the places and events they refused to leave. Come now Scout, why keep yearning for the past? Why cling to it? Forget it! You are lost and forgotten, sunk into oblivion long ago. Be honest with yourself. Even your best friend has not answered one of your letters for over six months. Do you really see yourself as being so important? Even your parents haven't sent you anything for months.

"But letters can easily go astray! And it takes months for one to get here. Twice now its taken months for a letter to reach me from home or Ankara," I tried to reason with the "spirit".

"You're just deceiving yourself," replied the "spirit". "Don't worry about the past. Live for today! You never know when your last hour will be. Make the best of every moment while you can."

"Listen, you child of the devil! The past, the memories, the encouraging words of those at home give me strength. And so does the thought of everything we will have to say to each other if fate chooses to bring our paths together again, just like we were before."

"You're a stubborn fool!" replied the voice. "A sentimental moron. Go ahead! Just live in the past. Mull it over, torture yourself, while others make the most of today's opportunities."

In the midst of this quarrel, I found myself back at the dorm, where I dusted off the old photographs. The figures stepped down, moved around me and spoke.

I grabbed my writing paper so I too might speak.

June 23, 1949

Sleep drove away the anguishes of my soul, and after a hearty breakfast, I set out to go fishing. I found two fishermen baiting their spiders on my cliff and so I had to try my luck elsewhere. The Goddess of Fortune, however, turned her back on me and one after another my lines snapped, my spiders fled, and again I had no fish to display in my pickle jar. Bored of the war with the fish, I devoted my dinner hours to enlisting the locals as I had planned to in the beginning.

I wandered the village beside our villas. At every turn I bumped into both legionnaires and members of the standing army, but rarely did I see one who had a creature of the fairer sex walking by his side. And those few samplings were so lousy that I would rather visit the village bistros alone. Beauties such as these were best eyed from a distance.

I abandoned all hopes having to do with the fairer sex and returned to the villa for a game of chess, some swimming and a movie. The feature presentation was a thrilling spy flick. The movie had a tremendous effect on the guy sitting in the row behind me because he clobbered me a good one on the head, not once but twice, and so hard that I all but fell out of my seat. By strike two, my interest in these blows to my noggin began to wane, and I whipped around, aimed my fist at the chap sitting behind me, and smashed it into his nose. I'm sure he wore a tumor the size of a potato between his eyes for a long time.

A mundane matter had it ended there, but the trouble was that I had not hit the guy who hit me. What started as a minor difference of opinion was raised to out-and-out combat. Two or three dozen legionnaires left the battlefield with blue and green bruises, tattered shirts, eyes adorned with lovely black circles and smashed noses. The casualties were escorted by the military police to the garrison jail. They thought nothing of life's little comforts in there because aside from strip floors, beds were not provided.

June 24, 1949

The victims of last night's combat were roused from slumber at 6:00. Collectively, we were a vanquished army who drifted out of the jail physically spent and in mighty rough shape. During the war, somebody landed such a blow to my mouth that my lips were swollen to three times their usual size and my tongue was temporarily out of commission due to a self-inflicted bite. Eating for the next few days would be an intricate affair. I made every effort to repair my torn shirt, but after the fifth needle stab to the finger, I ripped the shirt to shreds. I, thus, had to spend one hundred piasters for a new one.

It was pouring rain and we were confined to the dorms or the canteen. I tried to alleviate the boredom with a swim but left the water like a bat out of hell after the salt water stung the open sores on my mouth. The burn brought tears to my eyes, and all the way back to the dorms I muttered curses to myself. All the pain and frustration melted, however, when I saw a letter waiting for me on my bed.

"You see, you son of the devil?" I snarled at yesterday's evil spirit.

The letter had been written a mere two weeks ago – a miracle of speed had delivered so quickly. Two weeks ago today, these two pieces of paper were lying on the familiar dining room table.

There is more than some value in acting out the role of a sentimental fool who remembers home and cherishes the memories. I greedily devoured every last word while sensing the physical presence of my parents.

I read the letter from beginning to end three, four, five times. Almost every word was committed to memory, yet I read it again. The tiniest tidbit assumed gigantic proportions during the two week journey the letter took to reach me.

June 25, 1949

I wrote a ten page letter home. So much for today.

June 28, 1949

The holiday is over tomorrow. The thought of the ship arriving to take me back was torture. Tomorrow it was back to Gia-Lam, back to the combat zone!

June 29, 1949

"All things must come to pass. . . ."

So too, this carefree existence of mine.

Today marks the end of my holiday here and the beginning of the harvest season back home. This day, the day of Peter and Paul, the birth of new bread, is considered a holiday. Things will be different this year. No longer do my people have the exclusive right to the fruits of their labor. A slice of the loaf must be shared. Shared, with the Russian pack of thieves. What will remain of their toils? For the hungry children?

But life goes on. It goes on until the Lord decrees: Enough! Then accounts will be settled, balanced and squared once and for all. No choice until, but to fulfill the responsibilities assigned to each and all by the Lord. The order for the time being was to go back to Gia-Lam. Lord, why do these moments in life pass so quickly? Why do the bad times linger? I had barely arrived and I found myself mulling over the complexities of molding back into the life of a soldier.

No more lazing around until eight or nine. Although I didn't take advantage too often, with my getting up early to fish, but the option was there and I missed it already. How typical. When given an opportunity, a man chooses to ignore it. Come the time to get up at six with the squadron, we crawl out of bed like men to be put on the rack.

One last fishing excursion. Did I not now, of all times, have to catch a splendid fish? I packed my things after lunch and left on the 1:30 ship for Haiphong, and the next morning the 8:00 a.m. train to Hanoi.

Chapter Fourteen
Gia-Lam Revisited

July 1, 1949

I had just put my bags down when word came from Charlie of a mission for the next day.

"Don't you look well-rested and fattened up, my dear chap. Just the kind of man we'll need tomorrow."

"Why don't you all just go straight to hell. Same goes for the guy who didn't let me stay on for a another couple of days."

"It's only because somebody has to replace Joe Bristle."

"What's this? Don't tell me Joe is dead."

"Hell no! Devil wouldn't take him. He was transferred to battalion headquarters."

"Where? Battalion headquarters? What happened to him? Was he wounded? Did he fall on his head? Go off the deep end?"

"Nah. The Gorilla's (Duvallieux's nickname) batman bit the dust the last time out and Joe became his replacement. Who knows why Joe, but the

163

choice was up to Duvallieux, and Joe's got some big mouth ever since. I've heard him shoot off at the NCOs. So anyway, you're just in time."

I was livid, "Damn it anyway. Just my luck. Why couldn't this rotten mission be three days ago?"

"So what? What difference does it make? If it had been three days ago, you'd only find yourself in another. These little excursions are happening one after the other now."

"All right, all right, I know it doesn't make any difference. Just wish I hadn't dropped into it like some fly into a bowl of soup. Last time too, I was out jumping the day after my return from the hospital and here we go all over again. Same thing. And you wonder why I throw a fit?"

"You're whining isn't going to do you a bit of good, buddy. Their bark around here is pretty high and mighty, you know. This here's going to be our sixth mission since you've been gone. You've got no right to complain after missing five, so you just keep quiet. We've been cruising the streets of hell for the past two weeks while you've been suntanning your belly. It's about time you took your turn."

"Does me some good to get it off my chest if nothing else. By the way, do you know which way we're going?"

"Don't know anything except that we're off, but I suspect we're heading north toward Thai-Nguyen. There was some dirty work afoot in that area the last time around. On the other hand, it's quite possible we'll go toward Bac-Giang. We'll see. Unpack your gear old chap, so you can turn around and pack it up again."

"Yeah, yeah. I'm going to report to the Captain first. Maybe he's lost his mood for marching."

"Don't count on it!" came Charlie's voice after me.

I didn't find any one in the office except for the paper pusher, so I gave him my papers and went back to the dorms. Sergeant Mortier was standing beside Charlie and shouting out orders for the next day. When he saw me, he lowered his voice so that I couldn't hear what he was saying.

He walked by me on his way out and with a big smile commented on how well I was looking. Just the kind of man they needed tomorrow. (Charlie's words exactly. Maybe there was some great conspiracy in the making.)

"Hey Charlie! What's the big secret? Why the whispering between you and the Sergeant?"

"Look, you know that even the walls have ears around this place. The Vietmins know our plans even before we do."

"Are you trying to tell me that you were whispering so that the

Vietmins won't know that we're going on a mission tomorrow? What idiot would believe that the Vietmins don't already know? They always find out about everything before we do, you know that."

"That's exactly why the whispering. The higher ups have been trying to conduct these past few missions with the greatest possible secrecy so that for once, we might have the upper hand."

"But Charlie, any fool knows that in any given situation the first word is always theirs. We'd have to lie in ambush for days to trap them like they always manage to trap us. Remember Na-Long, when we waited for three days without one falling in the line of fire?"

"I do remember. That's why tomorrow, we're going as quietly as possible and at a most unexpected time."

"Any way we go, it's gonna be the same as always."

"Don't concern yourself over it. Just do as you're told.!"

July 2, 1949

Reveille was at 1:00 a.m. Charlie and Mortier went from bed to bed waking everyone up.

"Hey Charlie! Is all this so secretive that we can't even talk any more?"

"Don't worry about it. Just shut up and get ready!" he answered quietly.

After the lazy days in Do-Son I didn't know who or what I was any more. Amazing how little time it took before a pampered lifestyle turned into a matter of habit. My every move this morning was mechanical, a mimick of those around me. Not ten minutes later we scurried out of our rooms to disappear among the woodlands on the opposite side of the tracks. The conditions were partial to the prevading air of secrecy, for the moon was out of sight and not a single star shone. What struck me as peculiar about this whole affair was the absence of rations. The first task before any mission had always been the distribution of grub and here we were without so much as a solitary cracker. Good, it could only mean that the mission would be over by noon. The prospect cheered me up somewhat but if I so much as turned my thoughts back to the wonderful days in Do-Son, I just about broke into tears.

The troops quietly filed along the hardly used path through the forest. After what seemed like eternity we came upon a roadway where, to my utter astonishment, several trucks and the first section were waiting.

Hushed orders were given, telling us to do as the first section and occupy scattered positions until the third section arrived. I climbed aboard one of the trucks, sat down on its floor to wait and two days worth of rations were distributed.

Twenty minutes later, I heard the rustle of bushes and branches from the same direction we had come. A few minutes later, the third section arrived.

Plessiner assembled the platoon commanders for a brief discussion, then section by section we boarded the trucks. I, along with half of my section, was ordered to the lead. The motors started up, what compared to the dead silence of before created a deafening noise fit to wake the dead.

Slowly, we advanced down the scarcely used dirt road while the chauffeurs, straining to see through the black of the night, struggled to maneuver around potholes and protruding rocks.

The trucks stopped so that we might continue on foot. Day was faintly breaking and the first hint of light appeared through the trees ahead. Spread out in groups, we paced the paths of the straggling forest with the lieutenant, Sergeant Mortier and Sergeant Susse taking the lead.

The three sections marched in silence. The sun was just starting to cast its rays over the tree crowns above when the section was ordered to stop and consume our breakfast preserves. Then, forward again.

A short while later the forest abruptly came to a halt to reveal a narrow, rice field.

Experience dictated that to come upon a rice field such as this was to come upon the village it sheltered. Not this time. So without stopping, on we trod along the banking with Susse in the front, Lieutenant Mercier following, Sergeant Mortier after him and the rest trailing behind. All at once, from the forest ahead a machine gun opened fire.

Our response was automatic. Into the mire we lunged, taking cover behind the banking and returned the enemy fire. Sparks of flame and smoke defined the target and we fired with confidence.

"You idiot!" I said to Charlie, lying on his belly beside me and still groping for cover. "Was this the reason for all the secrecy? Told you, didn't I, that two days before we knew, they knew we'd be coming exactly this way today. Why else would they set up their weapons directly ahead and facing this way?"

"Don't tell me about it, old buddy. Tell them big shots in Hanoi. If you ever get a chance, that is, and don't end up like Sergeant Susse. Did you see that? He caught the first round."

The other two sections scattered along the length of the field in an attempt to dislodge the enemy position. The offense was strong and unyielding, and any effort made to gain on the enemy proved a failure. The lieutenant ordered the third section to the right and the first to the left to surround the enemy with fire from both sides and divert the bulk of the attack. We, the second section, tried to advance down the middle through the mud and waters but with little result. From here and there down the line came the wounded's cry of pain.

The full force of all available resources was engaged in defensive action. Thanks to the troops on either side who successfully called away the greater part of the onslaught, we forced our way through and silenced the enemy guns one by one.

It had taken almost two hours of battle to force the retreat, to occupy the Vietmin's emplacement. We found hide nor hair of either dead or injured bodies. Only weapons thrown in all directions, machine guns carelessly left behind, and cartridge hulls by the hundreds littering the ground. To have abandoned all this in the interest of carrying out only the casualties would indicate substantial losses.

Our losses, four injured and one dead, were comparatively light. Two of these were unfit to travel and there was nothing to do but carry them out ourselves.

Captain Plessiner nominated ten men and one lance sergeant to assume responsibility for carrying the casualties back to the trucks: Alex and I were included. To be acting like a hearse, yet again, was not at all to my liking. Still, I had no choice but to grin and bear it. The distasteful task was bound to consume four hours at least; time that I would rather spend in the company of those alive and well.

That only ten men were to come along did not make me feel any better, especially when I thought about the vulnerability of our numbers and the potential attacks along the way. Surely it would be late in the afternoon by the time we reached the trucks. Assuming of course, that we made it at all, and exempting similar circumstances to Dinh-Lap when it took five days to get back on track after we had gone a missing.

We pieced together three stretchers from the bamboo shoots, thin strips of liana and large, wide burdock leaves. With the body of Sergeant Susse and the two seriously injured in place, we hit the road. The other two wounded men limped along behind on their own while they could, and when no longer able they too were carried.

"Alex, ever done work as a paramedic before?"

"Don't even know what it is."

"Just what you're doing right now, you moron. Carting dead and injured bodies around."

"Oh I get it! Did plenty of that in Lang-Son, but not like this. Before, we always went to pick them up in trucks, loaded them on and drove them to the hospital. To haul them around for hours on end like this is a first."

Our breathing became increasingly labored with every mechanical step.

Sweat streamed down our brows. When we stopped to rest the overly exhausted were relieved by those who had attended to the security of the road ahead. As we sat in silence, we heard a noise creep into the stillness, a crackling of bushes and branches that seemed too intense to be caused by a mere breeze in the air. We listened as the sound spread and grew.

Our lance sergeant used hand signals to instruct us to conceal the injured men some distance away. The men were deported as per orders, we returned to the site, and just as we drew back on both sides of the road a native appeared a few hundred metres away, his shoulders sagging under the weight of his bamboo rod yoke. Six more natives followed him. We waited until they were right beside us then leaped out from behind the bushes to stop them. They stared at us, unable to move. We gave them no chance to come to their senses, but stripped them of their baggage, and lay them face down on the ground. A thorough search of the baskets revealed nothing but edibles and clothing.

Lucky for them, because they would not have lived to see the day after had we found weapons or ammunition. It was difficult to decide whether the groceries were explicitly for family consumption or on the way to Vietmins. While we were occupied with their baskets they, with faces drained of all color, followed our every move, especially that of the gun barrels levelled at their heads.

Their timing was perfect. We were not about to let them go. If help dropped out of nowhere like this, why not take advantage of it? Why not let them haul the stretchers? We took them over to where the stretchers were located. Now the natives were truly terrified, thinking that we wanted to wreak our vengenace on them. With an abundance of sign language, it sunk in that they were only to carry the stretchers, and that when the job was over they were free to go on their merry way. They were relieved and expressed their gratitude with bows so deep that their brows more or less beat against their knees. The natives lifted the stretchers in a flash and started off at such a spanking pace that the two wounded men were hard pressed to keep up. We thought it best to put them on stretchers too if we wanted to reach the trucks before dark.

The time we lost while preparing the extra stretchers was quickly made up by frequent rotation of the load. The sun was still tracing its light across the mountain side when we met up with the trucks. A group of partisans who had been dispatched from Gia-Lam surrounded the trucks. Here, the lance sergeant told us that we were to assume the responsibility of taking the casualties back and not the partisans. Wonderful, it would mean that we could spend the night in a real bed instead of under some bush in the great outdoors.

The hired hands were let loose to the wind while we stormed down the road, homeward bound.

The section returned to base late in the afternoon and immediately removed the casualties from the trucks. Alex and I lucked out after all. We were in the right place at the right time when Captain Plessiner selected the ten relief paramedics yesterday. Of the Hungarians in the section, only one was injured – Dinnes, who sustained a shot to the chest, and to compensate for our meagre losses, a bunch of Vietmins were brought back as prisoners-of-war.

"Hey Alex, you son of the devil. You were real lucky for being sent back yesterday. You think it was bad before you took off? Man, all hell broke loose after you was gone. I didn't even know where to throw me head."

"Doesn't look much to me like you were caught in some great showdown," retorted Alex. "If anything, you look just like a man returning from a Sunday stroll in the park while Scout here and I were breaking our backs trying to carry our casualties out."

"Yeah! So I heard. You guys nabbed some Vietnamese and they did all the carryin' for you. Hard work my foot. You were trapin' on behind and doing nothin'. Wish you was there last night. Man oh man, what a row! Should have seen them Vietmins running around like chickens with their heads lopped off."

"Did you maybe see them, Gypsy?" asked Charlie. "Because I sure as hell never did. For one thing, the attack broke out in the middle of the night, and the first section caught the full force of the first round, and that was at least two hundred metres away."

"So Charlie, what did happen? Was it really as bad as Gypsy says it was?"

"Well, yes and no. The worst of it was that we managed to settle down for the night in a spot that was swarming with Vietmins. 'Course we didn't know it at the time, but even so, twice as many guards were posted. That turned out to be our saving grace 'cause soon as the Vietmins started shooting, everyone was on their feet and shooting right back. You should have seen us! We were mowing them down left and right. Anyway, the battle lasted for a good hour. Caught a good many who gave our guns the slip, and made them pick up their own dead. From that I could see come dawn, there was more then plenty to pick up. The fields were strewn with enemy corpses. We were pretty lucky this time, I guess. Only nineteen injured and seven dead. Big deal. Tomorrow, it'll be our turn."

"You're a real source of comfort, that you are."

"At you service, *sir*! Your uniform is supposed to be a bullet shield, or didn't you know? You didn't come here to be caressed with sweet nothings, you know. Besides, you have no right to complain, what with a vacation under your belt. Wish the rest of us could say the same. So don't you say another word."

What could I say? He was right and I knew it. I gave the matter some thought and came up with an idea.

"Here's what, Charlie. If you really think that tomorrow it'll be our turn, then let's organize a mammoth rummy tournament tonight. What better send off to the hereafter then a smashing card party?"

"Good idea. Sounds a lot better to me than spending another night listening to the rattle of machine guns. Let's go over to Joe's after supper and win away his salary."

"That's not such a hot idea. I mean, to go over to his place. You know that wandering around in the middle of the night can be pretty dangerous."

"We'll stay there 'till the morning and come back before Mortier sounds reveille."

It was agreed, and off we went to Joe's, dragging Steve Bidon along as a fourth. Everything was going just great. Moods were bright or rather, might have been, meaning Charlie's and mine, had our calculations come to pass. We did not win Joe's salary, but he and Steve won ours.

July 4, 1949

Steve popped over to see me after lunch. Was I, perchance, interested in going with him to visit Dinnes in the Hanoi hospital and taking in a little dancing and maybe a movie after?

The response I coughed up was not cordial,

"Aren't you forgetting something important? In case you didn't know, and if your memory fails you, let me be so bold as to remind you that half my monthly salary is sitting in your pocket. Or have you so easily forgotten everything that happened in the past few hours? I ain't got a piaster to my name 'till the fifteenth. Charlie's in the same boat. I strongly suggest that you don't say a word to him if you have any intention of living to see tomorrow."

"But don't you see, that's precisely why I'm inviting you, because I know I won all your money. Joe wanted to invite Charlie along too, but Duvallieux assigned him tons of work to do, he's up to his ears in it. That's why I came alone. Come on! Everything's on me."

"What heart! It's my money!"

I was not about to let the enticing offer to recoup at least a portion of my losses pass by. First we stopped by the hospital to visit Dinnes who was sitting up in bed, propped up on pillows like some Turkish pasha. He was feeling not too badly considering that the bullet was still lodged in his chest. His grin was wide as he insisted that he got the better end of the deal. Here he was, smothered to death by the tender care of nurses and loving every minute of it, while we were reaping the benefits of mountain climbing. The last laugh would ultimately be his only once the bullet was removed, because for now, he was about ready to faint with every breath he took.

Steve and I were green with envy when a nurse came in to stroke his brow and make gentle inquiries as to his needs, and we all but broke out in a cold sweat. For Dinnes we wished an additional five bullets as we swept off the ward and left him behind rejoicing. On the way out, we swore up and down that we would make every effort to get injured so as to land in the hospital. Since prospects for a shot to the chest in the next few seconds were exceedingly slim, we sought out a dance hall where, our brows were not stroked, but where the utmost attention was given to lifting my money out of Steve's pockets. We quickly tired of the ladies money hunting craze and flounced out of the hall. The afternoon was proving to be quite patronizing, so after stopping at a cafe for two bottles of wine, just so the entire excursion would not go down as totally futile, we hit the road for home.

We put on the pace to arrive back in Gia-Lam in time for supper. I stood my ground however much Steve insisted on dining at a bistro in town. Ever since the poisoning incident, I dared not consume anything at a bistro or cafe that was not bottled and corked.

July 15, 1949

The entire company, except approximately twenty men who were left behind to tidy up the area, were dispatched on a three week mission. For me the ten day period brought absolutely nothing of virtue. I was on guard duty day in and day out. For that reason alone, I felt that I deserved a Legion of Honor decoration. Not only was I attending my responsibilities with the utmost care and devotion, but my nerves were dancing St. Vitus' dance night after night. If I stopped to consider that given a rough estimation, the dance was bound to play havoc with my nerves yet another hundred times, ten medals at the very least ought to be proudly dangling from my arrogant throat. Not to flatter myself, but for slaughtering mosquitoes by the thousands, thereby reducing their population and ensuring that fewer of the bloodsuckers were around to leave their mark on the sensitive skins of my comrades, I was worthy of a special distinction of merit.

One day the remaining section was ordered to the airport for military preparedness. The entire section, except me, who was left behind to tidy up the area. Something's not quite right here, all this imposed isolation, somebody up there does not like me. A broom was thrust into my hands and I was told to go to it.

To top it all off, not so much as a word had arrived from anywhere since that letter from my parents which came while I was still vacationing on Do-Son. And what a difference a few letters would make to my feelings of well-being. To bear the brunt of this sad destiny would be so much easier under the influence of caring thoughts from afar. Who knows? The welcome relief might even put a damper on the unceasing frantic convulsions of my nervous system. But if Fate so chose to single me out as the one to persecute, then there was no escaping it. My turn was up and there was little I could do to change the situation.

The day after the company left we moved our residences from the storage area over to the offices and officer's quarters so that those left behind, were all located under one roof and in a better position to implement defensive measures should an attack materialize.

The possibility of an attack and preparations for it were in itself nothing out of the ordinary. We'd been on the alert in anticipation of an offensive drive ever since we moved over here from Gia-Lam. But the Vietmins thus far had refused to abide; much as we waited they hadn't come around yet unless it was to mine the tracks. But shooting? Not a one. What the hell were they waiting for? Wish they would go ahead and get it over with. Or could it be that they were purposely withholding an onslaught, trusting that we might die a slow death in vain anticipation? No question that the impact of a cold war was often far more effective than days of actual warfare.

A French National Holiday intruded upon the monotony of our days. The ceremonial processions and festal addresses that normally marked such occasions were dispensed with in favor of gorging. That, however, was attended to with meticulous care. The officer in charge, the chief watchdog, delivered a short speech by way of observing some formality. Then we popped open a few bottles of champagne and toasted France. A fourteen course dinner followed the toast. Since it was a holiday, we were served a good quality wine in sufficient quantity to allow for at least two bottles per person instead of the customary cheap red wine that came from and was distributed by the barrel. I could see already that tonight, not my nerves but my feet would be dancing the csardas. As for the world at large, meaning in Gia-Lam and Hanoi, all was turned upside down today in festive celebration. Streets, squares and houses alike were adorned with, and saging under, the weight of an abundance of banners, colorful streamers and flags waving in the wind. The highlight was a visit paid by the Emperor of Indochina, Bao-Dai.

Those left behind, only because of our low numbers, were fortunately excluded from the usual banal processional and dress parade. The rejection spared us from a bake in the sun while that dunce of a footman paced up and down before the united front in assembly, or while his speeches lasting forever, killed the venerated audience off with boredom. In attendance were representatives of the various branches of military service who marched in procession by the thousands, while civil and military police together might cause a scandal to erupt at anytime. An assassination attempt by the Vietmins was not entirely unfeasible, and therefore, every precaution was taken to ensure that the Emperor's visit remain free of incident.

An entire company was sent to represent our regiment. The Emperor was held in low esteem, and after hearing the judgements passed, I was more than glad not to be in the Emperor's shoes.

From the early morning hours until late in the afternoon they marched in a row, cutting the route ahead of Bao-Dai and his entourage. No wonder that the royal party became subject to curses which included the stripping of all baptismal rights. Presuming that they were baptized to start with!

The Emperor also dared to visit Gia-Lam where he paraded his face in an open car while the masses lined the streets screaming and waving miniature flags. It was our good fortune that for lack of strength he did not make it as far as the station, thus leaving us free to pursue the idleness of the day undisturbed.

The Emperor's visit was then , the second "sensational event of worldwide interest" which lent a touch of variety to the sameness of our days. But emperor this and emperor that amounted to nothing as far as a festive dinner was concerned. No gala meal was forthcoming. The Emperor was a windbag a master at spouting verbal nothings, a ruler who ran short of generosity but never of words. There remained no room in his itinerary for treating those under his rule, those who had honored him here today with this splendid reception. Granted, he did, with the body of generals and high ranking officers, delight in an epicurian banquet to which we were not invited.

That millions of mosquitoes may nip his most Honorable Highness under the royal armpits!

July 16, 1949

The diversity of our lives was broken only by the minor casualties who one by one began to slip back from the mission. Symptoms included minor flesh wounds to arms and legs, physical and mental exhaustion, and mild cases of shell shock, all of which were easily treatable on the premises. Leo, who ambled in along with the rest, was more than capable of dispensing the appropriate medications, administering injections and securing bandages. The encounter was serious and according to Leo, there was hardly a man in the outfit who did not suffer an injury. With the wounded, truckloads of war spoils arrived; everything from silk blouses to heavy artillery.

Participation on the battlefield was not a prerequisite for nervous exhaustion. A serious case of frayed nerves could just as easily be acquired simply by walking up and down the tracks every night. This activity was capable of matching or surpassing any case of nervous strain secured in actual combat. However, the men on guard duty were overlooked in favor of those returning from the fields. Nobody stopped to consider that we were no better off than they. We were not considered a priority.

Due to either my nervous exhaustion or the multitude of mosquitoe bites, I woke this morning with a burning fever. My temperature had to be at least forty degrees. It took a good while before I could pull myself together so that I might drag my ailing body down to the infirmary. The doctor took my temperature, pushed and proded all over, ordered Leo to give me a handful of Quinine, then booted me out.

Well that certainly didn't get me very far! Though the quinine did drive my temperature down, I was not granted the respite from my graveyard shift on guard that I had hoped for.

"Darn it all anyway," I mumbled as I surveyed the length of the tracks. "Wish I'd gone along with the company. Wish I would have gotten a not so serious shot in the thigh so I could sleep in peace in my own bed."

What was most annoying was that there was no news from the opposite side of the world. Not a word turned up from Budapest, Ankara or Brussels. This was not due to any deficiency on the part of the postal system. Revered as always, the service ran smoothly and letters by the sackful poured in on a daily basis. None, however, were addressed to me.

July 22, 1949

I was witness today to an event that was both remarkable and inexplicable. Even today, some thirty years later, a plausible explanation of the incident escapes me. In the chapter where we moved out of Gia-Lam, I mentioned that behind the station was a huge tree whose branches spread to shelter a small pagoda.

The belief of the natives was that any tree standing beside a pagoda was sacred and not to be harmed. Anyone who assaulted or did willful damage to such a tree risked catastrophic punishment.

After landing on the shores of Haiphong, camp cots along with rods were distributed. These rods we erected in each corner of our beds as a support for the mosquitoes nets that were so essential for an undistrubed night's rest. From time to time, especially with all the moving around we did, the rods went missing and replacement had to be found. If by chance – supplies in the Legion never came by chance, some extras were to be found in the storeroom, the storeman handed them out upon the asking. But any reserve rods were usually serviced by the trees and bushes in the area.

Today one of the boys in the Third section had urgent need for one of these net supporting gizmos. He saw the large tree behind the station had exactly the sort of straight branches that would stand up to the task. He grabbed his coup-coup and up the tree he climbed to lop off the branches himself. The guardian of the pagoda was horror struck by what he saw.

"You mustn't harm the sacred tree of Buddha," he yelled to the lad, "lest misfortune strike you down. Buddha will punish you!"

The Emperor(centre) and his entrourage

Bao-Dai giving a speech

Elephants in ceremonial attire heading for parade

Seeing that his warning went unheeded and the boy merely continued his climb, the guardian ran into the pagoda where he lit a stick of incense and began beating out a slow, even rhythm on a drum. The young man all the while was chopping down the suitable branches and dropping them to the ground.

So, I thought, Buddha's sacred tree is being chopped to bits. If the legend is true, if what the natives believe is rooted in fact, then our man will pay for his sinful deed. Let me see. Not just one hundred, but mosquitoes by the thousands will bite him senseless because twigs from Buddha's sacred tree will refuse to perform. This furious woodcutter will sleep little once the bloodsucking monsters start running in and out from under the net. The mosquitoes will bite the hell out of him and drain not just his blood to the last drop but suck out his very soul, presuming that he possessed one.

By this point in my forecast, the woodcutter had secured enough branches and after flinging down his knife, he started his trek down the tree. Though clearly exercising a great deal of caution in doing so, hardly a few steps later and for no apparent reason, he plunged to the ground from about three metres up.

At that moment the pagoda guardian ceased his drumming, emerged from the pagoda and said to the wailing woodcutter, "Did I not tell you that Buddha would punish you for mutilating his sacred tree?"

With that, he re-entered the pagoda and resumed his drumming.

Scratches acquired on the way down and what covered his body were the least of his woes. The lad suffered from dislocated and sprained limbs, and some internal injuries on top of it all. Had I not seen with my very own eyes his calculated, deliberate and prudent steps from one branch to the next as he slowly climbed down, had I not watched him deftly clutch the branches with both hands on the descent, I would have said that carelessness caused his downfall. His technique could not be faulted but he took the spill even so.

It gave me the creeps. Contrary to the heat of the day, a chill came over me. Goose pimples crept up and down my spine, and gripping fear took hold of me. For the first time I truly felt that frequently alluded to quality of mysticism here. For the first time I honestly believed that it existed not just in the imagination. For of the many inexplicable incidents in the Far East, I was finally witness to one.

Well Scout, my boy, don't even think about climbing a pagoda tree to fell its branches, unless you want a hostile Buddha to come breathing down your neck. No reason to start a feud with the Buddha when there are plenty of Vietmins in the region to clash swords with. And should you have the need for a mosquitoe net supporting rod, don't try to get it off a pagoda tree unless you want to end up a rumpled mess lying in the hospital. (Actually, the thought was not altogether bad, meaning a stay in the hospital, as it would free me from guard duty for a couple of weeks.)

Dare I say that after this, nobody in their right mind had any desire to climb and cut twigs off the sacred tree?

July 23,1949

I had been asleep but four hours after an exhausting night of patrol when somebody started shaking me awake. I scraped the bottom of the barrel in search of vocabulary to heap on the head of whomever was responsible. I was about ready to fling a hand grenade at the offender when I saw it was Julius.

"Damn it all, you blundering idiot! Why are you waking me up? I 've hardly slept for four hours and you come around rousing me out of bed. I hope the sky falls on you, you idiot!"

"Hold it, Scout! I only did it because there's a whole slew of letters for you here. Just arrived." And he pressed the bundle under my nose.

My wrath evaporated at the sight of my letters. I felt as fresh as someone after three days of sleep, and my half-paralyzed legs of before just about started to dance. I apologized profusely to Julius, and to emphasize my sincerity, I pressed a bottle of wine into his hands. So what if the bottle was not mine, but secured from underneath the bed of whoever lived next door. (If the owner should come looking for if, well then – the mice drank it!)

In total, Julius pressed eight letters into my palms. Budapest, Ankara, Brussels, places that for so long now had been buried under a mist of silence, suddenly came swarming alive around me.

My present circumstances made no difference to the joy that was now mine. If only for a short while, the letters dissolved my feeling of abandonment and as always, I devoured every word. Two or three of the eight letters had roamed around Europe, Africa and Asia before finding their way here. The letters included all the wise counsel of parents and siblings miles away: take care to dress well and not catch a cold, watch that some wild animal doesn't tear you to pieces.

Most surprising was the news inside the letter from Ankara – my younger sister was moving to Brussels!

"By the time you read these words," she wrote, "I will be living in Brussels with our older sister. I tired of the Turks, of Ankara, but especially of the American attache's lowbred and not very educated trivialities. On top of all that I had to contend with most of the household duties. And so, my dear brother, the next letter you get from me will be mailed from my new home in Brussels."

How true, the words of Omar Khayyam: "We are but miniature pieces on the giant chessboard, tiny dots on the sprawling meadow that is life. Life shifts the pieces around back and forth, loses interest, knocks them out, then sets them back in their graves."

And so did fate shift my tiny family around.

That my initial goal was Ankara, that my second choice was Brussels was to no avail when life dictated otherwise. My square on the chessboard was Indochina, its stifling and humid air, its jungles swarming with Vietmins. At one time, I was almost standing on the doorstep of Brussels before a clever move swept over me to other side of the world.

These forks in the road were beginning to converge. Already, the separate paths of my two sisters had come to join together. Reunited by fate, on the same square they stood to await the next calculated move.

A fleeting second, then it was gone. The wailing and limping of injured men around extinguished all hope as quickly as it had come and my envisioned hairpin curve went up in a puff of smoke.

When misery was rampant it was easy to forget that these people counted among the more fortunate. If that bullet or splinter had struck a hair higher or lower, no longer would I see them hobbling around, no longer would I hear their whimperings. In a hastily unearthed grave they would be resting, or waiting out their intended fate after serving a life long sentence as a cripple. No question that I had to count myself in with the lucky ones. If those grenade splinters back on the Dong-Khe bend had blasted into my face half a centimetre higher, I would now be confined to some French institute for the blind and relying upon others to be my eyes in the reading of and responding to these letters.

I was so wrapped up in my letters that I failed to take notice of the dinner hour and everyone else's absence because of it. Only when they came back did I realize that I had missed the meal. According to Julius, I hadn't missed much because our cook had distinguished himself yet again and Julius ended up dumping half of his meal. However, Julius did bring me two bread rolls and half a thermos of wine.

August 4, 1949

The section was back. The strain of the past three weeks was evident on their unshaven faces, tired bodies and moods. Only a few were without a dressing of one sort or another. They told of battles, truck loads of prisoners and of the damage the war had had on the Hanoi garrison.

"So Gypsy," I asked, "how was it?"

"You wouldn't have to ask if you had come with us."

I thought it best to let him be. In his state he was bound to put a bullet through me. I tried to weasel the information out of Charlie instead.

"So tell me old buddy, do you feel tired out?"

"Just shut your face okay? Go for a three week mountain hike yourself, then try asking such a stupid question."

His disposition was even more snappish than Gypsy's. I was not surprised. Weeks of prowling the forests and mountains, countless encounters with the enemy, and backpacks for pillows would cause anyone to be in a sour mood.

Excepting Alex, all of the Hungarians evaded injury. Alex's injury was, however, the result of his own carelessness and not from battle. He had wanted to carve a walking stick and the sharp knife had slipped and sliced his thumb down to the bone. The wound was all but healed now, but he lamented over the absence of a medal of distinction after such a traumatic injury.

"You see Scout? A man sheds his precious blood and they can't even be bothered to pin a silver medal on his chest."

"Slice your neck open next time Alex, you'll get something for sure. If not a silver medal than work on a chain gang."

"Well you're certainly no different from the rest! You just don't feel at one with your seriously injured comrades."

"Don't I? Trust me, my heart goes out to you, but right now I have to go on guard duty and don't have time to feel sorry for anyone."

Just short of midnight I developed a fever again and my shift was terminated. I thought it a strong indication of malaria. If only something positive would come out of it, perhaps being booted out of the Legion. I would more than willingly put up with a case of malaria if the outcome were dismissal papers for being unfit for service on medical grounds.

August 5, 1949

The doctor completed a thorough examination and sent me over to the hospital for tests and diagnosis. The guard standing by the gate directed me to the admissions office of the Lanessan Hospital. The upcoming days held much promise and my mood was optimistic. I pinned my hopes on developing a bout or two of fever during the course of the examination. There was no question in my mind that out of the ordinary events were about to enter my life. The doctor of the regiment would not send me over for a complete check up for no reason. Clearly there was something seriously wrong with me and a discharge was practically imminent.

Inside the office I was received by a very old head nurse with whom I conflicted with in but a few seconds. All was not starting out well. The nurse spoke very quickly and clipped her words so I couldn't understand half of what she said. When she saw that I was not doing as I was told she politely reprimanded me, and two nurses rushed in to see what the bellowing was all about. I suspected that they were accustomed to the earth shattering voice of their superior and always came tearing over to aid the victim. One of the two nurses was extremely pretty, dazzling me with her jet black hair and blue eyes, she detected my enthusiasm right away and made fun of it with a jeering grin. The sarcasm did not escape me, and I, in turn, realized that at least fifty men were enthused by her every day. I saw the situation as hopeless and chucked any further notions I may have entertained.

The nurses put their superior's wishes into words that I could understand, meaning that I was to kindly go into a closet off the hallway, change into a hospital gown, then reappear for further instructions. With the help of my Venus, I found the cubicle, changed and returned to stand before her eminence who towered over me.

My medical history was taken, I was given a bed number and off I went to find it. I caught myself in the window and laughed outloud at the image. The housecoat and pyjamas were at least four sizes too large and I looked like a refugee who was waiting for the charity of someone to take pity on me. I had barely settled into bed when my Venus sailed in to take my temperature and blood pressure. She also handed me a sample vial which would be sent to the laboratory for testing. So out of bed I walked toward the door with the letters W.C. prominently posted on it.

I heard Venus laughing as I closed the door behind me. I returned to my bed, after I executed the order concerning the bottle, and discovered that during my absence Venus had dug up a new set of pyjamas that were practically tailor made for me. I waited for her to disappear so that I could change, but she did not and insisted I hurry up because she had better things to do than stand around here all day. When she saw that I was hesitant about it she pulled down my pyjama bottoms. Lucky for me the shirt hung past my knees and covered everything that was best left covered. I modestly accomplished the change with my back turned to her. Venus all the while was glancing around and looking bored. Not doubt that such a thing was as common place for her as washing my hands was for me.

After I had changed she ordered me into bed, tidied the sheets and then vanished in a flash with the full bottle and pyjamas made for the jolly green giant. Gazing at her disappearing figure I concluded that she possessed the attributes of a Venus not just above the neck but all over. The ward was separated from the adjoining hallway by a waist high window and because my bed was up against it, I was able to survey Venus' comings and goings, and the shapely curves of her full figure which the tight uniform made no bones about revealing.

I whiled away the time daydreaming about a closer relationship in which Venus played the lead, but because of one or two circumstances of little consequence there was scant chance of my dream ever coming true. I was, first of all, not a doctor, gold braids did not dazzle across my shoulders, my pockets were not bulging with money, and I was not exactly a splitting image of Adonis. Suffice to say that my one and only redeemable feature, my most beautiful eyes which sparkled as she busied herself around me, were not enough to entice her into a leading role.

Within ten minutes my personal nurse returned with a doctor whose bearing could be called anything but friendly. His manner, however, was in stark contrast to his surly appearance. He perched himself on the edge of the bed and launched into an animated conversation that was more fitting for buddies of twenty years. After a lengthy spell of chatting and joking he rose from the bed, ordered that I not be fed anything other than half a litre of milk for the remainder of the day, gave me a friendly pat on the head and with his arms around Venus' shoulders, turned and left the ward. I, in imitation of Gandhi, fasted for the rest of the day. I was, however, granted something else besides the milk. Venus laid me on my stomach and stabbed two injections which were administered with the sensitivity of someone flinging a dart from twenty metres.

August 6, 1949

I was subjected to a multitude of tests, my body was carted from one machine to the next and put to the test in every which way, and my temperature taken more times than I can remember. From all this and from the myriad of injections I developed stomach cramps, headaches, dizzy spells, and nausea. Everything but a fever. If only they had taken my temperature while Venus rumaged about me, and on me! That however went unrecorded on my temperature chart.

August 7, 1949

My friendly doctor submitted the results of his diagnosis around noon: nothing. He could find nothing wrong with me, and I was to return to the company. I was dejected to say the least.

"They couldn't care less about my virtually guaranteed discharge," I mumbled while changing. This time around I was not under the supervision of Venus. I waved goodbye to my snow white bed, the soft and velvety hands of Venus, the splendid cuisine and to my much envied roommates. If only our chef cooked your meals, none of you would last much longer than two weeks. I was as chestfallen on my way out the gate as I had been jubilant on the way in.

Fate had singled me out to harass and tease. Fever bouts one after the other at camp, and here, where I had dire need of it, not one. Luck was not giving me preferential treatment. And to think of how I had embroidered my mind with the vision of my cruise back to Oran! A welcoming delegation, a brass band playing, a two month holiday before civilian clothes again, then Brussels crescent. And here I'm trudging toward Gia-Lam.

Yes, luck was steering clear of me, and in my despair over it, I dropped into a bistro and tossed back two bottles of wine. Under its influence I decided to do away with all doctors. It was a crying shame that not one was willing to show favor toward a sickman stricken with malaria, that not one came forward to recommend a discharge. As I eagerly and maliciously mowed the doctors down one-by-one, I heard someone call out my name. I glanced in the direction of the voice and saw someone waving at me from the doorway. True, I was seeing double, but the goatee gave Charlie away.

Who was to know by what means, but they found me here in the bistro, sitting in front of the empty bottles. Charlie and Mortier had been cruising the streets suspecting I might have trouble finding my way alone, and thought it best to come looking for me and drive me back. There was a sliver of truth in this because waking up the next morning in my own bed in Gia-Lam I had difficulty remembering how I had gotten there, and further-more, found it curious that it was not Venus but Charlie who heralded reveille.

August 11, 1949

Day to day existence was colorless, the evenings alone provided interest and only if we got together for a little gin rummy party and a lot of arguing. Tomorrow, however, was a promising day; we were being thrown into combat as paratroopers. The Vietmins were acting up and we were about to be thrown into their laps. The Vietmins were likely to use us for target practice as we swayed back and forth on the gentle descent despite the Geneva Conference had abolished *practice shooting* of this nature. At least that's how I understood it, but since Geneva was a long way off, I couldn't imagine that the Vietmins were aware of any such prohibition. and even if they were, what did they care about decisions laid down at the Geneva Conference table?

I would have placed a ban on the bamboo rods tapered to needle sharp-ness which the Vietmins were inclined to plant over any territory known or suspected to be a target point for paratroopers. More often than not, they were better informed to the time and place of our jumps than we were.

The needle sharp rods were terribly dangerous, and a man was liable to damn for all eternity should he perch himself on one. On one occasion, before a paratrooper detachment existed within the Legion, a squadron of the French regular army was jumping over terrain studded with these rods and the majority were impaled upon landing. The very thought was enough to take a man's breath away. We were painfully aware that our jump tomor-row was to be over similar territory. How many of us would meet a parallel fate?

It was true that artillery had set up a campaign to scour the ground in question the day before jumping, but a few rods were bound to be overlooked. Poor Walter (Chesko) was once a victim of one of these forgotten rods. Lucky for him the rod was already tilted halfway over when he landed on it, its effectiveness was reduced by the angle and after half a dozen operations Walter was whole again. He was especially fortunate that none of his vital organs were damaged.

August 12, 1949

Reveille at 4:00 a.m. Mortier was subdued this morning, something that was not an everyday occurrence. It was likely that his mind's eye mirrored a row of sharpened bamboo rods lined up in battle formation. Slow as we were, the group somehow managed to get ready with a major mess left behind, we gathered in front of the main building where the Captain, in the company of Lieutenant Mercier, was standing-by.

Across the gentle breeze of dawn came the enticing aroma of freshly brewed coffee laced with rum. We lined up beside the coffee kettle, each man received his share and after its consumption we boarded the trucks. Waving goodbye to those held back to safeguard the area, we started out toward the airport. I was surprised to find that our destination was not Gia-Lam's airport but Bak-May, and from this, I presumed our bearing to be a northeastern one.

The joyride lasted for half an hour and we arrived at the airport after bisecting Hanoi. We disembarked and headed toward the warehouse to pick up our parachutes. We found the warehouse doors locked. According to Mercier, the Captain had to be present before we could collect our gear. As a rule, parachutes were always distributed immediately after arrival at the airport and so, we didn't really understand what all this was about. We broke into groups to discuss the plausible reasons behind this uncommon incident, perhaps Charlie knew. Was it possible the jump might be cancelled? The question was raised in anticipation of a postponement, that perchance that was the reason for the delay and certainly not because we had any objections to a termination of plans.

"How the hell am I supposed to know? I know exactly as much as you do."

"You go on over there and ask that lieutenant."

"Like hell I will, he's not going to tell me anything. He probably doesn't know anything anyway."

"Like hell he doesn't. How could he not? Why else would he have ordered us to wait?"

"Because he's waiting for his orders from Plessiner."

"What difference does it make whether we wait or not?" growled

Charlie. "the longer we wait, the more bamboo rods will be cleared away."

"There ain't gonna be no bamboo rods there today! Hell, nobody knows where we're supposed to jump. I'm willing to bet that the Captain himself is only now being informed as to the location."

"Here comes the Captain now! Get a load of that smirk on his face!"

The lieutenant had caught sight of the approaching Captain and ordered the men into formation. The Captain hastened to join the lieutenant and together while madly flinging their arms about, they made their way over to the hopelessly lined up contingent. They stopped in front of the assembly, argued for a while, then turning toward us the Captain announced his decision to cancel today's jump.

Gypsy was thrilled to pieces. "See you blockhead, Charlie was right. Them Vietmins can go ahead and wait. There ain't gonna be any bamboo rods today!"

"Oh no, certainly not old buddy! My rear end is gonna stay intact for another few days."

The clatter of the wheels against the pavement on the return trip to Hanoi seemed to strike up a merrier tune than it had on the way to the airport. Contributing to this tone was the rising sun. The early morning hours look of the stirring city presented a much more cheerful picture than it had earlier, when the streets were depleted of life and illuminated only by neon signs. The city was coming to life in a manner typical of any large metropolitan centre. Street sweepers, garbage collectors and delivery personnel were among the first signs of a new day. Not wanting to let the very early morning customers slip by, street vendors were busily pushing their business mounted on a two wheeled barrow, and rushing to occupy their stands before competing traffic became really heavy. After all, every piaster helped to ease the financial burden for daily existence. We were overcome with relief when it was announced that:

"The jump is cancelled."

Four words and an enormous burden was lifted off our shoulders. Nobody stopped to consider that this unpleasant event would come to pass with hopeless certainty in one or two days, or maybe a week later. Quite simply, nobody wanted to think about it. It was enough that for the present, the anxieties over it were lifted from body and soul, that everything around appeared more beautiful and encouraging In this relaxed state of mind we rolled back to the residence where we found Julius staring at us with his mouth open wide.

"What the hell are you guys doing back here? I would have expected you to have wiped out two thousands Vietmins by now."

"Anything or anyone else you'd like us to exterminate?" Charlie barked at him,

"What's this? Are we perhaps in your way? Did you feel better when alone than in our outstanding company?"

I added my bit to the argument. "You should be glad to be free of constant guard duty, you idiot, instead of being so resentful."

"I'm not complaining, old chum! I'm really glad to see all of you back. Now I don't have to do most of the work by myself and at night, I won't have to sleep with eyes half open, even when I'm not on guard."

Back in our rooms we put a lot of effort into cleaning up the mess we had left behind earlier. Instructions were bellowed out by Mortier, who likewise was positively effected by the jump's cancellation, and who had recovered his usual grating tone of voice as a result. When all was scrupulously clean and neat, we gathered in the small square behind the station for the hearing of the daily gospel. In addition to the usual routine a small group was nominated to go marauding. Charlie and I were among the fortunate participants to be included in this important campaign. In view of the fact that no other provisions were provided besides tinned food for lunch, we presumed that we would be back in time for supper. The foray was to be a local one that would take no longer than a few hours.

We headed toward Haiphong. The spacious rice fields which spread on both sides of the road were broken here and there by grasslands well-suited for grazing, on which rested a few wretched hovels and a scattering of shabby palms with torn leaves. We turned off the beaten track and continued the hike on the banking stretching between the rice fields. We looked through those hovels which lay directly on our path, and inquired as to whether or not the inhabitants had noticed any Vietmin activity in the area. Our questions elicited only meaningless gibberish or a shrug of the shoulders in response. To continue this line of questioning was pointless; language barriers aside, they were certainly not going to provide us with the necessary information even if they had been able to understand French.

We stopped at noon for a brief rest period and ate our lunch. This was easier said than done because our hands were constantly engaged in swatting at mosquitoes who, in this area, were much less friendly than those we had encountered back among the natives. We continued and found most of the hovels along the way empty because the inhabitants were out working the rice fields. A few naked children were seen running back and forth between the houses while the village elders, who watched over the naked tots, sat around looking bored.

We entered one of these villages and our attention was immediately drawn to a mound of dirt which looked to be freshly dug and seemed curiously out of place in the surroundings. The sergeant in command of the patrol, a fellow called Schulz, ordered us to round up the village. Four men, old and older still, two women and six children were all that we could find. Schulz ordered them to dig up the mound. They pretended not to understand; but when Giovanni kicked one of the *old gentlemen* in his behind, they set down to the task with such an enthusiasm, like they had done nothing but dig mounds of dirt their entire lives.

The reason for their initial reluctance became apparent once the job was done. The overlay of dirt had served to conceal machine guns, hand grenades and ammunition. We had stumbled across a Vietmin den, but what happened to the Vietmins? These four kindred spirits of Methuselah did not exactly look like people who spent their evenings in acts of sabotage or who wanted to mount attacks against us.

We did not see any point in interrogating them as to how the weapons and ammunition had gotten here or where the Vietmins had escaped to. We knew that no response would be forthcoming. Although, it was entirely possible that the Vietmins had not taken flight at all but were still in the vicinity, working their fields, and to take their machine guns along while doing so did not seem necessary. Then when the elders caught scent of our impending arrival they had hastily thrown the gear together and had shovelled dirt over it. Time must have been pressing, because the machine guns were not rolled up in anything and the barrels were completely filled with dirt. After the weapons were turned up, Sergeant Schulz sent Charlie along with ten men out to station themselves beyond the vicinity of the huts and pan the area in case of a surprise attack. One never knew, and it was better to be safe than sorry.

Sergeant Shulz grabbed one of the machine guns and pressing the barrel against the brow of one of the kinsmen, indicated to him that he was about to be executed. The man stood motionless.

While Schulz was busy trying to frighten warriors, myself and two others rounded up five yokes to carry our find. The four men and one woman, who appeared to be the younger of the two, would come as prisoners with us back to Gia-Lam. Our conscience would not permit us to take both women along because we didn't want those tots to be left on their own. Somebody had to look after them, 10 or 15 years would undoubtedly qualify them as splendid Vietmins.

We placed the baskets on the shoulders of the five captives, tied their right hands to the rods, and their left hands to each other. Thus we continued the journey and arrived at the highway after making a slight detour. We inspected the hovels we came upon along the way, but our luck had exhausted itself the first round. The return trip was made slower by captives who were not inclined to keep up the pace. We were the ones forced to slow down and match our pace with their's, and it was past the supper hour by the time we arrived back in Gia-Lam.

After depositing the weapons and prisoners at headquarters, we went over to Joe Bristle's for supper. The bottled wine, born of his generous hospitality, made up for the suffering we endured while trying to force down the terrible meal.

August 13, 1949

It was Sunday, no issuing of orders, no line-ups, we could take it easy. I should go to church, I thought. I glanced at my watch, it was only 7:30 and High Mass did not start until 10:00 or 11:00. It was about time that I went, especially if there was nothing else to do all day. I haven't been to Mass since I was in Do-Son. I'm going to give myself another half-hour of lazing around, then I'm going to get ready and go.

I should ask someone to come along so I don't have to go alone. But who? Alex? He doesn't even know what a church is. Never seen the inside of one in his life. Maybe Julius? He was even worse, with his ultra-refined spiritual complex. Charlie? A hoisting crane couldn't drag him out of bed before noon on a Sunday, unless he had to go on duty.

Duty? I hadn't stopped to think about it. Was I maybe supposed to be on duty today?

Nah. Don't think so. If that were the case, somebody would have reminded me of it a long time ago. I'm not going anywhere until 9:00, and if nobody calls me by then, then I'm sure I'm free for the entire day. Best if I don't say a word to anyone, not invite a soul and just go by myself. Nobody will miss me or even notice that I left.

After this extended monologue, the half-hour period I had set aside for doing nothing had expired. I quickly got up, pulled on my everyday work clothes and scurried down to the kitchen for a bite of breakfast. Back to my room where I changed into my Sunday best and hit the road for Hanoi.

I glanced down the side street which led to regimental headquarters just in case I should be spotted by an officer who may have decided to go out for a morning stroll. I wasn't particularly worried about having to account for my plans or explaining where I was going, since most of them couldn't care less about what we did on Sundays so long as we were off duty. A conflict of interest especially remote if the officer one came across was not associated with the person's own squadron. On the other hand, there was always the chance that a man might bump into an overly critical officer who took pride in making a mountain out of a molehill, or who just happened to get up on the wrong side of the bed and was looking to raise hell or to take his revenge out on somebody.

As it so happened, nobody was walking down the avenue this morning, but in front of the officer's mess was a jeep. Sitting inside was Steve Bidon, who wouldn't think of missing the opportunity to see me. Nor did he pass by the chance to ask, while yelling at the top of his lungs, "Where are you going, Scout?" The distance between us was not so great that it would have been a problem to hear him had he raised the question in an undertone. His timing couldn't have been worse. I wanted to plaster his mouth shut but since he was too far away for me to do that, I yelled back that I was going to church in Hanoi.

"Where did you say you were going?" he yelled in return, as if he were deliberately trying to bring the entire host of officers who were at the moment likely sitting at the breakfast table, down my neck.

"I told you, you deaf idiot!" I screamed back. "I'm going to church in Hanoi!"

It made no difference any longer whether I was screaming or not. Everyone within a one kilometre radius were aware of my plans. What they didn't know was that nobody was taking my departure for granted.

"Wait a second Scout. We're going into town too, so you might as well come with us."

"Who exactly do you mean by 'we'?" I yelled back, walking closer to stop this needless yelling which was bound to lure out half of Gia-Lam.

"Capitaine St. Etienne, Sergeant Du Brouxen, and me. We're going to the hospital."

Typical, I thought to myself, as my luck would have it. I was lucky only in that St. Etienne, who was not from our squadron, was not the type to be faultfinding and held a fondness for Hungarians. Ever since the time when Joe Bristle had told him that he bore the name of the first king of Hungary, St. Stephen, he acted much more friendlier toward any Hungarians he encountered. I saw little point in declining the ride offer. They would pass me before I was halfway across the bridge and then too, it was better to ride than to walk. I surrendered to fate and elected to ride.

We waited for no more than ten minutes for St. Etienne to emerge from the dining hall. He tilted his cap in response to my greeting and returned the greeting asking where I was going.

"To the Catholic church in Hanoi," I answered.

"Fine. We'll drop you off there."

That was it as far as conversation was concerned. Fifteen minutes later I was standing in front of the church, right on time for the 9:30 Mass.

When Mass was over I came out of the church and stopped at the top of the stairs to gaze out over the surrounding area, which was radiating under the peace and quiet of the Sunday morning. The few stores in the area were closed. Rickshaw pushing coolies were lounging in the shade, not engaged in their usual indiscreet shoving in front of the church, yelling for customers: "Pus-pus, monsieur?" In the stifling heat of a Sunday in August, the shade was worth more to them than slaving over a few lousy piasters. I had no choice but to walk back to Gia-Lam, something that in this paltry forty degree heat would feel soothing, unless I came down with heat stroke along the way. Noon was approaching, the sun's rays bore straight down and shade could be found only under trees, none of which were willing to accompany me all the way to Gia-Lam. For the better part of the journey, the soles of my feet would burn from the heat of the sand.

Only after I started down the stairs did I notice a black convertible parked beside the stairs with a European woman with black curly hair sitting inside. With one hand on the door and the other arm propped on the back of the seat, she was sitting facing the church and staring at me.

Was she really staring at me, or at someone else lounging around behind me? I looked around, saw no one else, and deduced that I was the target of her gaze. I stared right back, straight between her black eyes.

While pursuing this visual game of mutual adoration, I couldn't help but notice that the she was approximately fifteen years older than me. I found myself in a battle of indecision. To hell with fifteen years there or fifteen years here if it meant that I didn't have to walk back in this stifling heat. Not to forget that the others would be eaten up with envy if they saw me come rolling back in a private car with a European woman at the helm. However if I accepted the ride, I was taking the risk of not getting back to my squadron before some ungodly hour and in the interim, a search party could quite conceivably come looking for me. I could find myself in a lot of trouble because to take one's leave in such a manner without explicit permission would be classified as desertion. The staring game continued as the minutes ticked by. The lady in the car grew frustrated and tired of waiting, she pouted her lips, shrugged her shoulders and drove off.

Didn't I make a mess out of that one! Why the hell had I wasted so much time trying to make up my mind? I could have at least sat down in the car first and thought about it in there. I was so angry that I just about kicked myself. I did not, only because to have done so was in no way a guarantee of her reappearance. Instead I hit the road to home fuming.

August 14, 1949

I woke up to somebody shaking my shoulder.

"Scout! Wake up! We're going jumping!"

"Wh-what happened? Where are we going?"

"Into combat! Line up in fifteen minutes."

"Into combat? Jumping?" I was close to tears. "That's madness! Which idiot would think of such a thing?"

I glanced at the clock, it was only 3:30. No light except for that radiated by the moon and the stars. Since switching on the lights was not permitted, we had to fumble around and try to get ready in the dark. I didn't even know who was who, nor did I feel altogether with it, after drinking and playing cards until midnight over at Joe's. If three hours of sleep was less than sufficient for a rabbit, then what about a slightly tipsy legionnaire? Charlie and I helped each other stagger down the stairs and were the last ones in line.

"My head feels like it's going to come apart," he moaned.

"Don't you think mine feels the same way? Julius is lucky. He can stay home and sleep."

"Sure, but don't forget he's got a permanent limp. Personally, I'd rather go jumping than hobble along as a cripple for the rest of my life."

"Can't say there ain't some truth in that. Look. Maybe we won't have to take the plunge after all. Maybe it'll be cancelled again."

"Not today, old buddy. I heard Mortier say that this jump is really the same one we were supposed to do the other day. All that fuss at the time was purposely created so as to deceive the Vietmins. Today we're leaving from Gia-Lam's airport, not from Bak-May's."

"The only advantage for us out of all this is that the Vietmins won't have a chance to stud the entire area with those bamboo rods."

"That's the whole idea, my friend."

The hot coffee with rum helped to straighten me out a bit, but despite three cups of it, I still had not quite come to, even by the time we reached the airport. Charlie and I helped each other in putting on and adjusting the parachutes. Mortier rushed over to intervene so fast that had I not caught Charlie by the throat, Mortier would have knocked him right over. Because it was by the throat that I grabbed him, Charlie turned goggle-eyed and was gasping for air. Only when I released my hold was he able to catch his breath. He swore that he would wipe out my entire family. Lucky for me that I had no family in the area. Then it was Mortier's turn to turn on us both, to swear up and down while he adjusted our parachutes. Dawn was beginning to break by the time we reached the plane.

The Captain and Lieutenant came along with our group and sat closest to the door, followed by Charlie and I. Plessiner and Mercier were so cheerful and animated as they talked that one would have thought they were on their way to a nightclub instead of a jump. Their good moods were contagious. By the time we arrived at the jump site, the entire company was laughing and telling jokes. The sun had begun its ascent and by the time the pilot switched on the red light indicating that jumping was to commence, our positive frame-of-mind made us forget the gravity of the day ahead. The Captain stood up, fastened his lock to the strap and stood ready at the door. The Lieutenant followed his example, then Charlie and everyone else. Mortier, who was responsible for driving the herd, brought up the rear.

The Captain was first to disappear into the void, followed by Mercier, Charlie and I. The others came after me, while the plane was flying over the designated area. Many of those who had already taken the plunge from the plane ahead had touched ground by now and had taken up protective, defensive positions so as to divert a possible attack.

Our drop in on the Vietmins really did turn out to be an unexpected surprise because I heard only a few rounds of machine gun fire on the way down and fewer shots still after I had touched ground. The few Vietmins who were in the area at the time obviously thought it better to retreat than risk facing an encounter. Even so, we followed the example of those who jumped ahead of us and took up defensive positions, just in case. We waited as the planes circled over the area for the leftover troops to take their turns.

And so they did. We watched somebody plunge headlong toward the ground after his parachute got jammed up. Fortunately he had enough presence of mind to open his reserve chute. He completed the descent safe and sound. Barely did we have a chance to breathe a sigh of relief when we saw four others leap out from the plane only to discover that the threads connecting their chutes had been severed. Three were able to open their reserve chutes, but one had had his reserve threads severed as well. We watched the tragedy unfold and were helpless to do anything. Listening to his screams was the most dreadful thing imaginable. Unfortunately, he did not lose consciousness on the way down and felt his body be crushed on the ground.

The first death of the day. There would be many more. We consoled ourselves as we began to gather section by section and the planes disappeared in the direction of Hanoi. The Captain held a brief discussion with the platoon commanders, and each section then turned in different directions to scatter among the mountains and forest. After a few minutes of hiking, the Lieutenant signalled a halt in order to clarify our objective.

The target was a community twenty kilometres away. The goal, its capture and occupation. Our section was assigned the task of safeguarding the right wing and carrying forth the assault against the community from the right. Furthermore, we were held responsible for eliminating any Vietmin forces along the way. The exact time of the onslaught against the community would depend on the degree of setback, if any, encountered during the approach. No mention was made of an alternate course of action should, for instance, we meet up with Vietmins in large numbers who proceeded to wipe out half our forces. Presumably, we would simply continue to forge ahead until the entire section was annihilated, in which case the problem would take of itself. There's not much use in even discussing the matter. Nor was there any debate over what would happen if, for instance, the first section arrived at the designated area without delay, only to have to wait another three days for the third section to show up. I trust that our superiors had thrashed out these minor details and we were not to question.

When the Lieutenant had finished with his informative statement he divided the group into two and sent half the section ahead under the leadership of Charlie. Our mission was to reach the mountainside lying directly opposite about one kilometre away, survey the stretch from a defensive point-of-view and verify its safeness so that the rest of the section could follow. Should we perchance be met with an onslaught on the way, we were to try and hold out until the others came to our aid. To retreat was out of the question. And if we did reach the designated spot without encountering problems along the way, a short round of machine gun fire was to be a signal for those left behind to follow.

With Charlie in the lead, Alex behind him, we set forth to execute the task.

"Hey Charlie," I said, "Can you see that half overgrown rocky area straight ahead? If the Vietmins were wanting to attack, that's the only feasible place they could do it from. Don't you think it would be better if we scattered about before going on and use the trees for cover?"

"I think you're right. But that place is quite a ways off still. At best, only cannon could shoot that far."

"Or doucettes."

"Yeah, or doucettes, but these trees could easily hold off every last bullet. There's no way that they would find their mark, not even by accident. Don't worry. If there is somebody lurking over there, we're not posing as targets of any sort just yet."

"That may be, but if we keep going the way we are now, a few hundred metres down the road they're going to mow us down with their doucettes any way they please. This forest is not dense enough to shelter us. They can easily pinpoint us as targets."

"Of course I'm not stupid enough to maintain this position all the way. We're going to draw near by crawling on our bellies after the halfway mark."

After hiking some three hundred metres down the road, Charlie motioned us to scatter. Another two hundred metres and all hell broke loose.

We flung ourselves to the ground behind the trees and evaluated the situation. The bullets sounded from all directions. Neither the crackle of light artillery nor heavy machine guns mingled with the noise, thus from a weapons point-of-view they did not have an advantage. In numbers, however, they were more likely to have the upper hand. Before they could strike from anywhere else, all six of us started shooting in the direction of the rocky terrain: the retaliation was under way. From behind the trees and lying on our bellies we hurtled bullets upon the enemy, sporadically however, since the assailants were out of sight and we saw little point in squandering ammunition on the rocks.

Charlie, who lying about ten metres in front of me, turned and called back. "Hey Scout. See that dense bush about five metres ahead of me? Take those three pinheads with you and try to worm your way over to the thicket."

"What do you take me for? Are you nuts? You don't actually think that six of us can drive the Vietmins out from behind those cliffs! They've entrenched themselves so securely behind there that if necessary, they could hold an entire squadron at bay. Take it easy, and let's just stay put until the others get here. Forty men will get on better than six!"

"Like hell, I want to attack! You think I'm crazy?"

"If we crawl close enough, we might be able to drive them out with hand grenades," said Alex.

"Let's go for it," I replied.

"Do as I said, and go only as far as the bush for the time being!" yelled Charlie. "All I want to do for now is get closer so that we're in a better position to survey the terrain. We'll decide later whether or not we should go any further. Take your leave Scout!"

He waved to the pinheads behind me, indicating that they were to stay low and crawl forward. Using my elbows, I too motioned them to do the same. We started out as ordered, but in a flash it crossed the mind of one of the Germans that he could get there a lot faster if he ran. He leaped up, and by crisscrossing back and forth he ran toward the bush. A few steps later he was felled by a bullet and lay crumpled on the ground.

"You fool!" screamed Charlie. "Did you have to do that?" But he was already crawling over to aid the injured man. "Scout! Only as far as the bush! Stop and open fire on the Vietmins."

I crawled but a few seconds when the sound of gun fire from behind blended with the racket.

"Charlie!" roared Alex. "They're attacking from the rear too!" and he turned to face that direction.

Charlie stopped fussing with the injured man and took a firing stance against the enemy attack form the rear. While the other two pinheads continued their advance toward the bush in question, I turned back to assist Charlie and Alex.

"Corporal Red! We're here!" we heard the Lieutenant yell just in time, for we were just about to open fire on the stirring bushes.

We were so preoccupied with the enemy that the arrival of the assisting squadron had completely escaped our attention. Charlie in his eagerness had completely forgotten to post at least one man as a spotter who could warn the rest in case of a surprise rear attack. We had good fortune to thank that it was our own troops and not that of the Vietmins. The arrival of fresh troops and the five-fold increase in gun power must have made those lurking behind the cliffs see reason because the firing progressively weakened, then ceased altogether. Our lieutenant followed suit and called a cease fire. After a brief wait he divided the squadron into three so that from three different sides could we draw near, outflank and capture the enemy position.

We had no way of knowing if their submission into silence was a trap or not. Because it was entirely possible that they thought we would assume the post abandoned and expected us to throw all caution to the wind as we drew near only to wipe out half the squadron before we clued in as to what was going on. The two outer flanks exploited every means of cover as they advanced forward while the central group kept the enemy position under fire despite the absence of retaliation.

If there was a surprise to be had then it was on us, because we reached the enemy position without encountering any resistance and found nothing outside of several hundred cartridge hulls. The Vietmins had long since moved out of sight and were likely watching our cautious steps from a comfortable distance.

It was almost noon, and since our injured man had to be administered to, the Lieutenant thought it best to eat lunch then and there in case we had no chance to do so later on. He was also arranging for the return transport of the wounded man. After all, for us to have to carry him back the entire way was asking a bit much. Walk he could not because it was his thigh that was shot to shreds, and the efforts of the squadron doctor who bandaged the leg with great expertise were, nevertheless, in vain, for the man was in danger of losing his leg if he did not receive professional care in time.

After flattening our tin cans so the Vietmins could not make bombs from them, the squadron rested while the Lieutenant radioed Captain Plessiner, who was directing the course of the entire operation, details relating the return transport of the injured man. Leaning up against the trunk of a shade tree while waiting for orders to continue, I felt a shiver run through me and a fever coming on.

"Sergeant!" I called to Mortier, who was lying on the ground a few steps away. "I don't think I can go any further with the group. Another bout of fever just turned up."

"Out of the question. You're going to go as long you can stand on your feet."

Step-by-step the fever possessed me, and as its power increased, I was less able to perceive the happenings around me. Above me, I saw the trees strangely hovering and soaring away. A buzzing and a rumbling murmur enveloped me as I watched hazy figures looming over me. I plunged deeper and deeper into stillness until there was nothing, only silence.

August 18, 1949

When I woke I was free of the fever but terribly frail and weak. With the help of God and the medical staff I managed to survive this latest attack of fever. How much longer before I could not find the strength to compete? Would I follow those who had lost a similar battle?

August 22, 1949

Life in the hospital was infinitely boring. Not too long ago, when Steve Bidon and I had gone to visit Dinnes in the hospital, the two of us had fantasized about being in his place. If only we would sustain a minor shot in the chest or leg so that we too could enjoy the care of nurses. And now, here I was.

All in all, I am not exaggerating if I say that given my mild excuse for being here, I was sore about it. I know I would have felt altogether different had I been sent here because of an injury, not a serious one naturally, but something like the minor chest wound which had sent Dinnes to the hospital. If this were the case, the malaria would simply be instrumental in furthering the dreams I had woven at my last medical examination. As it stood, I predicted an end result little different from the last time. They will send me packing back to the squadron in a few days.

I was a soldier on pass today and as such, I was allowed to get up and stroll around the yard. According to my doctor, this way I would regain my strength faster and be able to return to my squadron quicker. Dare I express my yearning desire for this to pass? On the other hand, if I didn't partake of a little jumping or mountain climbing, how was I ever going to sustain a minor, but looking as though it was serious enough to warrant a discharge, injury?

So here I was, a soldier on pass. I was permitted an one hour walk in the morning and another after supper. It was during my morning walk that I strayed into the canteen and met up with two other men from my squadron. I asked them for a report on the mission I had been forced to abandon. Had they managed to occupy and seize that community in question?

"Of course we did," replied one. "Granted, it did take three days because the Vietmins were appallingly fierce with their defence tactics, but we did drive them out. We collected weapons, ammunition and the usual prisoners by the truckloads. Besides all that, we came upon a good-sized fully-equipped hospital complete with doctors and nurses.

"And what about our side? Did we end up with a lot of dead or injured men?"

"Only three dead, but almost everyone came away injured."

"Do you know if anyone was brought in from the second unit?"

"I don't think so. To the best of my knowledge, no one was seriously wounded from that unit."

Thanking them for this bit of correspondence, wishing them speedy recoveries - to which they replied they were in no hurry, I left them behind so that I could go to the pavilion where the injured men were housed. I was curious to see if anyone from our unit was in there, and if not, I thought I might come across a Hungarian.

Those of us who were in the hospital due to some illness were kept separate from those who were wounded in battle. Long buildings stood in a row, each separated from the rest by a small yard. In the building farthest from the entrance were lodged the sick patients while all the rest were reserved for those who were injured. These buildings were joined by a network of roofed sidewalks so that the nurses and doctors would not get drenched in case a torrential downpour came crashing down, when they had to go from one wing to another. Parallel to this sheltered sidewalk ran the motorway and on its opposite side was the canteen as well as the hospital chapel.

As I was crossing the street after emerging from the canteen, I saw one of the nurses waving me toward her.

I wonder what she wants? My hour pass isn't up yet. There's still at least twenty minutes to go.

"Why do I have to come in?" I asked. "My hour isn't up yet."

"Your doctor is looking for you."

"Why?"

"I have no idea. He just told me to find you and take you over to see him."

"What on earth could he possibly want? He saw me on his rounds this morning, asked some questions and did some examining, why would he want to see me again? Can't he at least wait until my pass time has run out?"

"I told you already that I don't know anything. You'll find out once you get there."

During the course of the argument we reached the clinic, where the doctor again dove into his physical and verbal probing. He then instructed the nurse who had brought me in to take me to the room where cardiographs were done and have an examination carried out. Not this circus all over again, I thought. The same thing was done last time and nothing came of it except that I was sent back to the squadron. There's nothing wrong with my heart! Why are they bothering with it?

It, my heart, showed signs of malfunctioning perhaps only when I bumped into a terribly attractive and self-sacrificing doll with a knockout figure and one who did not close her eyes when laid down. A touch of palpitations in the proximity of the fifth and sixth ribs was most certainly present during such times. I was thinking on my way over to the private room that this doctor, from what I could see, was obviously not content to let me be in peace. He was prepared to poke, quibble and twist things around until he achieved an outcome no different from the last time around. Today, a cardiograph but tomorrow Gia-Lam,

I wanted them to make up their minds and either cure me of this wretched malaria or grant me a discharge. This procrastination was starting to get on my nerves. After the fuss was over and the cardiograph was completed, we returned to the clinic and took with us the resulting slips of paper. The doctor gave the graph a thorough checking, and ordered me back to bed and told me that I was not allowed to get out of it for the rest of the day.

"Damn it anyway," I cried furiously on my way back to bed. "There goes my evening walk and a movie down the drain! I've got one dreadfully boring evening to look forward to, unless it occurs to one of those still at home to come in and visit me. And I doubt that that will happen. The nightly rummy parties over at Joe's take precedence over visiting a sick comrade."

In the afternoon, after the compulsory siesta was over, the nurse on duty brought in everyone's respective injections and medications. She informed me, after administering my shot, that I was to go to another pavilion the following morning in compliance with my doctor's orders. They were sending me to Dalat for a one month sick leave. I had to wait out the time until departure which would likely be the next day in the collective pavilion.

"Where's he sending me? To Dalat?" I asked. "Don't make a fool out of me. That's impossible."

"I have no intention of making a fool out of you. Why do you think it's so impossible? Those who are thought to benefit from the climate Dalat has to offer are always sent down there. The nurse on duty tomorrow morning will come and take you over."

"How am I supposed to go to Dalat when I have no clothes other than what I had on when I was brought in from the mission?"

"It's taken care of. Don't worry about it. Tomorrow or the day after, you'll be taken back to your squadron and you can pick up whatever you'll need."

With that she disappeared in a flash, leaving me both beset by doubts and nearly jumping out of my bed for joy. I was left alone with conflicting thoughts racing through my mind like a thousand bolts of lightning rocking the sky during a storm. Good Lord! They were sending me on a one month vacation, and to Dalat of all places! This was like a dream come true. Do-Son had been wonderful, but Da-Lat! This can't be true! I was so excited over this business of travelling that I could hardly fall asleep. I don't know how, but I did manage to drift off, and found myself startled out of sleep by one of the nurses on duty.

"Scout, what on earth were you dreaming about? You were screaming. What I would like to know is what, because I couldn't understand a word you were saying."

"If I was screaming and you couldn't understand me, then I was probably speaking Hungarian. I dreamed that I was in constant flight, during which I found myself plunging down at least five times. I was screaming out for help. But now, I would like to know when I have to go over to the collective pavilion."

"Right now. That's why I woke you up. Pick up your things and let's go."

In her hands she was holding my file folder, and still, I could not believe even now that I was actually being transferred over to the Dalat group. In the interest of clarifying this whole Dalat affair, I have to note that whoever found himself sent there was extremely fortunate. For such a glorious vacation to expire, a man had to be seriously ill first and then he needed the intervention of a sympathetic doctor.

I relaxed and believed that I was really going, only after I was accompanied by the nurse over to the pavilion and only once I was in the company of those who affirmed that this group was in fact on its way to Dalat. There were perhaps forty of us. The first thing I did was race around to try and find some Hungarians. Unfortunately, I did not find any.

I was summoned after the post-dinner siesta and told to go down to the gate where a jeep was waiting to take me over to my squadron in Gia-Lam so that I could pick up anything I might need.

Once back at camp, Julius, who was on duty, was the first person I bumped into. He greeted me with a wide grin.

"What's the matter Scout? Did they kick you out?" he asked with a touch of malice.

"They sure the hell did! And so hard that I'm about to sail all the way to Dalat because of it."

"Where? How far? Don't tell me they're sending you on a vacation again!" he asked, as he wiped the smirk off his face.

"You're damn right they're sending me! And for a whole month at that! I only came back here so that I can pack up my stuff."

"Damn you anyway!" he shouted. "What a fluke. You've got more luck coming your way than everyone else in Indochina put together."

Up in the office taking care of necessary official business, I could still hear Julius' blessings bestowed on me, ranging from an epileptic fit to a plane crash.

August 25, 1949

It was necessary to rise at 4:00 a.m. so that the group members could get ready in time for the plane's departure. We didn't have to worry about our luggage because it was shipped over last night. There was nothing left to do but eat breakfast and get ready. This, however, proceeded so slowly that I almost had a nervous breakdown by the time everyone was aboard the trucks, a good hour later than myself. It was 6:00 by the time we got to Bak-May's airport. We were to fly not aboard the usual J.U. 52 or Junkers, but on a Dakota. What made this painful was that this particular plane had the annoying habit of taking a one hundred metre nose dive in the most unexpected moments and for no accountable reason.

It was precisely 7:00 when the plane's engines roared to life. The plane taxied over to the starting line, where the engines were worked at peak capacity to attain a maximum speed down the runway. The floor of the plane assumed a horizontal position shortly after.

Since we were flying through dense cloud, and unable to see anything of the scenery below, we entertained each other instead. The company of men became louder and louder and roars of laughter came after the telling of a coarse joke. This kidding around went on for a while, but the nurses brought an end to the telling of the raunchier jokes, saying that they were an insult to their ears.

Not about to contradict its reputation, our Dakota took such a plunge that we just about beat our heads on the ceiling. The boisterous and cheerful crowd became silent, like a fish out of water, and the ashen faces rivalled that of a freshly plastered wall. Four among us were paratroopers, and though all were familiar with the Dakota's tendency to drop like this, we still felt uncomfortable after the event.

Slowly the plane wound its way out of the thick cloud cover. The sun shone brightly down upon the smooth, reflective surface of the ocean below and from up here, the fishing vessels sailing past looked as though they were tiny mosquitoes. A city reaching far and wide came into sight, what had to be wither Tourane (known as Da-Nang today) or Hue. Soon it fell far behind, and gave way to the beginning of a carpet of green, the dense and savage jungle that was sporadically broken by tiny clearings upon which were scattered circular huts with gabled rooftops. Excepting these tiny native villages, there was no sign of any life all the way to Saigon.

At precisely 2:00 p.m. the plane touched down at the Siagon airport. We sensed immediately the change in temperature, the shift from the cool and pleasant air of above to the intense and stifling one of below. Since the flight to Dalat was not scheduled to leave until tomorrow, we were to spend the night here. The ride to our overnight accommodation was a bumpy one that consumed well over an hour and a half because we had to cut across Cholon and the traffic on the streets was nearly indescribable. The old and broken vehicles most inappropriately labelled as cars were barely held together by a mess of thick wires and a miracle, and that they were still puffing away in this wretched condition was another insoluble mystery.

Filling up every last inch of space were a host of rickshaws drawn by coolies or mounted on three wheelers, throngs of people on bicycles, a swarm of ragged and dirty children, and a noisy crowd on foot rushing to and fro. Flung across shoulders were the inevitable bamboo rods, the baskets suspended on either end laden with heaven only knows what kind of goods.

Dogs and cats mingled in with this colorful outdoor commotion along with a few dozen chickens that had broken free of their cages and who, in their confusion and alarm, were madly cackling and frantically flying about all over the place. Chasing and trying to catch them were a few dozen children and adults, who scared the poor fowls even more and forced them to seek refuge in all quarters of the globe. The filth and garbage strewn all over the streets was likewise indescribable. Suffice it to say that on this stifling tropical day, an overwhelming stench emanated from the rotting garbage and saturated the air.

Our chauffeur did manage to scrape his way through this incredible and bizarre crowd, and it was with great relief that we made it to our military class accommodations, situated somewhere in Saigon.

It is only natural that when a man lands in a new city, or a strange environment, the first thing he wishes to do is familiarize himself with it. I too acted upon this unwritten law and within the space of one short hour did not know whether I was in Tierra del Fuego, South America or Shanghai. I sauntered aimlessly along down a wide palm lined boulevard, and on the other side, I saw two legionnaires walking in the opposite direction. I ran over to ask them whether they were French or German, thinking, that I would be further ahead if I addressed them in their native tongue. To which one replied that they were Hungarians, and at this, I proposed that we urgently look for a bistro so that we could have a drink to celebrate our chance encounter.

It was not necessary to repeat my proposition. Immediately, we started out on a bistro seeking tour. As we were walking down the boulevard, there suddenly appeared a lady with a stunning figure clad in a transparent white kimono. We could not help but comment outloud on her remarkably curvaceous physique. We came quite close to her and all the while, in Hungarian of course, we were not sparing in our compliments as to her walk, which we compared to that of a graceful gazelle, or concerning the curves of her body, which we eloquently described and sung the praises of. At this, the lady abruptly turned and made a sharp remark.

"Might it occur to you that I understand Hungarian?"

We stood there, rooted to the sidewalk, mouths gaping a metre wide and eyes almost popping out of their sockets from the shock. We waited for the ground to open and swallow us up so that we would not have to meet the angry and hurtful eyes of this gazelle.

The lady turned on her heels and dashed away, but not before adding, in a spiteful tone, that we should be ashamed of ourselves. We just stood there staring at each other like stuck pigs. When we came to our senses, with great difficulty I might add, we decided that this encounter justified not one toast but two.

My companions, after listening to the troubles of my heart poured out over drinks, proved to be completely supportive and offered to help in any way they could. Together we resumed our search for the camp after drinking was over with, but with not the best results. Contributing in part to the futility of our efforts was the fact that after drinking a toast to happiness for having bumped into a Hungarian lady, our legs were not exactly gripping the asphalt with any great degree of steadiness. After another hour of aimless wandering about we decided to invoke the aid of the local police, lest we pound and wear out the pavement of Saigon for another week and all for nothing. It was thanks to this suggestion that with the able assistance of five native police officers, by 7:00 p.m. I managed to track down our camp. The timing couldn't have been better because a sizable tropical storm broke out just as I arrived.

August 26, 1949

We rose at the crack of dawn because we had to be at the airport by 7:00. We made it on time, but the plane did not. It was still undergoing repairs in the hangar, delaying departure time by at least two hours.

Where else could a man waste two empty hours but in the airport lounge? Several others entertained a similar idea and in no time at all we took up all the available seats in what was, prior to our arrival, a nearly deserted bar. In comparison to the stifling heat outside, the cool and refreshing air inside had much the same effect on us as a mouthful of water. The decor consisted of leather couches, tiny tables and a thick, elaborate carpet. Time passed quickly in such a pleasant atmosphere, but no sooner did we stretch out on the comfortable couches than the plane's departure was announced.

As the plane taxied toward the starting line, I had a funny feeling that something was not quite right with the motor. After running the engines for about five minutes the pilot shut them off, and appeared through the cockpit door with a set of tools saying that there was a slight malfunction with the motor which he would fix in no time and we would be on our way. After hammering for quite some time the pilot started the motors again, but again, they were not quite right. He poked his head the small door a second time and told us to get off. This plane was not going anywhere today. At the same time, he assured us that it would be operational tomorrow and urged us to come back then.

August 27, 1949

I woke up with a start, glanced a my watch to discover it was 7:30. Good Heavens! Don't tell me they forgot about me! I was so afraid of that, I had trouble breathing. Dear God, these guys went and left me here! I leaped out of bed, only to see that the others were still sleeping.

"What happened? How come there wasn't a reveille?" I asked the guy next to me.

"What happened is, that there's no plane. They phoned over from the hangar and told us not to go out because they weren't able to repair the Dakota and there's no reserve plane available. The Dakota won't be ready before tomorrow, so we won't be leaving until then."

Well, another day in Saigon. Not that this didn't appeal to me; in a city so lively and animated, so colorful and interesting, and full of life it was impossible for a man not to have a good time in it. And besides, who was crazy enough to sit in the camp all day and stare at the walls?

There was only one slight problem. That being, that a good time did not come for free. And besides that, who was in any mood to prowl about alone? But then, the company of a lady was twice the expense. On the other hand, if I didn't feel like staring at the walls, I shouldn't begrudge the piasters. It just might be possible to solve this little problem regarding the excursion. Maybe I could have my cake and eat it too. With this thought, I hung around by the entrance to the camp and waited for a rickshaw. A voice called out behind me,

"Are you going into town?" asked one of the paratroopers from the group.

"Yes. I'm waiting for a rickshaw."

"Let's go together and split the cost."

"Sure thing." I was happy to grab this opportunity because even if not much, I was starting my outing by saving some money.

A riskshaw pulled up and wheeled us out as far as the depot, where the driver tried to scrounge double the going rate out of us. We tried to reason with him but he was so physically and verbally insistent that we thought it best to pay what he demanded in case he called the Police if we refused. If this continued I wouldn't have a lot left to throw away in Saigon. Oh well, I shouldn't begrudge a poor coolie the few lousy piasters he depended on much more than I did. A half dozen children in need of lots of rice were probably waiting for him at home. If I was forced to suffer a wrongdoing in the face of defeat this in itself was a small consolation.

When a man finds himself in a strange city and has a whole day to squander, what was more natural than to sit on a bench in a park, or beside a table set up on the sidewalk outside a coffee house, tavern or bistro and stare at the passers-by while sipping a bottle of beer. While any new place can theoretically have much interest to offer, that of a city in the far east especially so.

Here was the intermingling of a world.

Filling the streets on equal footing were blonde, blue-eyed Europeans; local citizens with their classic jet black hair; Arabs wearing turbans and Blacks with skin the shade of night. As for the oriental populace, their tendency to look alike made it difficult to differentiate between those who were in fact natives of Indochina and those who were Japanese, Burmese, or Chinese. The reason for the presence of the Europeans in particular was just cause for speculation. That I was here was owing to accidental misfortune. But what about, for example, that blonde gentleman clad in European attire sipping his cool lemonade three tables over? What was he doing here? And the many thousand more like him? What storm was it that picked them up and deposited them here? Could it be possible that they were merely tourists on an around the world tour? Is it not possible also that they just might be international swindlers, con men, or spies, operating under ideal conditions in the currently nebulous political and economic climate of Indochina?

So absorbed was I with my examination of the colorful commotion on the streets that I failed to notice my companion stand up and leave. Presumably, he had grown weary of the idleness. Nor did I notice the three Indochinese women occupy the table next to mine. Some sort of an invisible alarm bell must have swung into action in order to divert my attention their way.

When I did finally notice them, the devil would not let me rest. I racked my brains trying to figure out a way to join the table. What the girls had to say about the matter did not particularly concern me. Either they liked it or they didn't. Should it happen that the idea appealed to them, what then? What the hell would I do with three of them? It'll cost me a fortune! It was an agonizing decision. The devil in me was urging me on, while the good fairy was holding me back. It wouldn't matter so much if there was only one lady, though even then I would think twice before acting, but three!

I've done a lot of crazy things in my life, and one more or less didn't make much of a difference. I justified it also by thinking that time would pass more quickly in the company of others than by hanging out alone. The decision was made. I flagged down a waiter, pressed five piasters in his hand, then told him to go over to the ladies table and intervene on my behalf. Would they take offense if I changed over to their table?

After a short exchange of words the waiter turned to look at me, grinned, pointed to the empty chair, and indicated that my desire to advance with honorable intentions has been heard and granted.

Mutual introductions and a few minutes of conversation later, two of the girls got up and left. It suddenly occurred to them that they had pressing business to attend to. I was more than gladdened by this turn of affairs. After all, one woman was cheaper than three. The one left behind, Thran Thi, was about twenty with smooth skin and a fragile figure. Thran Thi, with her easy going manner, dragged out of me that this was my first visit to Saigon, that I had a whole day I didn't know what to do with, and that I would be flying on to Dalat the next day for a month long vacation.

The truth was out. She immediately offered her services as a guide when she realized that she was dealing with an inexperienced and naive newcomer. I accepted gladly. By her offering before my asking, I felt relieved of some responsibilty and less obliged to her. Had I suspected that my purely honorable desire for companionship would not lead to the finding of an entirely honorable guide, perhaps I would not have felt so elated. I was a bit slow on the uptake and by the time I hit upon the truth, a third of my monthly salary had wandered over into her handbag.

Lucky for me that I realized what my friendly, flattering, purring and most accommodating guide was up to. This way, the next day I would bid

Saigon farewell somewhat depleted of cash but not totally wiped out. To give credit, Thran Thi did work hard for my money. She was a most eager guide who showed me all over the place, from the exclusive and elegant European quarter to the Grande Marche area, where the traffic congestion was so scary that I desired nothing less than a way out as quickly as possible.

I felt ill in the midst of this native population where a european face was a rarity. The faces that I did see pop up next to mine especially those with whom I came eye-to-eye, inspired me to get out of there fast. I was almost using my guide as a body shield in front of me as I quickened my pace toward the quieter atmosphere around the depot. It was the most sickening of thoughts to imagine that instead of a spiteful glance which left no room for misinterpretation, a sharp dagger could conceivably come flying my way, and find itself lodged in my back or in the vicinity of my heart. This was easy and fair game for those who were masters in the art of dagger throwing and for those who had guts enough to fling a hand grenade.

There was no reason not to look around just because I was in a hurry. I took the time in spite of my haste to glance inside the odd store or look at the abundant varieties of edibles that were displayed along the sidewalk. The people had no reservations about eating food that had been spat on by filthy flies and pawed by thousands of hands. It was difficult to stomach the sight let alone eat any of the stuff. The ghastly throngs, the dirty stores and courtyards outdid everything in my previous experience. Having made it to the vicinity of the railway station, I felt like I had just stepped from a mud puddle into the crystal clear waters of a babbling brook. Just a few streets over and what a different world this was!

Since I had not given Thran Thi the opportunity of asking me to buy her some pretty item in one of the countless stores along the Grand Marche, she made a beeline for the stores around the depot so that she could continue what she had started in the morning – stripping me of money. So as to cut short her shopping spree before it ever started, I tried to bid her goodbye. She did not take kindly to my wanting to get rid of her and reacted with anger. She had every intention of claiming the one or two piasters left in my pocket for herself, and if I left her high and dry now, there was no way those piasters could ever find their way over to her. She put on her most charming smile, curled up next to me and purred with greater conviction than the most spoiled cat, but I stood my ground and held out against her seductive temptations. Late afternoon was closing in too, so I jumped into a rickshaw coming my way and waved goodbye to this money hungry huntress whose eyes by this time were flashing with hatred.

Chapter Fifteen
Dalat

Cao Bang
That-Khe · Dong-Khe
Dong Dang · · Na-Sam
Lang-Son ·

HANOI
Gia-Lam' · Haiphong
Do-Son

NORTH
VIETNAM

Tourane

SOUTH
VIETNAM

Dalat ·

SAIGON

August 28, 1949

A dreadful screeching woke me with a start. It was a rude awakening at best. There is no arguing that the deep and peaceful sleep of the early morning hours, say, between four and six, were the sweetest a man could come by. It was a luxury not to be startled out of sleep during these hours by the blasting of voices of two legionnaire sergeants, but to awaken slowly, yawning and stretching at one's own pace. This was a sheer delight. So for a second I thought that this was a call to combat, and in hot haste, I found myself grabbing for combat equipment and looking for the tunue combat. I did not find it anywhere. Only after my mind began to clear from the fog of deep sleep did I realize that I was not in Gia-Lam but in Saigon. The two NCOs whispered in their strident tone that in one hour we had to leave for the airport, where the planes were standing-by and waiting for our arrival.

The stars were still twinkling in the sky as we dashed through Cholon on the way to the airport. It was a relief to find, once at the airport, that we were going to fly not on Dakotas but on Junkers, a model that was less prone to pitching and tossing.

207

A view of our holiday resort

Our swimming pool

A cog-wheel railway

The number of men going to Dalat had multiplied during our one day wait in Saigon and two planes were necessary to accommodate us all. We split into two groups and boarded, I in the second group. The plane was one which serviced paratroopers, and thus, the comfortable seats had been dismantled and taken out. In their place were two long benches running the length of the plane. As a result, the only way to look out the windows was to kneel on the benches, or if a man wanted to wring his neck, from a seating position twist around so far that his neck stiffened. Kneeling was much more practical, though it was not too comfortable. And so, I kneeled on the hard wooden bench and watched the scenery below unfold and draw away: forest, tiny clearings, a few hovels, a couple of rice fields . . . forests, clearings, a few hovels . . . It was all so boring that I soon stopped looking around, besides, my knees were starting to complain about the hardness of the bench. I chose instead to listen to the others chattering away, adding my bit from time to time.

We must have been airborne for about half an hour when the plane suddenly lurched and lost altitude. We didn't even have time to get frightened. In an instant, we were tumbling over one another and ended up in a jumbled heap with the baggage. Quite audible were the loud ouches coming from those stuck at the bottom of the pile. I was not to be excluded. I managed to shake off the four or five canvas sacks that were piled on top of me. This proved to be unfortunate because the guy who was sprawled on top of the bags plopped down to take their place and proved to be much more of a nuisance, and far less comfortable than the soft and lightweight bags.

I don't know exactly what it was, but there was a hard object in the guy's pocket which wedged its way in-between my ribs. I came up with a good Hungarian blessing in response, at which he tried to peel himself off me by digging his elbows into my side. The plane chose this moment to lurch again and tip the other way and we all rolled to its far side. The plane rocked back and forth a couple of more times before it levelled out and continued on its merry way. Only when everything had returned to order, only after everyone had rid themselves of the unwanted baggage and bodies did we stare at each other with mouths gaping wide and wonder what the hell had happened.

The words stayed stuck in everyone's throats. In silence we sat on the benches, on the floor, on the luggage, wherever each man had landed after the last dip. And there we stayed while trying to untangle the mystery. The pilot growled into the loudspeaker that the plane's left motor had conked out without warning: "No cause for alarm. Don't any of you worry about it. The two working engines will get us back to Saigon where we will simply ask for another plane."

I wondered if this reference to "asking for another plane" was intended as a stupid joke similar to that made by our paratrooper instructors back in Philippeville when they had offered words of consolation prior to our first jump. No problem such as this to worry about, had we been aboard a Dakota. Given a similar malfunction, it most certainly would have crashed without a hope in hell of recovery.

Good lord "Judy" was uncomfortable at best and limped to get by, but at least it was reliable. So what if one of its engines gave out? It was still capable of drawing on the strength of its remaining two motors and piddling for a while. And so it was that we hobbled into Saigon, where another plane and its entourage of two doctors were waiting. We were given a hurried physical before we changed planes just to make sure that no one had sustained any serious injuries. Nothing was uncovered except the odd broken rib, scratches of various sizes and bluish-green bruises.

When we hit the road for Dalat the second time I remembered the dream I had in the Hanoi hospital, and Julius Mole's outburst after I had told him that I was going to Dalat for a one month sick leave. His wish, "If I can't be on it, I hope the damn plane crashes!" had almost come true.

We landed at the Dalat airport three hours late, but we landed thanks to our pilots whose emotions were under control.

The holiday resort was built around a large lake and in the midst of a forest some six kilometres outside the city. The climate here was terrific. It was pleasantly warm, unlike the stifling and humid heat up in Tonkin. The weather itself promised a glorious thirty days to come. And these thirty days flew by.

Swimming, fishing, chess, ping-pong, libraries and walks in the forest when it wasn't pouring rain lent ample variety to my days. Movies too, but for that we had to make a trip into the city. This in itself was not a problem, because cars that travelled regularly back and forth between the resort and Dalat were at our service. Saying the cars were ours alone was perhaps a bit of an exaggeration, because they were not engaged for our exclusive pleasure. In fact, if we had been the sole residents of the resort, perhaps the automobile service might never have been introduced in the first place.

Some distance away from our two storey barracks were private dwellings in which the officers and NCOs vacationed. And it was for them that service was instigated. We profited from it also, because the service spared us from having to walk twelve kilometres every time we wanted to go see a movie.

Much to my relief, I was not the only Hungarian in the camp. A small group was hanging around in front of the residences upon our arrival into camp, curiously looking over the new vacationers even before the trucks had come to a complete stop. The chauffeur hardly had time to turn off the motor before a voice broke free from the crowd to ask:

"Are there any Hungarians among you?"

"There sure are!" I answered. "Who's doing the asking? Where are you?"

Two figures detached themselves from the crowd. One, black-haired and stout; the other, blonde and lanky. Standing beside each other like that, they held a strong resemblance to Laurel and Hardy.

The stocky, brown complexed guy, who several years ago was wearing the uniform of the Royal Hungarian Mounted Police with the stripes of a sergeant, had a markedly scared face, which he suffered when a handgrenade blew up prematurely.

"They mangled my face but good, old chum," he kept repeating. His appearance was so frightening that I almost had a heart attack every time I looked at him. The poor guy had no delusions as to his appearance, though he did try to mask the fact for his own sake with a steady stream of jokes. He had another bad habit of making use of every possible opportunity to comment, explain, educate and instruct. On account of this irritating habit of his and the fact he had at one time strutted about wearing the uniform and feather cap of the Royal Hungarian Mounted Police, I pinned the title of "wise gerdarme" on him. We understood each other and got along well. And as we both enjoyed walking, went for many walks together in the surrounding forests. The endless excursions provided by his former job as a police NCO were so ingrained that only when roving about in a forest did he feel satisfied and truly in his element.

Not so the lanky blonde whom I shall baptize Zoltán could not be enticed to walk with a ton of gold.

"Listen you paratrooper!" he kept harping, "I do plenty of marching with the squadron. No way I'm going to do any more walking here unless it's to go to the bathroom."

True to his word, I never saw him take a walk. Even when going to the lake a step away from the swimming pool he drove, when that was really just a hop, skip and a jump away from our home.

One day the wise gerdarme and I decided to go for a long walk in the forest, something that we could contemplate with an easy conscience here because there were no Vietmins in the area, and the Moi's were friendly and peaceloving people who would not hurt a fly. These black winged critters, of which there were more than enough to go around, had a particular fondness for seeking out the Moi's huts and feasting upon the slabs of meat hung outside after a recent kill. And yet, the Moi's wouldn't think of shooing them away. It was meekness such as this which characterized these "barbaric" natives.

A Moi house on the edge of the jungle

Moi men discussing the hunt

Sewing boxes adorning the ears of a young Moi woman

During the walk I watched these barbarians as they sat idly in front of their huts, smoking, talking and laughing. Being witness to their carefree and peaceful existence, I reflected on who was more fortunate. We or they? Whose life was more settled? Whose flowed more smoothly? Ours or theirs? Were we the more fortunate just because the so-called modern world provided for everything a man could ever need or want, from a comfortable pair of slippers to a refrigerator to every luxury imaginable? Or was the lifestyle of the Moi's better, a people who were primitive in every sense of the word, wore little else besides a loincloth and hunted with bow and arrows? The Moi's couldn't care less about and wanted no part of the ravaging civilized world around them, the modern arms it provided, or all the wonderful things and comfort it had to offer. They didn't want any shoes or fashionable clothes or radios or refrigerators. Nor did they live in homes equipped with every modern convenience or sleep in soft down beds. They resided smack in the middle of an industrial world, had dealings with it on a daily basis, and yet, they chose to reject this world. But then, look at how much more content, balanced and happy they were than we. Their sense of spiritual fellowship and respect for each other was far greater than ours. To continue listing all of that which they had over us would not alter the final conclusion: I was jealous!

Although no weapons were permitted in the camp, the wise gerdarme did have a jackknife. "You know, old chum," he said, "I would just as soon part with my very own eyes than with this knife. I guard it like a treasure. And when you look at it, remember that it sliced my bacon and kept my company throughout my entire patrol along the length of Transdanubia. Treat it with due respect, for in it lies the blue waters of the Balaton and the forest murmurs of Bakony."

So with this renowned jackknife, we set out to discover but a small patch of Indochina's primitive jungle.

Although rumored to be in these parts, tigers and leopards were the farthest thing from our minds when we hit the forest trail. We ambled along the beaten track, wonder struck by the giant trees and the countless shapes of flowers dressed in as many different shades. True to form, the wise gendarme was incessantly explaining things. I was so used to the professor's lecture by now that I paid him no heed and tuned him out. On we strolled, gazing around, meeting up with some Moi now and again, who stepped out of the way on the narrow path to wait until we passed by, while exchanging friendly greetings in Moi to which we replied in Hungarian.

They carried baskets, arrows, felled animals and children on their backs. The latter were hanging from the backs of the fairer sex, who also had sewing boxes dangling from their ears.

The long walk left us feeling exhausted, so we sat down under a tree to rest and perhaps catch a bit of a snooze – presuming that the ants and other creatures permitted it. No sooner did we sit down when the wise gendarme broke into a monologue.

"Oh those wonderful days of patrolling the beat back home, when we sat down to chew the bacon under the cool shade of a acacia tree. With this knife, see? This very knife! Those, my pal, were the good ol' days. Boots beating the dust, cap feathers fluttering in the wind. . . ." On and on he went, while I quietly listened.

His story telling was shattered by a rifle crack. Then another and then a third, and always from a different direction. We stared at each other in astonishment, unable to fanthom the nature of this shooting.

"Hey you wise guy, I'd stake my life on that someone is out there hunting tigers or leopards."

"Well, if that's the case, then we're sitting ducks right in the middle of it. And if that tiger or leopard is trying to make his escape, then he's bound to be heading in our direction because the shots can be heard coming from all over the place. And judging by the sound of things, not too far away either."

We had both leaped to our feet with the urgency of one stung by fifty thousand ants and back to camp we tore at a speed so fast, that it made a cheetah appear lame.

On another occasion we drove into Dalat with Zoltán to catch a flick. *The Marriage of Frankenstein* was showing. Zoltán, from the very first minute on did not care for either Frankenstein or his marriage. I found no fault with the film, but then, there's no accounting for differences in taste. During the running of the film Zoltán whined and complained so much that I had trouble understanding any of the words.

"Hey Zoltán! If you don't shut you trap I'm going to kick you in the shin so hard, that you won't be able to walk as far as the bathroom anymore."

At this, he shut up.

Had I left him to sulk on his own, then maybe the evening wouldn't have ended so miserably. True, that we were not to blame for what happened later on. We were participants only. After the show, Zoltán suggested that we go someplace to eat. "Soupe chinois" would do if nothing else was available

Set up in one of the small squares we saw a few tiny canopied stalls around which lingered the aroma of "soupe chinois" and other Chinese specialties. We went into one that actually had benches in front of the counter. Meaning, that we would not have to sip the soup standing up. We bowed politely to the owner of the restaurant sat down by the counter and ordered some soup. He grabbed two large bowls from the dozens sitting on the counter beside a variety of other odds and ends, filled them with the soup simmering in pots behind the counter and with a wide smile, placed the soup, pairs of chopsticks and porcelain spoons in front of us. Both Zoltán and I opted for the chopsticks with which to attack the chunks of meat peering out from the bowl.

Simultaneously we put the meat in our mouths and simultaneously we spat it out. The taste was atrocious.

I suddenly recalled the parallel incident in Hanoi, the salad laced with poison which had a similar taste to this. Without a moment's hesitation I picked up the bowl and flung it at the master of the restaurant, who ducked just in time. The bowl missed his head and instead, landed on the shelf and splattered against jars filled with what looked like pickles and who knows what else.

As though Zoltán had been lying low and waiting for a chance just like this, he proceeded to sweep the bowls and everything else off the counter. The master of the restaurant began to scream at the top of his lungs when he saw the major mop-up, and in no time at all he was joined by no less than twenty of his kinsmen who entered into the screaming contest with him.

We wanted to get out of there in a hurry. After leaving twenty piasters on the shelf, we turned to discover the doorway was crowed by the screaming herd of kinsmen. The bench proved to be of great help in this regard. What luck that we had stumbled into a restaurant furnished with a bench! We picked up the wide, long bench, threw it into the fist shaking and screaming audience, dealt out blows right and left, then observing the "discretion is the better part of valor" motto, we rushed out of there in search of some place a little quieter.

As it turned out, we did not get very far. A jeep with four robust members of the Military Police appeared as if out of nowhere, and the cops had us nabbed in no time at all. They shoved us into the jeep, took us to the police station where we found, much to our surprise, that the Commanding Officer was Hungarian.

We were still standing outside the door when the Sergeant caught sight of Zoltán. He watched from his seated position behind his desk, as Zoltán was dragged inside by the Police who were restraining him on either side. He shot out of his seat like a cannon ball and pitched into Zoltán; "What in the blazes did you do this time?" The mumbled curses which followed gave credibility to his true Hungarian nature.

And as for Zoltán, to be greeted in such a manner proved beyond a shadow of a doubt that this was not his first *visit* to the station. He pointed an accusing finger at me, and pleaded,

"It wasn't me! He started it!"

"Who are you?" the sergeant whispered in a voice so soft that it caused shivers to crawl up and down my spine. "I haven't seen your face around here before, and I don't want to see it again, you hear? I don't need no troublemakers bothering me all the time."

I launched into an explanation, but I only had time to stammer out maybe five words, when the Sergeant quite impolitely screamed at me,

"Shut your face!"

He turned to Zoltán, and in a much more subdued tone of voice said this. "Listen, you henchman! To this day you alone were the source of all my troubles, and now, I'm stuck having to deal with two of you. I'll tell you, the entire camp taken collectively causes less of a problem than you alone. And here you go, hooking yourself up with another absconder."

He continued, turning to me, "You are no less of an absconder than this guy here who causes his mother never ending sorrow. And if I ever see either of your faces around this place again, you're both going to spend what's left of your vacations holed up in there." He motioned to the tombeau.

"So what did you destroy this time?" he asked Zoltán. "How much damage did you do?"

"I told you already, that I didn't start it! He's the one who broke the first bowl and two pickle jars."

"Just like that?" he turned on me. "Then be so kind as to tell me how much damage you did."

"I'm only responsible for breaking one bowl and those two pickle jars. Zoltán was the one who destroyed everything else."

"But we paid for all the damage!" he interrupted fervently.

I rallied in support. "I should think so! By all means we paid. God forbid that anyone think that we left without paying for the mess we made."

"So! You paid!"

"But naturally!" we replied. How dare anyone infer that we didn't pay! As to how much, well, that minor detail was not discussed. He did not ask, and we did not say: case closed.

"Go to hell, both of you. I don't want to see your faces around here again!"

Interestingly, after I immigrated to Canada and settled in Calgary, I met the Hungarian sergeant again. I was living with a Hungarian family in a house that had many rooms for rent. Shortly after I moved in, another tenant moved into the room next to mine. I met the new tenant as he was stepping out of his room and I was nearing mine.

I took one look at him and instead of saying hello or introducing myself, I simply said:

"You! I've seen you somewhere before!"

"It's possible," he replied. "I'd just like to know where, because this is my first day in Calgary. Don't know where you've been, but I've tramped around a good part of this globe."

"Well," I said, "after my discharge from the French Foreign Legion. . . ."

"You were in the Legion?" he asked. "Me too. Were you in Indochina?"

"Yes. For almost two years. I was a paratrooper. . . ."

The conversation flowed on until it weaved its way around to Dalat. Turned out that he was the very same Hungarian sergeant who, by way of parting in the Dalat police station, had said, "I don't ever want to lay eyes on your face again!"

And true enough, we never did meet up again, at least not in Dalat. But many years down the road and many thousands of kilometres from Dalat, fate reunited us again. What I saw was an altogether different person. This was no longer a legionnaire sergeant with a harsh voice and stern bearing, but a soft-spoken man with qualities of grace and charm.

We talked about the past for a long time, and had a good laugh over the incident in Dalat.

"So," he asked when we were ready to retire, "Out with it. Did you guys really pay that man."

"I beg your pardon!" I retorted, pretending to be hurt all over again. "You should know that a legionnaire always pays!"

It is curious how people can cross paths. After that particular incident I visited Dalat quite frequently, by myself or with friends, but not once did I meet up with this Hungarian fellow. True, I was not extended another invitation to the station because I made sure to give them no reason for it but still, we could have easily bumped into each other elsewhere in the city or back in camp, for that matter. But no. Years had to pass, and thousands of kilometres had to be put behind us before we were given a chance to meet again.

I have made reference already to the fact that the Moi clung steadfastly to their traditions and refused to be conquered by the civilized world they were surrounded by. I also mentioned, that those in the camp who had families lived in separate cottages. Each of these houses had a little yard to go with it, that had to be maintained. At one point, one of the residents decided that instead of breaking their backs with gardening chores and keeping the streets in order, or rather than having the wives do the work, it would be better to drum up a few natives from the area and pay them well to do the dirty work. This idea was acted upon and a short time later two dozen natives showed up, and willingly accepted the job.

The Moi set down to do the work, and admirably at that. The only problem was, that their attire consisted of nothing more than the usual loincloth, and this was not at all to the liking of several of the mothers. Specifically those that had adolescents. These mothers decided that they would organize a clothing collection and dress the naked Moi. The campaign was successful. They collected enough clothes, then told the Mois to get dressed. Trying to explain how was somewhat problematic but in the end, the near naked assembly were fully clothed. And so they continued their work for maybe ten minutes. The friction of the clothes against the skin which was conditioned to always being exposed to fresh air was itchy and irritating. One after another they began to peel off the shirts, the blouses, the pants. Not a quarter of an hour after getting dressed they continued with their work naked. The mothers led their adolescents into a back room and never again hired the natives to work in the camp.

It was tiny incidents such as this that added spice to our days. The more than three weeks up until now had passed gloriously. The wise gerdame was due to return to his outfit the day after tomorrow, and I two days after that. Zoltán had two weeks to go, since he had been granted a six week vacation. Once the wise gerdame leaves, and because Zoltán did not pursue walks beyond the bathroom, I will have no one to stroll with. And so, the gendarme and I went for one last walk through the forest. So familiar were we with one area that we were able to identify individual trees. The odd native greeted us like long time friends, and when they saw us coming, they invited us to come have a cigarette with them in front of their huts.

Once they understood what was going on, they expressed their deepest regrets and started wailing. When we felt that their wailing had spent itself, we bid them a touching goodbye and started off back to camp with the tribe hot on our heels. We walked for a quarter of an hour and they were still following. We had to end the parade and wave goodbye or the Moi would have followed us all the way back to camp. We let it be known that enough was enough and that it was time for them to go home now. We waited until every member of the escort party had their backs turned and was walking the other way, and only then did we bolt down the path back to camp.

September 29, 1949

My second last day in Dalat. Like everyone else who was returning to their outfit, I had to go for an examination. The physical we had to undergo was very thorough so that in case it was deemed necessary, the vacation time would be extended.

The wise gendarme left yesterday, tomorrow it will be my turn!

Since I could not persuade Zoltán to join me for a walk through the forest or even to help me kill my last afternoon with a trip into Dalat, we went swimming instead. Actually, I went alone. That lazy idiot ended up waiting over two hours for a car to come his way when, even if he had crawled over it did not take more than fifteen minutes to get to the lakeshore. I was long since sitting on the shore, spent from swimming and especially from the snakes who refused to give me a moments peace, when Zoltán, like a lord stepped off a jeep.

The snakes in the pool were of the perfectly harmless variety who, exempting the frogs which were their main source of nourishment, did not hurt a single living thing. So what did it matter if I knew they were harmless? Even so, I just about went off the deep end every time I went swimming and felt one of these innocent creatures worm its way up and down my leg, only to stick its head out of the water and come to rest on my shoulder. Never mind the times when they made an appearance in front or beside me. That was not too upsetting, I merely swatted at them, either hit or missed, and they disappeared. But it was another matter altogether when one of them decided to tag along for the ride by wrapping itself around my waist. Swimming would have been much more relaxing if they hadn't been so tame, if they had showed some fear of us rather than the other way around. It was for this reason that including today, I visited the pool all of three times during the entire month.

I should also mention that the jeeps were not always driven by men. We had two female drivers as well, and it was with one of them that a small scandal occurred.

It happened on a day when neither Zoltán or the wise gendarme were willing to accompany me to Dalat, since I was leaving in the morning and returning in time for lunch. No way they were going to come along for such a short time, so they said.

I, on the other hand, wanted to go so that I could get a color picture of myself. This was necessary because one day, I don't know how or where, a Hungarian newspaper was delivered to camp, and in it, I found the address of two Hungarian girls who wanted to correspond with Hungarian men living abroad. The paper was over six months old, but still, I knew I would have no luck unless I tried. Whether or not these girls included legionnaires into their category of "Hungarian men living abroad" remained to be seen when a response arrived, if it came at all. And, one of the conditions stipulated before serious communication could commence, was that the writer send a color photograph. (A black and white photograph would not do!)

There were two addresses in the paper, one to Vera and one to Eva. An argument started as to who should write to who. Zoltán voluntarily withdrew from the battlefield, saying that he was not crazy enough to squander his money on women uselessly. That left the wise gendarme and I to argue over Vera and Eva. Fifteen thousand kilometres between us and two women we had yet to see and here we were fighting over them. Both of us wanted Eva.

The gendarme, probably because Eva's father was a doctor and he was hoping that if and when he made it home, Eva's dad could help patch up his scarred face. But I stood my ground and won out in the end. Eva was mine, and that's why I had to go to Dalat to get a picture made.

How typical of women! Even if they were only seventeen-years-old, as this Eva from Nyiregyhaza, acquired after a long battle was. She lived on the other side of the world, I truly couldn't be sure that she existed at all, and yet, she was already parting me from my money. And seeing that the paper was six months old, who is to know how many men she's been in contact with already. But if I didn't try, I'd be out of luck. For now, all it was costing me was a picture. Greater things have been lost!

Anyway, I, alone, stood on the road, waiting for the next jeep which rolled by a few minutes later with a woman at the helm. The two of us hit the road for Dalat, passing through shady forests and along the way I got mixed up with her. She was, heaven only knows whose, life long companion. Granted, I did find out a few days later, but that was like crying over spilt milk. News of the incident leaked out, though how it ever did remains a mystery to this very day. I can only be glad that I managed to escape by the skin of my teeth. I have only the lady chauffeur to thank for my narrow escape. The ride through the shady forest was so much to her liking that even her partner, who was out for blood, could rejoice that the ride ended as smoothly as it did and with the least amount of scandal. Especially when we returned from Dalat after the picture-taking with the same lady chauffeur through the very same shady forest where we again enjoyed the softness of the grass.

September 30, 1949

What happened to the weather? When I went to sleep at three this morning the sky was full of stars and the moon was shing bright. And now, a thick cover of black cloud enveloped the sky. If it was the intention of somebody up there to let loose a liberal rainstorm, could he please wait another two and a half hours, because that was when my plane was due to depart for Tourane (Da Nang). The cars were already waiting and the officer on duty was going from room to room announcing the names of those due to return to their outfits today.

At 11:30 the Dakota darted down the runway and Dalat was a thing of the past.

Sunset in Tourane

Charlie Red

With injured Hungarians in front of
the Tourane hospital(author standing in middle)

Our good old Dakota remained faithful to itself and demonstrated its ability to plunge many times over. Our stomachs leaped back and forth between the top of our heads and the things we were sitting on and our faces shifted color from pale white to flaming red, all depending on the whim of the plane at the time. We hauled the pilot over the coals, and all the while, we were scouting the terrain, looking for Tourane. We could hardly wait for it to appear on the horizon. Unfortunately, nothing much was visible beyond the converging thick carpet of green. The jungle was broken sporadically to reveal a clearing with some huts in it. Not much consolation as far as we were concerned. I imagine that the Jews were no less exalted when they saw the promised land then we, when at long last, saw in the distance the much longed for city of Tourane.

The landing was a bumpy one. Up above, the air had been cool and refreshing but down below, a tropical heat wave pervaded the air. When the plane stopped in front of the terminal and the door opened, the burning air hit us like a burst of flame. And what is more, we could look forward to enjoying life in this crater for a while because en route, the pilot had announced that we had a temporary stopover of perhaps two to three days or until the plane was deemed mechanically sound. It was likely that the necessary repairs were of a more serious nature than the pilot made them out to be. It's quite possible that we again ended up on a plane that was on its last legs, one that had hobbled its way as far as Tourane but was hard pressed to go any further. Apart from this, the few days spent here might be useful in that I could adjust to the change in climate gradually, and not be hit with it suddenly once I was back in Hanoi. If I could condition myself to a heat which was far worse than that up north, I would not find the temperatures in Hanoi so intolerable.

Early afternoon, a good many hours to go until supper and an unfamiliar city. Becoming acquainted with it promised to be a far easier task than finding my way around Saigon (Ho Chi Minh City) was, especially since it defied comparison with Saigon in terms of sheer size, and furthermore, our accommodations were nearly in the hub of the city. A ten minute walk took me into the centre of town where shops, bistros, a movie theatre or two and entertainment hot spots abounded. Amazing, how all cities were made alike. The same picture done up in different colors and forms presented itself everywhere I went.

My experience during that night in Saigon taught me a lesson, and I proceeded with caution lest I again end up in a bedroom and find myself stripped of my money. If I saw one, two or three kimono clad sexpots standing about idly or sitting by the bistro table while sipping lemonade, I turned around and walked the other way. The devil perched on my shoulder and whispering in my ear that, "Hey, it's you they're waiting for!" was wasting his breath. I heeded instead the wise counsel of the good fairy sitting on my other shoulder who warned, "Listen to me! They're not waiting for you! It's only your money they're after!"

I did as the good fairy told me to do, and worked my way down street after street, thereby avoiding any and all potential occasions of sin. While steering this way and that, my attention on one street was drawn to a very noisy and active bunch of legionnaires. I swore that I heard Hungarian in the snatches of conversation. One person stuck out like a sore thumb because he was a head taller than the rest and because he was gesticulating wildly. His back was turned to me, but I was willing to bet anything that this lanky fellow was none other than Charlie Red from our squadron.

"Hey Charlie!" I yelled at the top of my lungs.

At this, the gangling brute turned around. It really was Corporal Charlie from Gia-Lam. We were very glad to see each other but especially I, him, since I presumed that he knew the ropes and knew of a place where a man might have a good time without worrying about being robbed. And besides this, I knew that Charlie was the type of person who would not allow himself to be cleaned out unless he got his money's worth in return.

"What the hell are you doing here my friend?" he yelled on his way over. I, at the same time, headed off in his direction. Both of us knocked over some pedestrians who were in our way.

"My vacation time in Dalat is over, and I'm on my way back to the squadron," I yelled back.

"And you, Charlie, what on earth are you doing here? Don't tell me that you too were sent on vacation!"

By now we were standing side-by-side and there was no need to yell. The friendly pat on the back which Charlie gave me almost forced me to spit out my lungs. I tried to return the gesture but was not quite as successful.

"Vacation you say? Me? When they bury me two metres underground that's when, and not before. I was sent here to take a refresher course for paratroopers. We're studying freefall, but for what and why me of all people, God only knows. But to hell with it. It's better still than slugging it out on those missions up there."

"So what's new up there?"

"There? Not a hell of a lot, my friend. The usual crap. We went on operations a few times. The usual dead and injured here and there. Leo was promoted to the rank of a corporal chief, Bracco's now a sergeant, Mercier's a first lieutenant. Seems like I'm the only one they forgot to promote. So what do the fools do instead? Send me here to go jumping. Oh well, I still say that it's a lot better here than marching on missions up there. But I still say I should have been a sergeant long ago!"

"Charlie, the day you become a sergeant is the day I become a captain. Never! Plessiner knows very well that if he promoted you to a sergeant, then everyone in camp from the sergeant's down would be made to feel uneasy. He knows all too well that you're wild enough as it is without carving a sergeant out of you. It's better for everyone concerned if you remain the corporal that you are."

"I'm gonna shave some of that big mouth of yours off just as soon as I get back to camp!"

"See how you're talking? Trust me. It's with the best of intentions that I'm trying to make you understand what a fool you are and why they refuse to promote you. And instead of repentingly bowing your head and admitting that I'm completely right in saying that you really are a madman, you sit here and threaten me with shaving away part of my face. Besides, how do you expect to become a sergeant when you've never taken an officer's training course?"

"Leo didn't take any such course either, and he still became a sergeant."

"Yeah, well that's all well and good. But you're forgetting, my chum, that Leo is busy playing the game of Mr. Doctor. You think they would have promoted him if he didn't deserve it? His three years spent at the University of Vienna were not in vain. He's making use of his knowledge and he deserves his stripes."

"But listen pal, I'm deserving too. I've fought enough, haven't I? And furthermore, I'm nearing the end of my five year stint, and I've never gone on vacation during all that time. Not like you who's already been twice."

"You don't hear me complaining over lack of a promotion, now do you? And I've gone through an injury whereas you haven't."

"You're not referring to that speck of dust which hit you up there between That-Khe and Dong-Khe are you?"

"You bet I am. First of all because you didn't even get that much, and second, because if the speck of dust as you say had landed a mere centimetre and a half higher, I wouldn't be standing here talking with you now. I'd be feeling my way around an institution for the blind somewhere in France. And how do you know that you won't be given a higher rank after you finish this course? Maybe that's why you were sent here."

"Who knows? Mercier did mumble something or other but you know how these things are. Often they're just frequent promises that don't mean a thing. Anyway, let's get out here before we're stomped to death. I know of a good place. Nice and cheap. Good women who won't rob you. Good music too. We can sway to the rhythm, dance to our heart's content, and hold the sexpots close. I assure you, these ones ain't gonna scream or punch you out."

Off we went to this supposedly wonderful spot. I took a good look at the sexpots and decided that most of them looked like alley cats. We had a good time despite the fact. The place really was very cheap and the entire party didn't cost us more than a few hundred piasters. Charlie gathered everyone that he knew there and we kicked up such a row that in no time at all the band was playing for us alone. And that's what started the commotion. The local regulars who were likewise guests on the premises did not take kindly to the fact that we had all but taken over the joint and that the band was providing us with exclusive entertainment. They expressed their dissatisfaction with the situation with a few choice words. These words were directed at Charlie, because he was the loudest and most disturbing of the lot. I should really say that his singing was the loudest, but I think that shouting was closer to the truth.

It was a stupid move on the part of these regulars to direct their sarcastic and vicious remarks at Charlie. Charlie was not amused, he leaped out of his seat, grabbed one of the regulars, and threw him out the door. The attack was so unexpected that the poor guy didn't know whether he was on the moon or on earth. It was easy to pick him up and throw him out because he was a puny little guy. Now the row really got going. Within a scant half an hour, Charlie and I with the help of our chums in tow had totally cleared the place out. And after we were done, not a soul dared to complain about the band playing only for us. On they played until who knows when, because the next thing I remember was someone shaking my shoulder and calling me to breakfast.

The partying stretched into the wee hours of the morning, and my head was swimming when I went down for breakfast. Only 8:00 a.m. and the sun was already pouring forth its heat. Imagine what it's going to be like around noon and in the early afternoon. But, I had to admit that Charlie was right. It was still better here, where there was only the heat to contend with. Contributing to the heat up north would be a touch of mountain climbing spiked with a few million mosquitoes. I hardly noticed the tiny critters here. I was bitten only a few times, though I slept without a mosquito net. In Gia-Lam, so many of them crawled the sides of my net that it sounded like the Legion's version of Beethoven's Fifth Symphony; played, or should I say buzzed?

I decided to find Charlie after breakfast. It was then I realized that I had forgotten to ask him where he was staying. How stupid of me, I could think of no other solution but to look for the bistro, though how I would ever find it remained a mystery. I wandered for hours up one street and down the next, but every bistro I came across looked the same. If only I would have bothered to take note of that stupid place's name! And I did not dare enter one of these places alone. I was in a strange city and who was to know in which they did not take kindly to legionnaires. I had no desire to meet the same fate as those we cleared out yesterday. Better to be afraid than to be sorry, I thought, and I continued my search.

It was 2:00 in the afternoon and I was exhausted from the heat and from all the walking. I wanted both Charlie and the bistro to go to hell, neither held any significance any longer. On the other hand, I would willingly have given half my kingdom for a park bench under a shady tree. The heat was enough to knock a man down. In my search for that bench in the shade, I found myself standing in front of the hospital. Where there is a hospital there are Hungarians, I thought. Ten minutes later I was sipping a cool bottle of beer in the hospital's canteen in the company of three injured Hungarian comrades.

Back at the residence we were informed that we had to stay on for another few days because repairs to the plane were on hold until tomorrow.

The situation was a pain from a monetary point-of-view. I was not about to wait out the time until that rickety old wreck was fixed by sitting on the edge of the bed, somehow or other I was bound to find Charlie and those other guys from the bistro, and I knew that I wouldn't be able to escape scot-free. Money does have a way of slipping through one's fingers when a man is having a good time, even in a cheap place, and I was worried because it was the beginning of the month. What I failed to understand was why they couldn't simply supply another plane as a replacement. Why did we have to wait for this particular old broken down Dakota? But, the administration knew what they were doing, I guess. We, meaning myself and those like me, were considered a bunch of morons who fulfilled our obligations but had absolutely no say in anything.

Just as I predicted. Waiting for that stupid wreck to be repaired really did do me in. I found Charlie, and as a result I could have easily turned my pockets inside out, not that all that many piasters would have fallen out. Despite the fact that most of Charlie's days were taken up with training, he still found time to visit the cheap bistro every night.

I split my time during the day between visiting the Hungarians in the residence and those at the hospital. I was forever in search of a cool canteen because it was so stifling that the air danced above the road, and only a beer or an ice cold lemonade promised relief. For how long? Only so long as a man was sipping it and then the sweat would start streaming down his body all over again. Oh well, I still took the time to visit my injured comrades. It made no difference, I bathed in sweat.

During the nights I slept less and less mainly because the partying at the bistro lasted longer and longer. When I left on October 8, I was so physically, mentally, spiritually and financially depleted that the journey was redemption. Even if it was aboard the Dakota! Had the repairs lasted a few days longer, the Hungarian contingent in the Tourane hospital would have increased by one.

Chapter Sixteen
Return to Gia-Lam

From the Bak-May airport, the car drove me only as far as the office of the battalion to where I had to report. Who was the first person I bumped into there but Joe Bristle.

"So, the chief of holiday goers, came back, did you?" he asked in a voice that was not entirely free of sarcasm.

"You're a fine one to talk! Ever since you've been assigned to Duvallieux you've done nothing but vacation yourself. Those two little boys do all your dirty work for you while you go shootin' off your mouth like you were the battalion commander or something. What I'd like know is how come he hasn't given you the boot yet. If it were me, I would have thrown you over to some penal squadron long ago so you can learn what it really means to be a soldier."

"You're talking? And what the hell are you? Nothing more than an ornamental soldier!"

"Who? Me? Just because they sent me down to Dalat for a few days?"

229

"A few days! The whole squadron collectively has gotten less vacation time than you alone, and you have the gall to say just a few days?"

"Why don't you catch as many ailments as I did, you twit, and you can go to Dalat too. You really think it's some earth shattering pleasure sweating and shaking through those malaria seizures? And there was probably something wrong with my heart besides, else they wouldn't have fooled around with all those cardiograms."

"Heart trouble my foot. You're a good faker and they fell for it."

"Oh sure, Weber's gonna be the one to fall for it, when he's the one who kicks 'em out of the hospital a dozen at a time. And now he went and threw me to the back to the squadron because I'm such a good faker. Sure. See this file? It says, 'Repos Complete!' You can't be so stupid that you don't know what that means, but in case you don't, it means complete rest. and you think that Weber of all people would write something like that on a man's file if he was faking it? Is Duvallieux in? Weber told me to report to him first."

"He went to Hanoi. Something's up. In the past few days there's been a lot of whispering going on between the Gorilla (Duvallieux's nickname) and the Squadron Commander. Some head honcho from Hanoi has been coming out day after day, and the talks go on behind closed doors for hours. Something's brewing that's for sure."

"If that's the case, I'm gonna go out to the squadron and report to Plessiner."

The squadron sector was a good kilometre away from the office of the Battalion. To have to drag my heavy trunk all that way in this heat was suicide.

"Hey Joe!"

"What is it?"

"Would you lend me those brats so they can help me carry this trunk over to the squadron? I'll give them five piasters each."

"It would be an honor! Might you also require a half-dozen virgins clad in white aboard a ceremonial carriage? So the gentleman from the Legion requires the services of a valet, does he? No way! Carry it yourself. You're not going to die over it."

"Oh come on. Quit bugging me. You know how seriously ill I am."

"Of course I know! See, my heart's bleeding for you. But no valets!"

"You just wait Joe, the Almighty Lord will punish you but good for your heartlessness. Can't you take pity on your suffering comrade? May ten thousand fleas and mites nip you in the armpits!"

While showering blessings on Joe, I dragged the trunk over to the squadron, where it was Sergeant Mortier who offered a ceremonial welcome.

"You look just like a fattened hog! I'll take care of that extra fat of yours in a hurry. Leave it up to me to shake you back into routine!"

What's his problem?

"Sergeant! Here's my file from the hospital." I eagerly pushed it in front of him. "See? Dr. Weber has written complete rest on it."

"Don't worry. I'll make sure that you get your complete rest. Let me see that file!"

He flipped it open, glanced at it, read it through, closed it and calmly told me to get changed within two minutes and report to the officer of the guard so that I could relieve Legionnaire Schulz.

"But Sergeant! According to Dr. Weber's orders, I'm supposed to get complete rest."

"Quatre jour! I report only to Captain Plessiner."

Well this was starting out just fine. "Quatre jour" meant four days in the station house. "What a thing to come back to!" I mumbled. First Joe and now the Sergeant was picking on me. I didn't see a soul on my way over to the beat. The sleeping quarters were empty save for the man on duty, Zimba, who was swearing a blue streak while fumbling with something.

"What's your problem? Were you fed some poison too? What's going on here? Where is everybody?"

"Where are they? Where are they? Where the hell could they possibly be? They went on a mission. Gone a week already. Hardly six of us left behind, and we're on guard duty day and night. There's no escaping Mortier. He'll have your neck if you don't disappear."

"I've already had the good fortune. He's nailed me with four days because I complained about having to relieve Schulz of guard duty so soon after coming back."

"Well then, you can play guard around the clock for the next four days. The rest of us are dead on our feet, and besides, you've been doing nothing for the past month."

Well! Here was someone else who was not exactly thrilled over my month long vacation. On my way over to the guard room I saw Schulz standing there waiting. Not surprising, since he looked like death warmed over. This kid's certainly had a rough go of it. He could have benefitted from the thirty day vacation in Dalat as much as a beggar from ten pennies. The officer of the guard all but gave me a hug when I stepped into the guard room.

"At long last I see a well-rested man! Go quickly and relieve the guard, he's been walking the beat for more than four hours."

I went outside and saw that it was Julius Mole who was staggering alongside the tracks.

"Scout!" he shouted with joy. "You came back after all! At last somebody will relieve me. I've lost all feeling in my legs."

"Finally somebody is glad to see me," I said. "It seems like everyone I've come across since I got back has been out to get me, so what's this? Did everyone swallow poison or what?"

"There's not been a moment of peace since you left, old buddy. One row after another, everyone's gone crazy, one guy's in a mood more murderous than the next. Don't say a word to Mortier, and if you value your life, don't go near Plessiner,"

"But I have to report ot him. Weber ordered a complete rest."

"A complete rest around here, Old buddy, is granted only if you're dead."

"I could see that by the way Schulz looked, he's halfway there."

"And he's been in that shape while on guard duty for the past five days straight."

"When are you expecting the squadron back?"

"When? An hour, a week? Who knows?"

With this, Julius waved me away and went off to sleep. I began the slow and leisurely pacing along the tracks from the station to the storage area converted into residences, while keeping an eye on the opposite side. I remembered Dalat, and thought that perhaps it might have been better had I not gone at all. It was so hard to regain the sense of routine in Gia-Lam, especially after Mortier's promise that he would be of assistance to that end. Thank you very much but no, I'd rather he didn't help. Somehow, I'll manage just fine on my own.

It was late in the afternoon. The sun's heat was diminishing and judging by the clouds covering the sky, rain was on its way. Good Lord! For me, everything looked overcast above and below. Things were starting to look grey when the officer of the guard came out to tell me to stay on for another two hours, if I could handle it, because the others couldn't even get to their feet. Well okay, I'll stay for two hours though I've already been pacing the road for more than four hours, during which time I've personally introduced myself to each of the bushes on the opposite side and asked them to please refrain from concealing any Vietmins because I was in no mood for shooting. And so, out of desire to repeat my performance, I promised two more hours of my time. Night was nearing which meant that the number of guards should have been doubled, and I was brave enough to mention this oversight to the officer of the guard.

"Just leave that up to me. I know when the guards have to be doubled. All day that's when. But what can I do if there's not enough of us? Give birth to some guard types?"

"Sure, if you can stand it!"

October 12, 1949

The squadron returned from the mission almost at same time as Charlie Red, who successfully completed his free fall training in Tourane. That the squadron was back did not in the least help our situation, because not one among them was anything less than completely exhausted. As I looked them over, I had to conclude that they were in much greater need of rest than us. Gypsy was quick to concur.

"Them no good Vietmins didn't leave us alone for a minute, may they rot in hell, didn't even let us eat in peace. We sit down and they fire a round down our necks, and we have to chuck the grub to run and chase 'em."

"So how was Dalat? I can see that they fattened you up. We were sweatin' it out on missions while you was stuffin' your face and suntannin' your belly."

"Let it be, Gypsy," interrupted Alex. "Not to worry, he'll get his share. He'll climb so many mountains that it might even kill him before he's through."

What was coming to me had already begun. Since my return I've been on guard duty day and night, an activity that in itself was not exactly life insurance.

October 15 – 16, 1949

Mortier and Charlie went from bed to bed quietly giving the ready for battle order. It was 3:00 a.m.

Half an hour later we were aboard the trucks, heading in the direction of Bac-Ninh. Considering that only our section was going and that only two days of provisions were provided, we were not about to encounter anything all that serious. We were in the vicinity of Bac-Ninh when per the Lieutenant's orders two of the three vehicles diverted from the original route, took a sharp turn north and continued on in that direction while we, aboard the third vehicle and under the leadership of Sergeant Mortier, continued on toward Bac-Ninh between the seemingly endless stretch of rice fields. Before we had even reached Bac-Ninh we disembarked and likewise assumed a northerly route along the dirt mounds between the rice fields.

Though a few stars were left twinkling in the sky, by now the crack of dawn had replaced the blackness of the night. With visibility thus improved we were able to advance across the slippery terrain much more quickly. A few bamboo huts came into view in the distance, but since no attack was forthcoming from anywhere, we remained on the course set out by Lieutenant Mercier. Suddenly we saw, perhaps one hundred metres in front of our position, three bamboo huts sitting on a small clearing. We detected no trace of man or animal, most suspicious was the lack of livestock. Judging by the cultivated rice fields in the surrounding area, we thought it quite possible that the huts were uninhabited. On the other hand, if the cultivated fields were a sign of inhabitants, considering the absence of animals, those inhabitants had to be none other than Vietmins.

Mortier signalled us to get down on our bellies and take cover. Silly of him to say so, because what kind of cover could anyone find inbetween rice fields? Making the best of what was available, each man submerged himself. Then Mortier waved Charlie closer, and I overheard the Sergeant tell Charlie to take the two of us and close in on one the huts.

"Scout! Gypsy! Come on!" Charlie called.

"Like hell! Can't you pick on someone else?"

"Shut your face Gypsy or I'll kick you in the ass. Get going!"

Stooped down to the rim of the dirt mounds, we advanced behind the mounds through the murky waters of the rice fields. At the halfway point we were hit by a round of fire coming not from the huts, but from behind the third or fourth rice table dirt mound to the right. Gypsy sustained a slight injury to his shoulder. It was more a scratch than a wound but he laid into Charlie because of it. Charlie's chapeau was blown off, while the tins of food in my backpack were shot to bits. That in certain situations a man was not particular in the least was proven beyond a shadow of a doubt given our current predicament. While silence reigned, we had taken every last step with the greatest of caution, and now, we slammed down into the mire as if it was a down comforter.

And then, as if Stokowsky himself had led us in, we each opened fire on the enemy. At the same time, in groups of two's and three's we stumbled through the muddied waters of the fields and tired to advance upon and silence the enemy. This was an intricate affair, seeing that they were comfortably crouched and firing from behind the dirt mound, where they were anything but a visible target. At the same time their position was to our advantage, since they dared not rise above the mound and their range of destruction as a result was considerably weakened. It was imperative that we finish with them quickly before reinforcements arrived. Mortier was clear on this, and he divided the fortified squadron into three. One group was to close in from the right and one from the left while the middle group was to tie down and try to wipe out the enemy using hand grenades. This business about the hand grenades was well-thought out, but the effectiveness of the plan was dependent on being within throwing distance. And getting that close to the Vietmins was a touch problematic because in order to do so we would have had to crawl over the dirt mounds and pose as ideal targets in the process.

While the middle groups was doing everything in their power to occupy the enemy's attention, Charlie from the right and I along with four others closed in from the left. I was fortunate in that on my side a trench was cut across the first dirt mound, so that water could flow freely from the yet to be cultivated field over to the cultivated side. At any rate, we did not have to crawl over the mound, which not only saved us some time but made the advancement upon the enemy far easier. The Vietmins likewise split their forces into three once they were aware of our plans to surround them. But with this move, their firing weakened to such a degree that our middle group successfully crawled across two paddies without sustaining a single loss, and silenced the enemy with hand grenades even before we could finish surrounding their position. The Vietmin losses included six dead and two not seriously injured whom we took as prisoners. The losses on our side included my tins of food. I couldn't help thinking about what I wasn't going to eat for the next two days.

The injured Gypsy was cursing Charlie.

"See, you idiot. This here's all your fault! Couldn't you have picked on someone else?"

"I'm gonna take a shot at you, Gypsy, if you don't shut up."

But instead, since the Gypsy was standing in front of Charlie with his back to him, Charlie tipped him over, and the Gypsy slipped down into the rice plants where he sat like someone getting ready to bathe.

We attended to the injuries of the two Vietmins, collected their weapons, hooked them up on a bamboo rod. We lit a fire under the huts and waited until they were completely engulfed in flames before continuing on our way.

We arrived at the main highway heading directly north well before nightfall. We were supposed to meet up with Lieutenant Mercier and his group there, but of course they were nowhere to be seen despite the fact that we were over two hours late because of our clash with the Vietmins.

We drew back off the road to seek a place that offered good protection, a place where we wouldn't have to worry about a surprise attack. We found an area densely overgrown with bushes and shrubbery, a terrain that offered ideal camoflage and from where we could keep an eye on the road at the same time. We tied together the hands and feet of our two prisoners and in the interest of security, we further secured the rope to the thick branches of a larger bush, just in case they might be harboring thoughts of escape. Mortier was prepared for all emergencies and ordered twice the usual number of men to stand guard in all four directions. Those not standing guard, took the time to rest or eat their supper rations.

I was scraping by, begging for handouts.

The sun had long since relinquished its place over to the moon and stars, but Mercier and his group were still nowhere to be seen. I was lying in a dreamless stupor up against my backpack promoted to the rank of pillow, when I heard Mortier telling Charlie to take six men and head south along the road in case Mercier and entourage were waiting there.

"I'd rather take one man along, " I heard him reply. "Six will create too much noise."

"Okay," said Mortier. "Then just two of you go."

"Scout! Where are you?"

I thought I was going to have a fit. Now I cursed him, like Gypsy had before. But I did not answer him. I lay silent, pretending to be asleep.

"Scout! Can't you hear me?"

Nope! I can't. You can't see me in the dark, so you'll just have to take someone else along. I "slept" like a baby. Even snored. And that caused my downfall, because that's how Charlie, may he rot in hell, found me.

"Come on Scout! Let's go find Mercier and his group."

"You're nuts! How do you expect to find them in this pitch dark?"

"First of all, it's not even dark. The moon's shining. And second, Mortier ordered us to go down the road a kilometre or so in case they're waiting for us somewhere along the way."

"Mortier's exact words were, 'a ways. . . .'" I wanted to bite my tongue, knowing that I had just given myself away.

"So, you weren't sleeping! You were just pretending."

"Of course I wasn't sleeping. Can't you take someone else along with you? Why are you always picking on me? The place is swarming with feather brains!"

"They can't be trusted."

"Scared that they're gonna shoot you in the back, aren't you?"

"Don't be so lippy. Come on!"

The upper dog was always right, so I had no choice.

We reached the guard posted on the south side. Charlie told him where we were going, so he wouldn't mistake us for Vietmins on the way back. Two of us were leaving and two of us would return, using Gia-Lam as the password. What we didn't count on was that another guard would be in his place by the time we got back, and that guard would have no idea what Gia-Lam was supposed to mean because the guard he replaced forgot to tell him.

We started out down the brightly lit highway. We stayed drawn back on the side of the road where we were hidden by the shadows of the trees. Charlie suddenly came to a dead stop after about two hundred metres.

"What is it? Did you hear something?" I asked in a whisper, while lying down in the grass.

"I didn't hear anything, my chum, but let's sit down by these bushes and wait."

"Wait for what?"

"Nothing. We'll just wait for half an hour, then go back."

"What about Mortier's orders?"

"What about them? He told us to go down the road a ways, did he not? And so we have. And I'm not about to go any further. I'll take care of Mortier and give him a full report."

"If you say so. You're the boss. But what if, say, Mercier and his group are waiting four hundred metres over, and what if they tell Mortier that they didn't see us anywhere? It's easy to put two and two together, the time we were gone and the distance, which equals very simply that something in our story doesn't ring true."

"We did as we were ordered. He wasn't very specific. He said 'a ways,' which could mean two metres or two kilometres. We'll wait out the half an hour here, them go back."

We sat in silence, without saying a word for about ten minutes, when we heard gently trodding steps and subdued voices. If we were quiet up until this point, we now held our breaths while attentive to the source of the noise. We saw some dozen Vietmins heading in a southwesterly direction, stepping carefully, so not to make any noise. Charlie and I flattened between the bushes, like pheasants who knew they were being hunted. Since the Vietmins were employing such precautionary measures on their approach, we suspected that they were aware of our squadron's presence in the area, but dared not attack because they were weak, or maybe, because they were gathering the forces of a stronger contingent with which to surround our squadron. When Charlie and I were certain that the Vietmins could not detect us, we headed back toward our resting squadron so that we could warn them of the impending Vietmin attack.

Once we were within earshot of the guard posted on the south side, Charlie quite audibly said to him:

"Gia-Lam!"

The response? A round of gunfire, what prompted us to want to hide under the grass had we only known how.

"Don't shoot, you fool!" screamed Charlie. "It's me! Corporal Red!"

The entire squadron, drawn by the sound of the gunfire, raced over, with Mortier in the lead, thinking, naturally, that the Vietmins were attacking.

"Sergeant! It's me, Corporal Red!" yelled Charlie, from his hiding place under the grass.

"Cease fire!" yelled Mortier.

"Did you see Lieutenant Mercier and his group?" he asked Charlie, once the confusion was cleared up.

"Not them," he replied, "but along the way we retreated deeper into the forest and saw a smaller Vietnamese unit moving westward. Chances are likely that they were preparing to attack."

"It looked like they wanted to surround the squadron."

"Why do you think that?"

"The twelve or so men were proceeding with extreme caution, which leads me to believe that they know of our position here. If not, then why not stay on the highway and head directly north instead of painstakingly trudging west through the forest? And if they really were preparing to attack then by now, every group is in position and they could move into action at any moment. The men that we saw are no further than four hundred metres from here."

"Charlie! Triple the guards in all four directions!" said Mortier. "Maybe Scout is right. Use the extras to alternately relieve the posted guards at half an hour intervals."

"I'll call you once the others have taken their turn, old buddy. Go and get some sleep for now."

I didn't need to be told twice. I put my "pillow" under my head and moments later found myself harassing the Vietmins in a dream world of rice fields.

With the arrival of Mercier and his group the forces swelled so that space became really tight. The "general headquarters" which we had "rented" out for ourselves proved to be sorely inadequate; therefore, moving commenced across the board. First we moved the two Vietmin's from their comfortable places under the bushes over between the tall grass and weeds much closer to the road. However it was not just the Vietmins who were forced to rely on the weeds for cover, many of our men could no longer adequately entrench themselves and pinned dry stalks of weed to their caps for camoflage. Triple guards were posted not in four but in eight places so that those men who were camoflaged by weeds alone would not feel at the mercy of a potential attack. Mortier gave the lieutenant details of the tour Charlie and I had taken and the discoveries we had made, telling him too, that we could expect some sort of an attack at any time.

"You don't have to worry about any attack of any kind. The men they saw were probably among those that we defeated some two hours ago," answered the lieutenant.

By the time the truth of the matter was unraveled and everyone had settled down in their places, there was hardly any time left to rest or sleep.

I don't believe I snored more than three times when someone violently shook me awake.

"Scout, wake up! It's your turn!"

"Wh-wh-what turn are you talking about? What do I have to do?"

"Go on guard."

"Okay, okay. You don't have to shake me out of my pants. Who's after me?"

"Zullner."

"Where's he lying?"

"How am I supposed to know? Find him yourself."

It didn't matter in the long run because by the time his turn came up, not only Zullner but the entire squadron including the two Vietmin prisoners were roused out of sleep and within five minutes, the camp was continuing its northward march along the main road. We filed down both sides of the road in a long row for about half an hour, when the lieutenant signalled a halt and called the troops to assemble. He waved Mortier, Charlie and two other corporals over to him. I saw him produce a map and go into a pointed explanation. The conference ceased, and they told us what was cooking.

Approximately three kilometres from our position was a tiny settlement reputed to be not only a gathering place for the Vietmins but a repository for their ammunition and provisions. It was our mission to approach the settlement, launch a surprise attack, and make a clean sweep of the area. The terrain leading to the settlement, though sparsely forested, was overgrown with bushes.

The pursuit was on. The troops split into six groups, each of which started out from our current position at ten minute intervals. Each group, in turn, waited for the one following to catch up before advancing for another ten minutes and again, waiting for the group behind. Should any one group clash with enemy forces along the way, then plans to attack the settlement depended on the strength of the attacking forces to be reckoned with and driven back.

Now this was what I called war strategy. But did anybody stop to take into consideration the natural features of the terrain we were facing, the distance we could conceivably cover during those ten minutes, or the number of Vietmins along the way who, though not interested in attacking, might pass the dope and warn their comrades to take heed because the paratroopers were coming? We could, given this possibility, arrive on the scene to find that everyone had vanished or, be greeted by a dozen heavy machine guns from the right and and another dozen from the left ready to mow us down as we filed in. And what to do with our prisoners who were otherwise much too small in stature and skinny to be employed as body shields?

As it turned out, I found out what was to become of the prisoners right after the departure of the first group. Following Mortier's orders, we tied them together like a butcher might do with a deboned piece of ham in preparation for smoking. About fifty metres from the road we found a sizable depression filled in with tall grass and weeds, and in it we laid the prisoners after securely stuffing their mouths. Just to make things more interesting for them, we tied one's right leg to the left of the other. Then, in case they tried to flee in such a tied up condition, they would have to do it three legged. A disgraceful but nonetheless often serviceable procedure, and one that would prove to be far more entertaining than having all four legs at their disposal. By the time we were finished tying them up, so neatly were they packaged that only a five thousand franc stamp pasted on their foreheads was missing, in which case we could have mailed them at the Post Office. We concealed their weapons at a respectable distance, lest they fall into temptation and try to recover them.

By the time their weapons were safely stored away, it was my group's turn to lead the way. Along the way, I racked my brains thinking about what might happen with those two unfortunate prisoners if the entire squadron should pass on into the hereafter. After all, nobody outside ourselves knew that beside the road was a ditch in which two tied together "Easter hams" were waiting to be resurrected.

We reached the third group who continued on while we stayed to wait for the fifth. The first group, I surmised, must be fairly close to the given location by now.

The ground beneath up until now proved to be smooth, even and free of jolts. Only the bushes had smacked at our faces once from the right and then from the left. The fifth group arrived precisely ten minutes later, at which point we continued on to meet up with the third. Everything was going according to orders so far. Exactly forty minutes later, we caught up with the already assembled first three groups. But the Vietnamese settlement was nowhere in sight, no matter how hard I strained my eyes to see.

"Hey Charlie! Where's that Vietmin nest? Did they clear out in the meantime, or what?"

"Mercier says that it's supposed to be sitting where the forest gets thicker on the other side of this here clearing, maybe another six or seven hundred metres away."

"Well then, what the hell are you waiting for? Why don't you go on?"

"Mercier wants us to hold off until all six groups get here. He wants us to launch the attack from here by closing in from three sides. You know, like he always does. A right wing, a left wing and a central flank. That's his craze."

"Fine, but what's it gonna be if those Vietmins just happen to fall outside of the right or left wings? They'll either do away with the weaker wings, or take off. Then what's Mercier planning on doing?"

"Ask him not me. I'm not in charge of this circus."

"Well, I'm curious to know what's going to come of all this."

"Me too, old buddy. But don't worry about it. We'll see. All we can do is receive our orders and carry them out. The rest is none of our business."

Mercier selected ten men, appointed a corporal to assume leadership and sent them ahead as a reconnaissance. The rest of us stayed behind and waited. No trace of the advance guard could be found when Mercier again signalled for us to use the forest overlay for cover and continue our advance toward the Vietmin settlement. We caught up to the reconnaissance group, but of our target, there was no sign. The forest increased in denseness if anything, and not a clearing or hut or Vietmin was in sight. The lieutenant called Mortier over to him and went into an explanation of sorts, as a result of which three more reconnaissance groups were formed and ordered to head out in three opposing directions.

"See, what did I tell you?" I said, turning to Charlie. "I told you he has no idea where those Vietmins are! We're taking great pains to go left, all three wings all the time, and I'm willing to bet my life that we should be going right."

"Why don't you tell him?"

"I'd be crazy to! I'd look like a fool if maybe he's in the right after all."

Fifteen minutes later, all three envoy groups were back. The report? No Vietmin settlement anywhere.

Mercier was extremely irate by now, knowing that he had made a miscalculation somewhere along the way. Then too, he understood clearly that we had noticed his mistake, and what bothered him most was that he had made a fool of himself. He took out his map, studied it for a few minutes, whereupon we changed course from the southwesterly route we had thus far been following to a directly westward one. Not twenty minutes later, we stopped again.

"Hey Charlie, what time is it?"

"Ten-thirty."

"That's impossible. That's what my watch says too, but my stomach is telling me that it's already supper time."

"Food will have to wait. Mercier's so furious that he's ready to explode."

"There's no doubt about it that he made an error. We should have been on top of the Vietmins ages ago. It don't take four hours to cover three kilometres."

"Either that, or this supposed Vietmin settlement doesn't even exist."

At this point the lieutenant split the squadron into two, and sent one off in a slightly northerly direction. When that group was about one hundred metres away from us, we too started off, but heading toward the extreme west! Ten minutes later we again divided in half, Mercier taking one half with him slightly off to the north while the other, under Charlie's leadership, crossed through the dense forest slightly off to the south.

Not fifty metres later, the sound of pistols and automatics firing broke the silence. That half of the section which had attacked initially received the bulk of the frontal attack. We, as far as circumstances permitted, raced to their aid, but our pace was quickly broken by the enemy fire, which forced us to the ground and reduced our speed to a crawl. Slowly we gained on Mercier's group, who were firing in all directions for lack of a target. We joined forces and scoured the terrain ourselves with gunfire from the base of the bushes to the top of the trees. The first group must have side-stepped us past the Lieutenant and his group, because we found ourselves somehow ahead of them rather than they ahead of us. We closed the ranks and the machine guns and automatic pistols of fifty men were emerged in reaping death all around.

At the same time we forced our way through, step-by-step, looking for the Vietnamese nest which still refused to materialize. We had been firing at the enemy for perhaps fifteen minutes when Mercier ordered a cease fire. We stopped, but the Vietmins did not. Their firing was, however, considerably weakened and much more chaotic. Hearing this, the Lieutenant and those around him doubled over and pressed ahead, able to establish a quicker pace, while the others, excluding the few injured who were unable to keep up, followed suit.

We continued forging ahead when all at once a tiny clearing with several huts appeared directly ahead. We were so surprised that we just about crashed straight into the huts. We had only enough time to hit the ground before we were fired at.

If nothing else, we now knew the source of the blessings being bestowed upon us and where to send them back. The tables were turned and this time we held the advantage. The trees provided us with excellent cover, while the Vietmins were holed up in a mousetrap. Furthermore, their close proximity allowed us to throw hand grenades at them. They continued to fire at us relentlessly, but their efforts were futile. Our retaliation was all the more effective. We could have easily done nothing else besides aim at the foundation and blast away the bamboo rod flooring, causing the walls and roof to cave in on the Vietmins trapped inside; but this we could not afford to do because our ammunition was running short. Instead, we used hand grenades to topple the walls and found that the blast brought down a section of the roof as well.

In an hour we were done with the Vietmins. Among the huts there was silence and no sign of movement. Either they had all passed on to their eternal places of rest, or, they saw fit to make themselves scarce. Before nearing the huts, we spread ourselves in order to minimize potential loss should somebody be alive after all and fire at us. We reached the huts minus any problems, only to find absolutely nothing. Not a corpse or wounded man anywhere! Blood stains were plentiful. Blood soaked rags littered the floor, as did a vast number of cartridge hulls and a few weapons left behind but rendered useless.

Once the Vietmins realized that their situation was hopeless, they had forced out several bamboo rods from the rear wall and escaped through the opening taking their dead and injured along. The blood stains of varying sizes visible at every step were testimony to the fact that their injuries were numerous. We collected the weapons left behind and then burned down the huts. Not that this served much purpose, because we could count on them to build others within a few days. If anything, we were doing them a favor because they didn't have to bother with taking down the ruins. Now that our job was done, we continued on the same road we had come. Our injuries included four arm wounds and two shoulder wounds. From time to time we changed their dressings as we helped them make it to the highway. Along the way we freed our prisoners, who were so numb they could hardly move, from their ropes. Here, we were granted a meal combined with rest.

Similar to yesterday, I had dinner due to the generosity of handouts. True that the donations were more suited for a breakfast meal but it was food. The ground coffee was nice but little use without the dry twigs and fire needed to boil water and there was no time for such formalities. I managed to collect three tins of food, so the Ministry of the Interior was adequately stuffed and had no reason to grumble. The Lieutenant was pressing the men for time because it was already 3:30 and we still had a long way to go before reaching the trucks. We asked the prisoners to please carry the weapons we had plundered. It was Alex and the Gypsy who did the asking in not so many words, from which they landed flat on their bellies. After this, we pressed on to reach the trucks waiting for us. We did not get very far though, because the two men with shoulder wounds were struck by such severe bouts of traumatic fever that they could not continue. There was no other solution but to throw together two stretchers to carry them. Assembling the stretchers cost us another forty-five minutes and boosted the nerves of the already high strung lieutenant. But what else could he do? Leave the two injured men behind? Because of the delay, it would be perhaps seven-thirty instead of six by the time we arrived at the rendezvous point. We rotated the stretcher carriers at frequent intervals so that the pair carrying the stretchers would not get exhausted.

We had another two hours of carrying the injured men when the Vietnamese attacked again. We uncovered the Vietmin's hiding place and blasted away the entire area within minutes. The result of the attack was more injuries. The squadron leader who was responsible for dispatching the trucks must have sensed that we were in trouble and did not wait for us to reach the meeting place but came out to meet us. After we had sent the Vietmins running, we had barely covered one hundred metres when the trucks arrived. We all gave a shout of victory at the sight of the unexpected assistance. It was evening by the time we arrived back in Gia-Lam.

October 17, 1949

Lady Luck did not abandon us today. The first section was sent on guard, the third was dispatched on a mission, while we slacked off and took it easy. An off season like this was most welcome. For those who were inclined to do so it was a chance to catch up on and answer a backlog of letters, tidy one's belongings, attend to business in the area; what the leadership saw as worthwhile even if we did not, then wait for the afternoon or for supper, and go into Hanoi to idle away what money we could find in the chest of drawers on entertainment.

With regards to the entertainment, a slight problem involving Alex Bofort emerged. During lunch earlier in the day, Alex had thrown his bowl at the cook's head. This was not catastrophic in itself but the bowl was filled with steaming hot soup. Alex was not the only one in disgust, but he was the quickest to lose his temper. The cook was immediately sent to the hospital while Alex raced around the camp and had to mop it up three times over. His condition was so weak by the time he finished that he hardly had the strength to collapse, yet alone come with us to Hanoi.

Charlie and I spent a wonderful evening in Hanoi. I don't even know how anymore, but Charlie made the acquaintance of a Hungarian family who lived beside the theatre square. The husband, was a geology scholar in the service of the French government. His wife, unlike her husband, enjoyed the company of others. Considering this Charlie and I showed up at the most opportune time. We were like a godsend because we were young, Hungarian and not opposed to anything that might lead to an escapade. Especially not when the issues at hand were dancing and drinking in the company of an attractive young Hungarian lady.

The three of us organized a splendid evening, but keeping within the strictest bounds. However, when we took the wife home at 3:00 a.m. we upset the peace of the household. Frankly, the scholar was the one we upset the most. He was outraged. His verbal disapproval had just about reached its peak when Charlie and I were brave enough to announce our intention to spend the rest of the night, because we had no desire to rickshaw back to Gia-Lam at 3:00 a.m. and risk arriving with two or three daggers in our chests. Finally, the determined young lady stepped forward on our behalf, we were given a place in the husband's lab. True, on the floor, but it was still better than in a coffin.

When we rejoined the squadron at around eight the next morning, all hell broke loose again. This time it was not caused by the husband but by Mortier because Charlie was supposed to have been on duty the night before. Charlie, however, had serious personal entertainment business to attend to with what's her name – within the strictest of boundaries. Charlie, however, had a peculiar knack for being able to soften up the hardest of souls. As a consequence, within five minutes Mortier had no idea where he stood, and the night of merrymaking was no longer a topic of discussion.

October 18, 1949

We woke up to a vulgar day. Charlie, to make up in some measure for his absence the previous evening was urging everyone at twice his usual volume, though he was not quite sure as to where or why. The point was to scream as loud as he could, and to make sure that Mortier heard how eager he was to do justice to his calling as a corporal and exercise his duties.

Sitting on the edge of my bed I waited for him to pause for a breath of air so I could tell him where to go and what to do once he got there. Since the pause was not forthcoming, I left him there high and dry and went down for breakfast. Since our chef was still in the hospital, thanks to Alex, the breakfast we got was outstanding. And since Captain Plessiner was the first to sample the coffee, it had to be good.

Returning to Charlie and his attempts to make up for his absence, within half an hour he was so hoarse from all that shouting though in all fairness the previous night's entertainment was also a contributing factor, that as far as Sir Corporal Charlie was concerned, we could look forward to a quiet morning.

After the impeccable lunch we settled down for a siesta, during which the mail came and went respectively. Among the many letters one was addressed to me. It came as such a surprise that I was in seventh heaven. It recalled my vacation in Dalat, even though that was a thing of the past. I mentioned writing a letter from there to a certain Eva, from the newspaper ad. It was she who this letter was from!

I never expected my letter to reach her. Even less did I expect a response. Yet here it was, complete with photograph. She struck a very friendly tone, as though we had known each other for years. The letter, written in honest and childlike simplicity, made me so happy that I was beside myself with joy. I would have received a Vietmin in this jubilant state I was in, but to my good fortune, nobody thought of the idea. She ended her letter by saying, "I'm hoping to get a letter from you." I set down to comply with her wishes immediately and wrote nonstop until evening and stopping when I did only because I had to go over to Joe's to celebrate his birthday.

We took turns with these celebrations, when opportunity and sufficient money presented themselves. Today's party drowned in a huge scandal, because we noticed that Leo wanted to cheat at rummy. We refrained from beating him half to death only because he had pull in the infirmary and cheated there as well when he could, but to our benefit. He had this to thank for escaping a thrashing and to show his gratitude, he swore on our health never to cheat again.

October 25, 1949

The three days of lazing around became ten days of lazing around. Thank god, it's our turn to go on a foray.

Reveille shall be sounded very early (when wasn't it in cases like this?), and we were told to prepare for the march before we went to bed. Come morning, we would be leaving right away and not have time to do anything but pull on our tonue combat gear.

Curious how promises of this sort were always kept to the letter, but when the promise in question was a favor to be granted or an out of turn promotion, then it became lost in a hazy mist of fog before it was ever realized. True to form, nobody forgot about the current promise and reveille was sounded at 2:00 a.m. – much earlier than usual.

The picture was the same as it always was on these missions. Board the trucks, get off the trucks, scale the mountains, come down the mountains, slipping and sliding here and there through the marshy and slimy waters of the rice fields, and by the time we stopped to rest, most of us looked like well bred hogs just after their daily ritual wallow in the mud.

We stumbled along for hours. Dawn was breaking when Mercier called for a rest period and breakfast rolled into one. We made a fire and boiled water when all at once a shot resounded.

Everybody stopped to wait for the next shot, but nothing came. That solitary shot was perhaps not intended for us. More than likely it was meant as a signal between Vietmins warning each other that there were legionnaires close-by.

Nothing happened all day. Nothing that is except that we burned down a few deserted huts. These could be nothing other than an evening refuge for the Vietmins. By burning the huts, it would be at least two days before they had another opportunity to take cover under a roof in the vicinity. More would be built by the third day. On the other hand, we did possess a selfish streak in that if we chanced upon two such deserted huts just as night was nearing, we didn't burn them down as of yet. We used them ourselves to spend the night in, and only in the morning were they eaten by flames.

We continued to comb the area after the fireworks were over. Somewhere along the way, we came across a puny little village where we were welcomed with open arms and accorded a cordial reception. To our great surprise it was not just people old as Methuselah who greeted us, but several young couples and their children. This smiling reception, because it was so out of the ordinary, aroused our suspicions.

Those we had encountered in the past were usually acting under the coercion of some higher authority. We were not willing to trust these smiling villagers, and it was thanks to this reluctance that we turned everything upside down. We found nothing. We felt bad about it by the time we were done because having been lucky in finding a sincerely friendly village for a change, we ransacked the whole place in gratitude.

To set things right and make up for our error, we distributed cigarettes to the elders and a few piasters to the children.

The forest came to an abrupt halt a few kilometres from the village. We found ourselves up to our knees in grass and weeds on what appeared to be a banana plantation. Taking advantage of the offerings, we picked some ripe bananas and made headway through the palms while munching on the fruit. Along the way we sustained an attack from one side. Judging by the sporadic shooting, we deduced that those responsible were a few Vietmin stragglers who just happened to be passing through.

The Lieutenant signalled us to let them keep shooting and not return the fire. Either they'll tire of it or press on. When and if there was a specific target to aim at, we would welcome them with loving kindness. We waited for a while but the Vietmins showed no inclination to either stop shooting or draw nearer. Mericer sent a message to those in front to advance in two's and three's, and not to shoot unless there was something to shoot at.

It was only after the eighth such unit had started their belly crawl forward that the lieutenant's prediction came true. The Vietmin's grew bored of the shooting and silenced their weapons. We heard voices and the rustling of tall grass. The enemy was retreating!

We leaped up and heaped a round of fire on the retreating Veitmins. The impact was immediate. One after the other they fell. We dashed off in pursuit of the ones who escaped, but it was easier for them to run barefoot then it was for us in considerably heavier garb. We sent another few rounds after them, and then, we scoured the area.

We found five dead and four seriously wounded. We left them, knowing that the escapees would come back for them. We arrived at the outskirts of Hanoi, an area engulfed by rice fields.

We stopped in a small clearing for dinner and a short rest before continuing our walk home. The men working their fields either waved or stopped to stare. We stopped to peer in huts which fell in our way, just to be sure that there was nothing lurking inside that was not to our liking.

We arrived back in Gia-Lam at dusk, but it was midnight before we got to bed. Exhausted from the day's trampling, covered in dirt and mud, and in clothes that radiated a less than pleasing odor, we had to clean up and have supper before we could crawl into bed.

October 26, 1949

It was like waking up in Dante's inferno. I was ablaze with fever one minute and shivering with cold the next. The small cot shook in time with my body as I shuddered from the cold. Everything converged, I felt someone put me in a car, take me somewhere and put me down again. The ice blocks and flames of hell were diligently alternating with each other. I plunged into a deep sleep and in my feverish dream, monsters attacked from all sides.

"Do you feel any better?" asked the nurse who gave me a shot.

She changed my night gown because it was soaking wet. Then another nurse came in to change the bedding which was likewise soaked through.

"You're past the bout," said one. "You'll sleep much more peacefully now."

I hardly heard the tail end of her words. I was asleep. When I woke up in the morning, the first person I saw was Dr. Weber. He was making his rounds and had just come to see me.

"Are you here again? Seems like the vacation in Dalat and complete rest I ordered did not bring about the results I was expecting."

"Dr. Weber, I was not permitted the complete rest which you ordered when I returned from Dalat, because . . . ," and proceeded to explain what had happened when I got back to the squadron.

"Well okay, just rest, get yourself together and I'll see what I can do."

He then continued his rounds. A few minutes later a nurse came in holding another shot, and who should it be but Venus! I was so glad to see her that I just about jumped out of bed. The dreams I had weaved months ago were set to continue I thought with joy. True, she gave no sign of recognition, which led me to believe that my plans would fall flat on their own. All the more when I saw her pitiful stare, put two and two together and realized that I must have looked like a lemon squeezed out fifty times over.

Venus administered the injection, took my temperature, fixed my pillows and blankets, then left, not saying a word. I was deeply hurt. After all the intricate plans I had weaved, who wouldn't have felt hurt? She could have at least said . . . I don't know! Something!

All that talking with Weber, the activity and the shot put me to sleep again. I woke up to someone speaking to me harshly.

"Scout, you lazy bum, get out of that bed! Out of this donkey den!"

Leo, Alex and Charlie were standing beside me. Alex, in his usual kind and friendly tone, was the one responsible for reveille.

"Here you are again, trying to get out of a jaunt through the rice paddies and a round or two of friendly shooting. How the hell do you do it? Here we go again. It's been three days already. . . ."

"Oh, come on!" I cut in. "I've been here for three days, you say?"

"Look at this! Now he wants us to believe that he doesn't even know how long he's been in. Hear that, Charlie? This guy thinks we're a bunch of fools"

"Guys! Seriously, I don't know. Since I was hit by that bout of fever in camp, I've been out of it until today. Weber checked me over this morning and gave me a shot. I fell asleep from it, and would have probably kept on sleeping 'till tomorrow morning if you guys hadn't woken me up now. What time is it?"

"It's after six," said Leo.

"I've slept through the entire day. No breakfast, lunch or supper."

"Should I call the nurse and tell her to bring you something?" asked Charlie.

But at that moment the night officer on duty stepped in and when he saw me awake, he asked if I wanted something to eat.

"I didn't wake you for supper because Dr. Weber told me to let you sleep. But if you want, I'll bring it to you now."

I wanted it desperately.

"Well then, old buddy, you just go ahead and eat. We're going to go hang around town for a while, then go back. Another three day mission slated to start early tomorrow morning."

"Hmm, so I've been in for three days." I turned the thought around in my head while eating. "What was it that Weber said? That he would see if he could do anything. Might he have meant that he would recommend repatriation?"

A faint glimmer of hope came alive again!

During the medical examination the next morning, Weber worked me over so thoroughly that there was not a square centimetre left untouched on my body that had not been subjected to repeated rapping, pinching and pounding. I found myself exhausted from all the orders. "Sit up, stand up, lie down, get up, walk, turn around, breathe this way, that way, not at all." By the time he was finished with me, I could hardly move. But don't think that it was all over. I still had to go and fuss with all that cardiogram stuff.

I cheered up only when I found out that Venus was to accompany me over to the machine, whose needle would today jump around like a billy goat. This I was convinced of even more when Venus, while securing the network of wiring on to my body had to, a couple of times, reach across the raised bed and so I came into contact with her breast.

Well, I thought to myself, if that machine doesn't get short circuited today, it never will! The cardiologist instructed me to stare at one spot while the machine was in operation. What else could I do with Venus sitting directly across from me in a tight uniform which had worked its way up.

The cardiologist collected the strips of paper after the examination was completed, hemming and hawing while doing so. Then, he told Venus that we could go. A short circuit was avoided when there was every reason for it!

At my next visit the doctor told me that I was to stay in bed for three days: complete bed rest. And to hold me to it, pills by the handful were shoved down my throat so I slept through almost the entire three days. On the fourth day I was given permission to take three walks totalling no more than an hour. On the fifth day I was allowed two hours and by the sixth day, I was free to move about as I pleased. By now I was so fed up with all this confinement to bed that I spent the entire day lounging beneath the palms in the garden. Medications were dispensed with, the effect of those I took earlier had worn off, and that I went to bed at the prescribed hour was to no avail. I could not fall asleep. I tossed and turned this way and that, sat up, sat down, but nothing helped. I, bored of the hour and a half struggle, went out for a walk around the yard.

It was a typical evening in the tropics. Stars twinkling overhead, the moon shedding a penetrating light, the banana palms gently swaying in the mellow evening breeze . . . and suddenly, Venus appeared in the doorway at the end of the hall that opened on to the yard. One light lit the entire length of the hallway. The moon cast its light on her white uniform, while the light from behind outlined her figure. And where those two sources of light met, it produced the illusion of a halo encircling her entire being. The sight was more bizarre than entrancing.

The spectacle started speaking, but in a tone of voice that was not becoming of such a glorious apparition. What did a mere mortal expect from such a haloed and moonlit figure but a tender and mild voice. She used a commanding voice to ask what I was doing out in the yard when I knew that wandering around, especially in the yard, was not permitted after lights were out.

"I can't sleep."

"Come inside. You're not supposed to be hanging around the yard in the middle of the night."

An order was an order, so I walked down the hallway and Venus went back into her office.

For lack of anything better to do, I kept walking in circles. The palm leaves reaching through the open windows of the hallway looked as though they were waving when I passed by. How I would love to wave goodbye back! A face appeared between the waving palm leaves. One face, one hand, that was waving goodbye from the opposite side of the world, from that window of the small apartment in that big city. Other pictures took their place alongside that face and hand. The physician's clock tolled 1:00 a.m. and brought me back to my senses. The visions between the palm leaves vanished and behind me a voice spoke:

"Get to bed this minute!"

Venus was standing behind me in a very commanding pose. I thought it best to go to bed without putting up any argument.

The next morning Dr. Weber came in with another doctor. Two doctors instead of one to try out their medical knowledge on me. They finished and took off just like that. The nurses too told me nothing besides that I was an outpatient and did not have to keep to my bed all day if I didn't want to. I walked until I almost collapsed from exhaustion, rested, then walked again. I bumped into another Hungarian along the way with whom I talked and played chess the whole day through, under the shade of that palm tree.

November 2, 1949

A thunderbolt struck! Dr. Weber announced that he was sending me back to the squadron.

Was this the wonderful, "I'll see what I can do?"

It would not be fair to blame Dr. Weber entirely, the fault was partly mine. Yesterday the nurse who made rounds after supper got caught up in a conversation with me and stupid me told her that I would love to go back to the squadron because it was terribly boring here and all the idleness and nothing to do was starting to get on my nerves. My wish was immediately fulfilled. By the afternoon, the jeep was already there to take me to Gia-Lam.

I reported on arrival to the Captain, who said that since Dr. Weber had ordered complete rest, I would be transferred in a few days to the officer's mess room at battalion headquarters. That glimmer of hope which I deemed to see with a possible repatriation melted away.

I fell into the old groove and my days with the squadron passed. The others did not take kindly to the fact that I was walking around with my hands in my pockets all day. I quickly put a stop to the nagging of a couple of NCOs by telling them to report to Plessiner if they had something to complain about. These guys were well-informed as to the situation, but liked to interfere just for the hell of it. I tried my best to avoid any and all situations that might give rise to conflict. However, I was not without sympathy for these bullies because while I was basking in the sun, they were slaving away. Into the fifth day of this hostile state of affairs, I received orders to move over to regimental headquarters.

November 7, 1949

I was busy with moving when Joe Bristle stood in the doorway to review my pompous entry with great expertise. Once I finished unloading the jeep he asked:

"Just where the hell do you think you're going?"

"And what business is it of yours? Might you be the one to say who will be assigned to the officer's mess room, or is that the Commander's job?"

"Oh! Would you be the newest assistant boss?"

"What kind of boss?"

"There's a Dutch guy here whom everyone despises. He's one of Lieutenant de Carvalho's assistants. The Commander mentioned last week that he'd like to get rid of him and bring in someone else. So, might you be that person? I can tell you one thing, You're going to have problems with that guy so long as you're working together."

"Why would I have problems with him?"

"Because he lays into everyone whether he has reason or not. Not a day has gone by since I've been here when we haven't gotten into a scrap over something or other. I help out too during dinner and supper, and he always finds something to bug me about."

"Why do you let him pester you? There's no way I'm gonna let him pick on me. I'll teach him how to be neat. You just wait and see."

"If that's what you think, my chum, you may as well turn around right now and go back. His room is like a pig sty, and you have to live with him. God only knows how many times Lieutenant de Carvalho has punished him because of it, but nothing has helped. You teach him? Write it off!"

"Well then, if that's the case, either he stays on or me. I refuse to live in a pig sty. And if the situation becomes unbearable, I'm sure de Carvalho will do something about it. Show me where his office is so I can report."

"Why don't you move in first? He usually takes a nap after lunch. Better if you go see him later."

"Okay. Then show me where the pig sty is."

When Joe showed it to me, I thought I was going to faint on the spot. How could anyone live like this? This room was separate from the staff's main building, because there was a small storage area which could only be accessed by going through this room.

There was ample room in it for three beds but the Dutchman and his lifestyle proved to be too many. The place was cramped, without a patch of free space to spare. Every available inch was taken up with things thrown all over the place. It was furnished with two beds, one desk and four chairs. Everything was flung in a heap, except for his bed that looked like it hadn't been made in days. There was no room to step on the red brick floor. Untidiness like this required a special skill.

The Dutchman was not in when I moved in. I picked up everything I could find lying around my bed and dumped it on his. Similarly with everything on the shelf above my bed. Our acquaintance could begin with tidying up, I thought, if it was my intention to have something to sleep on tonight. Here's your first chance to lay into me. I truly didn't want this to happen, but somehow I have to teach you how to be neat.

No sooner had I finished housecleaning when my roommate stepped in. He all but turned into a pillar of salt when he saw me and his things thrown all over his bed. I was quite surprised when I say "him" because based on Joe's description I was expecting a face that resembled Lucifer's, while his was almost exactly the opposite. But when he opened his mouth, what came out surpassed everything. The mass of words he heaped on me in a jargon that put to shame every last resident of Angyalfold left me speechless and stunned. I sat on the edge of my bed and waited for him to finish with his torrent of abuse. This took a while, because my restrained composure merely added fuel to the fire. When he ran out of wind, I told him that I was going to report to Lieutenant de Carvalho, and if he dared throw something back on my bed, or beside it, or on my shelf, I would immediately report him to de Carvalho. With this, I left him so he could go on fuming.

Lieutenant de Carvalho gave the impression of being a friendly and direct man. He seemed to be the kind of man who insisted upon being treated with a respect befitting his rank, but one who did not give the cold shoulder to others just because they held a lesser rank.

I reported to him and explained why I was here. For a few seconds we looked at each other steadily in the eyes, then he slowly gave me the once over, got up from his chair, came around the desk and extended his hand. His handshake convinced me even more that this was a man not just decent to the core, but that I was standing eye-to-eye with one who did not have an inflated opinion of himself and did not look down on others with disdain.

"Come. I'll show you around your barracks."

"I've already moved in and met my roommate. In fact, we've already had our first argument."

"Not the best of beginnings. What was the argument about?"

"Well strictly speaking, he was the one doing the yelling, because I threw everything from my bed over to his, plus what was scattered around my bed and on the shelf, thinking that I would force him to tidy up a bit if he wanted to sleep tonight. I don't know if I got anywhere with it or if I got my point across. All I wanted to do was bring him to his senses a bit."

"You're not going to get very far with him! But I'll tell you this much, try and get along with him because if you don't, then it'll be my headache and both of you will have to answer to me. Tell that to the Dutchman too!"

"Yes, Lieutenant."

When I returned to my room I saw everything imaginable piled up on my bed. The Dutchman was not in. I turned right around, went back to de Carvalho and as promised, reported the incident.

"Let's go have a look," he said and set out for the dorms.

When he opened the door to my lodging the Dutchman was there, eagerly in the process of trying to put the table on top of everything else already on my bed. When de Carvalho saw this the Dutchman was in jail two minutes later.

De Carvalho looked around the room, and said, "These are your new quarters."

He started to go, but called back, "Ask Joe to explain everything you need to know. There's still two hours until supper, that's plenty of time for him to roughly brief you and outline your agenda."

With this I stepped into a new passage of my life as a legionnaire, one that would prove to be the last.

I found Joe in the the Commander's office, absorbed with tidying the desk. The Commander was in Hanoi, and had left everything scattered over everything. Not that this was the first time, but no matter how upside down his desk was the Gorilla knew where everything was and if he needed something, he found it without hesitation. The Gorilla would skin Joe alive for putting things in order because this way he wouldn't be able to find anything.

"Joe!" I yelled just when he happened to be standing with his back to the door.

"Yes Lieutenant!" he replied, turning around and standing at attention. "Scout, I'm going to kick you so hard that you're gonna go flying right back to That-Khe and land smack in the middle of the Vietmins. What the hell are you pestering me for? Can't you see that I'm busy?"

"Sure I can see, but can I have a word with you anyway? You can keep doing whatever it is you're doing while we talk."

"Fine. Say what you have to say."

"Lieutenant de Carvalho said to tell you to tell me what the Dutchman can't"

"And just exactly what is it that the Dutchman can't tell you and why not?"

"You have to explain what I'm to do around here because the Dutchman is locked up."

"Wait a minute until I get these papers together."

"The Gorilla is going to disembowel you."

"He's not such a bad guy. Sure he threatens me enough, but he never does anything about it. Actually, he's glad when I clean up his desk. The only time he's ready to tear his hair out is when he can't find what he needs. At any rate, after I tidy things up I try to be on hand to help him find whatever he is looking for. That's when he always threatens to skin me, shoot me or throw me from a plane without a parachute. All right, let's go."

Joe showed and told me what I had to do. And thus, I became a waiter, steward, bartender, busboy, assistant supervisor, kitchen supervisor, bookkeeper, accountant and storeman rolled into one.

My first day was disastrous. Can't say that I was an experienced waiter and my stab at the job in the first few minutes was a series of never ending mishaps. One of the reasons for my problems was that the dining hall was divided into two sections. Officers ranked captain and higher dined in the smaller area, or room, while the larger section, containing a bar off in one corner, was the domain of the remaining officers. There was an opening between the two areas but no door.

Beside this opening was a table where the four first lieutenants sat. I was coming in with a large plate of meat as Joe was going out, and in my attempt to steer clear of him I bumped into the doorway and dumped the plate down one of the first lieutenant's neck, or more specifically, on top of his head and the sauce slowly dripped down his neck.

The Lieutenant gave out a scream that clinked the empty glasses over the bar. That the Lieutenant didn't skin me alive was thanks to Lieutenant de Carvalho who assessed the situation and stood up for me saying to the Lieutenant that it was my first day and accidents were bound to happen and he would give him a clean shirt if he came up to de Carvalho's room.

While Lieutenant Meyer was away attending to his needs, Joe and I, with the able assistance of a couple of sympathetic lieutenants, rendered the dining hall fit for eating again. When Lieutenant Meyer returned after cleaning up and changing his shirt, he went to sit in the farthest corner of the dining room where he would not be endangered by flying saucy dishes coming at him, or me. At the same time, nobody was brave enough to occupy his former seat.

It was thanks to this incident that I got some help. I told de Carvalho that this inconvenience could have been avoided if we didn't have to race in and out so often. I suggested that with a little more teamwork we could be more careful. If somebody from the kitchen brought the food out as far as the hallway entrance and handed it to Joe and I there, we could take over and speed up service at the same time. He admitted I was right and authorized the enlisting of extra hands.

I entrusted the mess hall cook with bringing in three kids around thirteen I promised him that they would have to help with dishwashing not just with serving the tables, a broad smile came over his face upon hearing this. Finally, he would not be solely responsible for washing the vast quantity of dishes.

November 12, 1949

This is the fifth day I've spent trying to settle into my new appointment. The going was rough but with Joe's efficient assistance, things were working out just fine. My three apprentices proved to be sensible lads, and the meals flowed more smoothly and peacefully with every passing day. Contributing to this was the Dutchman's absence. Following his release from jail he was transferred elsewhere. Joe was gracious in dispensing good advice, which I gratefully accepted. Being familiar with all the officers, he knew who was of sound mind and who was deranged. I was introduced individually to them all by Joe, each introduction laced with a sprinkling of comments about the person in question. Fortunately, those of sound mind prevailed.

My three apprentices and I did a superb job of returning things to an orderly state in the warehouse and in my own room. I purchased drapes, rush matting and cloths for the shelves. When everything was sparkling clean and standing in rank and file, I called in the chief supervisor to show him how and why I had put things in place in the warehouse.

All the canned goods were arranged neatly and stored separately, and inventory was taken and the list hung on the wall. Naturally, he was compelled to cross through my room and only a blind man could fail to see its cleanliness. Inside the warehouse he examined everything inside out, passed back through my room on the way out, and left without saying a word.

What the hell, I thought. He could have at least said, "everything looks pretty good," or "very tidy in here," instead of turning around and leaving without a word.

I staged this exhibition immediately after dinner so that the chief supervisor would have plenty of time to survey everything and express his opinion. His behavior threw cold water on my enthusiasm and left me completely dumbfounded. I went to sleep to wipe out the crushing defeat. I had already dozed off when the door opened and in stepped de Carvalho. Behind him, the entire staff platoon, with the Dutchman right in front. Carvalho showed them my room and the warehouse. After everyone had properly reviewed everything in sight, de Carvalho said this to them:

"Just goes to show you what a legionnaire's room can look like. It doesn't have to be in the same filthy condition yours was!" This last remark was clearly intended for the Dutchman's ears.

If I was dumbfounded before, now I was openmouthed with astonishment. Naturally I was expecting some sort of acknowledgement, but this, this public recognition? I was not counting on something so impressive. This gala performance was intended as a commendation, unfortunately de Carvalho did not stop to think that perhaps it did me more harm than good. I have to say that the acknowledgement itself made me feel very good, I just wish he would have left the platoon out of it. Murderous glances came flying my way especially after the Lieutenant announced that from here on in, he wanted to see every place within the sector look just as neat. Lucky for me that I was completely separated from the rest and living in my own little world. This way, they could only badger me from a distance and wish me all those wonderful things that I hoped the Good Lord would grace them with in return.

November 14, 1949

The crowd was starting to straggle down for breakfast while my three apprentices were busily setting up the tables with necessities for the morning meal. I was ordering them about from behind the bar counter, where I was putting out liqueur glasses in a long row. Quite a few of the men liked to prepare the way for the coffee with a couple of shots of cognac. Joe was among the stragglers appearing in the dining room doorway. He came down the hall, up to the bar door and called:

"Scout, today's your birthday!"

"That's out of the question, it's Steve's turn. I celebrated mine Friday of last week and if I remember correctly, that was the fourth time since I got back from Dalat."

"That may be, but today it really and truly is your birthday. It's November 14."

"Stop fooling around."

"Here's the calender! Look for yourself. I brought it along on purpose."

"That's no good! I hardly have a few piasters to my name."

"We can improve on that. Just be careful how you portion out the liqueurs."

Twenty-six portions had to be measured out of every bottle. What was left over the bartender could keep, if he was clever enough and didn't get caught. So I did my best to pour cleverly. With this plus the little money I had, we'd get by somehow.

"Well then, let the herd know, and tell them that it's my birthday."

What a flukey guy Steve was, getting out of his birthday like that. I kept on pouring the cognac diligently. More was consumed this morning than was the norm, almost as though everyone sensed the difficulties I was wrestling with. To such an extent did the cognac flow that when Joe came back an hour later, I was happy to report that all our problems were solved if the drinking bout at lunch and supper kept pace with this morning's.

"More so, since of all the guys around here who drink like fishes, only us two are left," he said.

"How come?"

"Because Steve and Charlie are on duty, Alex is in jail and I can't find Leo or Walter. Only two fiendish pranksters left of seven and the money we have will be plenty for two."

I was tremendously lucky at lunch. One of the sous-lieutenants was promoted to lieutenant and in the midst of all the congratulations, bottles were emptied one after the other. Well Joe, I thought, are we ever going to celebrate tonight! These guys aren't the only ones. True that for the most part bottled wine was consumed during supper, with which no amount of cleverness did any good. But when Joe and I did our calculations after supper, it turned out that we had enough to hire ambulances to bring us home if need be.

I entrusted the cook and my three apprentices with the after supper clean up chores, padlocked the warehouse and bar doors and hit the road leading to Hanoi. We passed Steve Bidon on the way out, who just happened to be on guard duty and laughed him into the ground. We had not even gotten as far as the bridge when one of our jeeps caught up with us. It too was heading into town so we hoisted ourselves aboard, and fifteen minutes later, we were sitting by an outdoor table belonging to one of the cafes lining Rue Paul Bert and sipping cool beer.

Joe pointed out, while eyeing the pedestrians, that this day might be made more memorable if it were spent in the arms of two dames.

"This dame stuff is not such a hot idea."

"Why not?"

"First of all, I wonder if they'd be worth the money we'd have to spend on them, and if we get involved with them, there's no way we'll get back before dark. Don't forget we're unarmed, and you know what it means to prowl the streets without weapons at night. Not to mention what might happen if we found ourselves in an obscure area."

"Well then, let's go to the Hollywood. It's a good nightclub. Plenty of dames and you can always dance there."

We acted on the impulse, flagged down a rickshaw and ten minutes later it pulled up in front of the Hollywood. We selected a quiet corner of the bar to sit in, one that was removed from the main floor. This was easily accomplished because there were hardly any legionnaires or civilians idling about the night club. It was too early yet, and the place was still quiet. The orchestra was not exactly putting itself out either. The music they were playing was slow and quiet enough to put a night guard to sleep.

I refuse to set out in detail the drinking and dancing. What is there to detail about this? Suffice to say that we started off with an aperitif, followed it with champagne, and in the interim completely forgot about our intention to return before dark. So much so, that we came to our sense to find four muscular waiters helping us leave the premises. We didn't really understand what the big hurry was all about, or why the bar was so empty, when now and then we had seen so many people swarming around us.

In short, we were helped in finding our way outside, where one of the waiters and quite politely at that, said:

"Gentlemen – it's closing time!"

This meant I supposed that we miscalculated the time, by a mere five or six hours. Not to be disconcerted because of it, we set a course directly for Gia-Lam while belting out *Je t'attendre* at the top of our lungs.

We were enraptured by the exquisite quality of our own voices ever so briefly, when a car pulled up beside us and we were surrounded by machine pistols levelled at us from all sides. Apart from the fact that both of us stood our ground quite adequately, the words got stuck in our throats faster than the time it took for them to surround us. Shoving us into the car, however, took even less time. The whole thing happened so fast that between, finding ourselves surrounded and finding ourselves shoved in the car, there was no time to ask our attackers what they wanted. Scared we were not, the large doses of aperitifs and champagne had supplied us with enough courage to confront not just the six we counted now, once we had the chance, but a thousand Vietmins if need be.

Sitting on the floor of the car, I began to wonder why the hell that gun barrel, or whatever it was, was pressed against my head when I had done nothing wrong. If anything, by drinking champagne and what not, I was boosting the economy of Indochina. Spending our hard to come by piasters, added to the wealth of the Vietmins and what thanks do I get? A gun barrel crushed against my scalp. Such ingratitude! What was going through Joe's head as he was crouched down I don't know, but I surmise his outlook on the future to be no brighter than mine. Certain circles existed whose members considered it a deadly sin to be a legionnaire and if it was one of those circles we had landed in, we were in deep trouble.

While the car was taking us to wherever, the fog started to lift a bit, at which point I saw, or thought I saw our attackers wearing the uniform of the local police.

"Hey Joe! These guys are local cops."

I could not understand what Joe mumbled by way of a reply because one of the seated men turned on me rudely and snarled, "Be quiet!" In truth, he did not express himself quite so eloquently. "Shut your face" was more like it. To stress his point, he stabbed that rotten gun barrel even closer to my head, when it was no further than a millimetre away before I had opened my mouth; or at least, that's the way I saw it. As a consequence, it took me no longer than a split second to shut up and withdraw.

"Scout, where are we?" spoke Joe at last.

"Haven't a clue."

"Shut your traps!" two of them shouted.

And again. Gun barrels levelled even closer.

A short time later we stopped in front of a building. I glanced out the window and saw a lit up sign over the entrance with POLICE written on it.

Joe and I had now reached the stage where we were able to size up the gravity of the situation. We had no idea what got us into this mess, but we knew that if these men were indeed members of the local police force, they had absolutely no right to lay a hand on us, not to speak of treating us in the manner they did.

We got out of the car, went inside the premises and found that it was in fact a guard room of the local police. This made it clear once and for all that we held all the winning cards. Sitting beside one of the desks inside the room was someone who looked like an NCO. Joe put him on the spot at once by asking him why we had been dragged in here like this. The guy was no more polite than those who had brought us in, and in a similar tone he read our alleged crimes.

One street over from where we had been arrested, the night patrol had come across the dead body of an Arab. The body still warm and the blood oozing from the slashed throat was proof of the fact that the murder had taken place just prior to our arrest. The night patrol began to comb the area at once and it was just our luck that we were the first ones they bumped into. It was only natural that they make the arrest.

We changed our tone and adopted theirs and demanded immediate restitution, and headed for the door. Not halfway there, four policemen blocked the door and levelled machine pistols at us. This was the last straw as far as Joe and I were concerned. We jumped back to the NCO's desk, and pounded our demand that he release us at once.

The NCO leapt out of his seat, his face flaming red with anger and flew into a rage, "Only if and when the matter gets straightened out," he screamed.

Beside the desk was a bench which Joe picked up and wanted to fling it at the NCO's head. Fortunately I was able to grab his arm, take away the bench and stop him before the policeman had a chance to pounce on him. Had Joe knocked the chap on the head, the result would have been fatal for sure.

"What do you want to straighten out?" screamed Joe an octave higher "You know very well that we didn't do it. It was one of your Vietmin buddies who took a hike and is probably laughing up his sleeve right now. We had just left the Hollywood a few minutes before we were arrested. No way we could have been anywhere near that Arab!"

At this the NCO picked up the phone, called the nightclub, and began speaking in a foreign language.

Now it was my turn. I slammed down the phone and yelled at him, saying, that under the circumstances he had no right to converse in a language he knew very well we did not understand.

"I want you to call headquarters at Gia-Lam at once and speak with Commander Duvallieux!"

"Geez, anyone but him!" interrupted Joe in Hungarian. "If he finds out I've been out all night without his permission, that'll be that end of me!"

Now it was the NCO who was infuriated because we weren't speaking in French now it was he who could not understand what we were saying.

"If you think," I answered, matching his tone, "that you have a right to speak in your language, then we certainly have the right to speak in any language we please."

And just to show him that we were not to be trifled with, Joe and I continued our argument over who should be contacted in Hungarian. Finally we settled on lieutenant so and so, who, because he was always the one held responsible for interrogating prisoners, was obviously assigned to some special secret section of service. Twice already he had taken me to task and forced me to answer for my actions. Why was I keeping a diary, and why in Hungarian? Was I perhaps giving classified information away to the Vietmins? He didn't bother me again once the contents were translated and explained to him. and then, we were also aware that he could not stand the natives be they Vietmins or not.

So it was his name we gave to the NCO and demanded that he call the lieutenant at once. He did just that and five minutes later, after profuse apologies, the car was taking us back to Gia-Lam. Our heads began to swim from the hot and stuffy air inside the car, so we asked to be let out and continued on foot. This was at the railroad bridge, and by this time, it was starting to get light out. We joined forces in raking the entire populace of Indochina over the coals. It was their fault that we had lost an hour of what was to be peaceful evening just because one of them had decided to hack open the neck of an Arab. The abuse was noisy and similar to what had gone on in the guard room. When we stepped on the bridge, we were sure that we woke up the guards on the Gia-Lam side of the bridge.

The return trip had proceeded smoothly up until then, until that half-witted Joe elected to cease with his berating and prove his democratic leaning by walking in one shoe only and donating the other to the poor. And to prove that he meant what he had said, he immediately took off one of his shoes, swung it in the air, and hobbled along in one shoe and one thin sock. Naturally, every little pebble cut into his sole. We were thus forced to stop after every ten steps to discuss this intolerable situation created by the existing pebbles. We were on about our tenth stopping place when we decided to dispatch an urgent letter to the office of the Paris Sanitation Department, and demand the immediate allocation on the premises of street sweepers on the condition that they be French because the Indochinese were not worth a grain of salt.

A few stops later I managed to talk Joe into starting his penchant for democracy tomorrow because at this rate, we would surely miss breakfast and likely not get back to the cadre before nightfall. And if the Gorilla couldn't find Joe when he woke up, Joe may as well lie down and take the place of the Arab with the slashed throat. Hearing the name "Gorilla" brought Joe to his senses. Joe picked up his shoe and put on the high gear for Gia-Lam. We would have arrived with no problems if along the road there wasn't a pond. It was by a stroke of fate that just as we reached the pond a large rat ran across the road. The rat vanished in the waters of the pond on the right, but not quickly enough. Joe spotted the rat and he sat down by the pond and tried to cajole the rat back out so he could give him one of his shoes to chew on. He went so far as to remove a shoe and beat the surface of the water with it, scaring the rat half to death in the process.

"Joe quit fooling around. Come one and let's go! The sun is already up. The rat isn't going to come out anyway. You're scaring the poor thing half to death with what you're doing. I'll bet he's already departed from this world."

"That's impossible, he couldn't have left because he knows he belongs to me. Come out, here's my shoe. I want to feed you. Here kitty, kitty, here's my shoe."

"Listen Joe, If you don't come along right now, I'm leaving you here. I'll report to the Gorilla and tell him that you can't be there for breakfast because you had urgent rat feeding business to do."

The name "Gorilla" again made the desired impact and we tore off for the cadre. We got there just in time. The cook was busy in the kitchen while the three apprentices were setting tables in the dining room. I stood behind the bar with a head swollen to the size of a barrel and waited for the arrival of the customers.

I no longer remember what provided the inspiration, but one day, a strong force compelled us into a poetry writing craze. for days on end we made use of every spare minute to compose. Monsters came to light one after the other, and for quite some time, the evening of cards and drinking traded off with poet's nights on which we laughed ourselves silly. These evening sessions were almost always held in my room, it being the only self contained suite.

We made so much noise one evening with our roars of laughter that de Carvalho, who had already gone to bed, came down in his pyjamas from his upstairs room and hit each of us with quatre jour, because despite it being 11:00 p.m. we were kicking up such a row that he was unable to fall asleep. This brought an end to our literary career aspirations, and sent us scurrying back to cards, that wicked tool of the devil.

When I became injured during the battle of That-Khe, I never thought my second injury would take place smack in the middle of the battalion's officer's bar. One day, one of the officers decided to drink champagne. I had never opened a bottle of champagne. That being the case, I set down to the task with the greatest of care. More than once I examined the bottle from top to bottom, front and back, thinking about the best way to go about it, and in this way I managed to shake up the wine inside.

For good measure I smashed it against the back of a chair in the bar at which it promptly exploded. The slivers of glass flew in all directions. One large wedge found refuge in the palm of my left hand. As a further consequence of the explosion, the white walls of the bar turned crimson within seconds.

I would never have thought that a champagne bottle could explode just like that. At the sound of the explosion, many heads turned to the bar and when I let out a muffled scream, three men stood up, came over to the bar and observed the blood spraying all over the wall.

"Maybe we should call the Captain (the Battalion's doctor) over and ask him to administer first aid."

"Fine, go call him!" urged another.

"Isn't Joe around so he can do it?" asked another.

"Looks like he isn't."

"Do you need some help?" asked the third.

"No thank you, I'll bleed to death just fine on my own." I replied, while trying to stop the bleeding by applying pressure to the vein.

"Well then, I'll go call him," said the first. He stepped off the bar stool leaned against the doorway and told the Captain what had happened.

The doctor stood up at his leisure and my blood continued to drip. He ambled over to the bar and looked in.

"Did you cut yourself?"

"Hell no. It was just a champagne bottle that blew up in my hand."

"Is there a surgical dressing case here? Come on out from there. Everything's covered in blood and I don't want blood all over me."

A surgical dressing case turned up and while the doctor was applying the dressing, the three kids cleaned up the bar. When all was said and done, everything went back to normal as though nothing had happened. I continued my work as waiter/bartender with one hand, but I was not about to open another bottle of champagne. I gave the bottle to Lieutenant Lambert and asked him to open it because the one stab I had at it was more than enough.

Walter

Steve

Leo

The next morning I was just about to go over to the infirmary so Leo could change the dressing on my hand when in stepped the Commander with three unfamiliar officers. Since Joe was nowhere to be seen I was obliged to comply with their request for cognacs, and I used my teeth in place of a corkscrew. The Commander and his three guests gazed with intrigue at my head twisted at an awkward angle, trying to force open the bottle. The bottle was still almost full, and when the cork finally popped out, a good portion of the contents spilled out. Well, I thought, I will have that much less to show for my foxy feats of skill. I handed the leadership of the bar over to Joe, who turned up in the meantime, and went to get my dressing changed.

Maneuvering corks out of bottles with my teeth, a procedure the Commander kept track of with great interest, lasted for about a week. These frequent visits of his to the bar truly surprised me, because up until now he had always taken his drinks back to his room or had Joe take them over to his table. During the course of the week he had sat around four times, watching me pull out the corks with head bent over. Looks like he wants to learn the trade of extracting corks in this manner from a master craftsman, I thought. Once my hand healed and I dispensed with the technique, the Commander failed to come around any longer.

The days flowed in their usual fashion until one morning when de Carvalho told me to dress in full uniform after breakfast and appear before the Commander during morning report. I was scared as a mouse suddenly finding itself in front of a cat.

My Lord what have I done? Could they have found out about my clever tactics at the bar? You're about to be denounced, Scout, by that hunchbacked Beelzebub and that lame Lucifer.

I suddenly became so extravagant with the dispensing of drinks that within ten minutes I had overfilled the glasses of four extra portions worth. Dear Lord, please don't let them drink a lot today or I'll be ruined.

"Joe!"

"What the hell do you want? I don't have any time. The Gorilla's in a frenzy."

"I have to ask you something very important.'

"What is it?"

"The big boss told me to appear at morning report. Did you by chance hear something? I thought maybe you'd know why all hell has broken loose."

"I haven't heard a thing," he mumbled and he was gone.

Joe had said the Gorilla was in a frenzy. If I escape with anything less than a chain gang I can be happy. I successfully over measured eight more portions by the time breakfast was over. To hell with it, I was done in.

A dozen delinquents were waiting their destiny when I stepped out in the yard. Before the Commander appeared the NCO took me and two others aside which gave me another fit of hysterics because only those condemned to die were separated in this manner. My one consolation was that I was not alone.

Then the Commander was coming straight to me, de Carvalho right behind him. My knees were shaking like mad and what gave me strength to stay standing I don't know. When the Commander stopped in front of me I sprung to attention and almost broke me heels. I was hoping that maybe he might include it as an extenuating circumstance; meaning, the sudden springing to attention. And then I could not believe my ears, I had just received a promotion. Owing to my exemplary attitude and conduct, my services rendered over and beyond the call of duty and so on, I was promoted from a legionnaire of the second class to a legionnaire of the first class.

From the box he was holding, de Carvalho removed two green stripes, handed them to me and followed the presentation with a salutation and handshakes. A huge weight fell off my shoulders. After the other two with me were likewise honored de Carvalho dismissed us.

"Scout, what happened?" asked Joe as I entered the dining room.

"Look at this!" I said showing him the two stripes.

"Don't drive me mad! You? A first class legionnaire? Don't tell me you're going to be the next commander of the battalion!"

"Watch your step from now on because you have yet to face such an imposing master as I. I'm prepared to saddle you mercilessly with 'quatre jour's'!"

It was easy to be a corporal or sergeant in the Legion, six months of training and anyone who met the requirements could become a sergeant. Much more difficult a task was it to become a legionnaire of the first class. This was a position that had to be deserved. And as hard as it was to come by, it was easy to lose. One false step, the slightest serious misdemeanor contrary to the rules and the green stripes fell.

It must have been nearing the end of November when Duvallieux ordered the entire squadron out on a practice jump. For days the survey had gone on in the Hanoi area to guarantee a trouble free jump. Those who touched ground first formed groups and waited for those behind to jump. The paratroopers were filing through the doorway of the plane when the chain snapped and someone's parachute did not release from the strap it was locked on to. Somebody had applied more than one silk thread to the chute!

The "Scout"

Author as chief accountant

In a rare moment of repose with Steve Bidon
Centre- unfamiliar comrade
Background- officers' mess hall

The air current threw that poor fellow around as he dragged behind the plane. The pilot slowed down as much as possible and shut the left engine down completely while the troopers inside pulled the man back into the plane. This maneuver unfortunately did not proceed swiftly or simply. The plane jerked the man for almost forty-five minutes before they were able to pull him inside. As we later heard, he was conscious the entire time and that was part of the problem. If he had fainted he wouldn't have known what was happening to him. The poor guy was half-crazed once he was on board again.

Ever since my transfer to this company I haven't felt like I was in the Legion. For my part, the transfer had brought to an end the missions and the time spent on patrol. In its place I was taking inventory of canned goods, portioning out drinks, fighting the cook and when I finished my duties as a bartender, I nominated myself as head bookeeper. I settled the daily accounts and submitted them to de Carvalho and I was done for the day. If the *Devil's Bible Society* was unable to gather for some reason, then I wrote letters. If I could talk myself into it, that is, something that did not occur very often. And as the days passed, the time came for my second Christmas in Indochina. We began preparations days before, by hauling in a huge Christmas tree. We could have set the tree up in one hour and not the half day that it took if not for the twenty men bustling about and taking orders from three NCOs. It was a typical case of one hand too many. When the tree was standing and everyone had dispersed, I picked up three discarded branches, tied them together, placed them in a glass jar and put them in my room, just to give the place a touch of pine scent.

Decorating the tree was the next thing to get underway, a job which took up two entire days owing to the presence of not three but five NCOs ordering everyone around. We had to climb up on the roof so that the top of the tree could get a smattering of ornaments. Setting out the gifts was next and took place on the fourth day. Miracle of miracles, that this was accomplished by only three men and without the meddling of any NCOs. As a result, everything was in its place within two and a half hours.

This Christmas of 1949 turned out to be the most memorable holiday of my life. The supper on this festive occasion began with a short speech delivered by Commander Duvallieux. Officers, NCOs and troops were gathered at tables set up in the yard. Gifts were distributed after the meal. We lit the bonfire and sang Christmas carols around it. I went up to my room for a few minutes and lit the five candles on my little tree. Five candles, one for every member of my family. I sang *Silent Night, Holy Night* in Hungarian, then rejoined Steve and Joe for more drinking and singing.

Apart from the three of us, there was another Hungarian in this section of battalion headquarters, I have not mentioned him before, because it was as though he didn't exist at all. It's been over a month and a half since his transfer here, but during all that time, I only saw him twice and we had exchanged a few words only once. Never did he seek out our company, nor did he try to make friends with anyone else. According to Steve, he was a completely reserved and withdrawn man who sometimes did not communicate with another soul for days on end. Nobody knew anything about him. He did not get any letters, nor did he write any. Rumor had it that he was descendent of an aristocratic family whose members had no idea that he was in the Legion. Similar rumors surrounded anyone who was likewise shrouded in secrecy and enveloped in silence. His tendency to withdraw did not ease today either. He drew away from the crowd, sat alone at one of the tables and came to life only when he was called over to receive his gift.

We three sat around a table, singing each with a bottle of wine in hand. We felt it needless to ask the Aristocrat to join us, knowing that he would refuse the invitation. As a result, our surprise was great when he came over and asked if we wanted to go with him to midnight Mass. This coming on of his was so unexpected that for a moment we were left speechless.

"Well, do you want to come or not?"

"I'll go with you," I replied, almost against my will.

Joe and Steve drew a large gulp from the bottle before answering that they did not want to go.

"In that case, Scout, come on, because the car is waiting for the church goers, and it's going to leave pretty soon." (It also surprised me that he new my nickname.)

I tried to strike up a conversation with him on the way over, thinking that if he lossened up enough to invite me to church with him then he might want to open up even further. Maybe he wanted to let down that secretive wall which up until now had made him unapproachable, maybe the mood of the Christmas season spurred him on to become more talkative. I was wrong. To my few questions which had nothing to do with family, his reply was a curt "no," so I gave up trying any more.

The church was crammed by the time we got there. Nevertheless, the Aristocrat and I fought our way through the crowd and stood over by the pews near the front. The liturgical ceremony began a few minutes later. In those days, Mass was still conducted in Latin, even to the prayers of the priest, the organist responded in Latin. The place in the Mass arrived when the priest prays quietly to himself, parishioners silence their song, and only the subdued sound of the organ played by the organist is audible in the background. We listened to the organ and stood staring at each other. We could not believe our ears, we could hear the quiet strains of *God Bless the People of Hungary*.

Slowly, and with dignity, the *Hungarian National Anthem* rippled through the nave of the church and cut the silence. The two tall, pale-skinned Hungarians stood out among the oriental-featured crowd, and just stared at each other with tears streaming from their eyes. Fifteen thousand kilometres from home and we listened, standing at attention with teary eyes in the midst of a Chinese crowd, to *God Bless the People of Hungary*.

Where is the vocabulary with which to express my emotions?

Nobody in the whole world outside of the Aristocrat and I received a Christmas present as precious.

After the last strains were sounded we looked up to the chorus hoping to spot the organist. No such luck. We then tried to cut our way through the mob, this too did not work. We were given disapproving glances for disturbing the peace. We had no choice but to wait until Mass was over. But by the time we got to the door leading to the organ loft it was locked. We never did find out who was the organist who gave us this unforgettable Christmas gift of 1949!

That one week between News Year's Eve and Christmas glided by quick as a day. Officers of unfamiliar corps came as guests day after day, and kept Joe and I so busy that we hardly had time to breath. Clearing of accounts took me twice as long because of the string of visits. The advantage of it was that the upshot of my clever tactics behind the bar multiplied fivefold, and my pockets were stuffed by the time New Year's Eve rolled around.

"Hey Joe! Are we going to see the old year out at that nightclub down by the lakeshore?"

"If you have enough money. That place is not the Hollywood, you know."

"No problem on my part. Question is, how do you stand?" I asked as we passed by each other he on his way out and I on my way in with a vegetable platter.

"I have a few hundred, but I don't think it's going to be enough in that place. At least not for one evening. Do you think you could lend me some?"

"I'll see."

"Don't be such a tightwad!" he called after me, while waiting in the doorway leading to the dining hall's kitchen for the apprentices to bring him out the food ready to be served.

Despite the system, I found myself looking around the kitchen quite often, overseeing the cook with regards to his clever handed tactics, because certain individuals complained about the portions being too small. He was often up to his tricks, and I always managed to catch him redhanded.

Nothing came of my frequent promises to slash his neck, and he knew all too well that my promises were exactly that and no more. I also had to be careful that no more food for us six be set aside than what was authorized. I frequently collected the small plates which the cook had put aside and so carefully concealed thinking of leaner days ahead.

"Look here!" I said to him for the thousandth time. "Whatever is left over at the end of dinner or supper is yours to keep anyway, so why are you forever hiding things all over the place when you know very well that I'm going to find out about the deficiency?"

I may as well have been talking to a wall. He went on hiding and I went on finding.

The fact that Joe accused me of being a tightwad injured my pride and I decided that would not give him a single piaster.

"So you don't have enough money?" I asked. "Somebody who has no money is in no position to entertain thoughts of having a good time, especially not in the lakeshore nightclub."

"You don't understand, I didn't mean to say that I don't have enough for myself. For my part alone, I can easily get by. What worries me is how much you're going to guzzle down. Because you know me, I'm incapable of ignoring a thirsty man in time of need."

"Hey Joe, why are you trying to befriend me? Didn't you hear me say that I have enough to spare?"

"Okay fine, but it can fall out of your pocket, can't it? If you give me a thousand or so now, there'd be less danger of it. You know I've always shared everything I own with you. After all, two good buddies like you and I can't just stand by and ignore the other in times of hardship. And if your money really did fall out of your pockets, what would you do? Don't misunderstand! I'm serious and I'm mentioning it as a possibility. If you gave some of it to me, you could demand it back. Aren't I right? But naturally only on the condition that it fall out of my pocket."

"What a bunch of baloney! You're full of hot air Joe. Just as mouthy as Popocatepetl. You could talk a kid out of its mother's womb."

"Okay fine! You don't have to bring the Pope into this."

"Who made any reference to the Pope? I said Popocatepetl, it's a volcano in Mexico."

"So who needs a volcano? I need fifteen hundred piasters."

"Here take it. Now shut your mouth," I said.

"Scout, We're going to have a grand old time tonight!" said Joe while I counted out the fifteen bills into his palm and a Mephistophelian smirk flashed across his face.

It being New Year's Eve, supper was scheduled an hour and a half earlier. At best, one-third of the officers took part in it. Within the space of an hour everything was wrapped up. No sooner had Joe and I finished with supper when in came Walter, Leo and Charlie. I set out two bottles of wine, when Steve also popped in. His arrival necessitated another bottle of wine.

"Hey Steve! Didn't you call the Aristocrat?"

"What for? That chap isn't normal. Besides, he wouldn't come anyway."

"Well I'm going to go up and call him down."

Joe turned on me. "Leave that fool alone! He's not going to come anyhow."

"But at least he can see that we were thinking of him."

The Aristocrat's room held eight beds. He was alone in the room, lying on his bed and staring at the ceiling.

"Come on down and join us!" I said to him. "All the Hungarians are gathered. We're going to throw a little New Year's bash and bid farewell to last year."

"Thank you for your consideration. I appreciate it a lot, I really do, but I'm not going to go." By turning to face the wall he indicated that as far as he was concerned the case was closed.

"Okay, so the Aristocrat is not willing to join us."

"I knew that calling him was a waste of time," said Steve.

"But at least I tried, so he could see that someone was thinking of him. Okay, so what's with the carousing at this lakeshore nightclub? Who's coming and who isn't."

"What's your big rush?" asked Charlie. "We're all going. But first, we'll finish drinking this wine that you set out, then go back to the sector to change. We're going to spruce ourselves up and then we'll conquer the lakeshore nightclub."

"And just who do you expect to conquer with that goatee fit for a chimney sweep hanging down your neck?" asked Walter.

"Don't forget, buddy, that women fall into a frenzy over bearded men."

"The woman who sinks low enough to fall into a frenzy over you, deserves what she gets!" replied Walter.

"Listen," I interrupted, "too much chatter! Slurp up that wine and let's go. The nightclub is going to fill up fast and we won't get a place."

By the time the guys got ready and were reassembled at my place and by the time the consumption of another few bottles of wine was done with, the hour was so advanced that every last jeep had departed for Hanoi and we were forced to walk. It was around eight p.m. by the time we reached the night club, and as I had suspected, the place was already jam packed. According to the person who was standing by the door welcoming guests, only one empty table remained. The price of acquiring it was a heap of pleading compounded by a good size tip. It was not a good table, it seated only four and was directly beside the stage on which a jazz band was going great guns. The musicians were honking and pounding away at the top of their lungs so that if we wanted to talk we had to scream to be heard. No wonder that nobody wanted to sit here, nobody had any desire to start the new year deaf, but we were glad that someone was available if only that particular one.

The waiter came to take our order once we were squeezed in beside the table. The proprietor too found his way over and saw that we looked a little squished. He must have had figured that in such cramped conditions we'd have trouble drinking not to speak of eating if maybe that was our intent. Since this might mean a loss of business for him, it was to his advantage to provide us with a larger table. The idea was a good one, but its execution was no easy task. The table had to be dragged across the dance floor. We hustled about until the small table was taken out and a larger replacement brought in. After we had so wonderfully succeeded in stirring up the peace in the joint, we finally got so far as having a bottle of cognac brought over.

"Guys! Let's empty the first for our loved ones back home. Let's drink not just to their health, but to the promise of a carefree New Year free of dread. May God grant the restricted people of Hungary a freer life!"

"Long live Scout! Let's stand up, whisper a quiet Apostles Creed, and empty our glasses for the people of Hungary!" said Steve.

The second shot we were brave enough to drink to our own health. Only after this did we look around to see, after all, what sort of a party and people we had wound our way into. The appraisal put us in a spot, and left us feeling embarrassed, because sitting at the table next to ours was a partisan first lieutenant with his wife and two daughters, and we had not even bothered to say hello to the Lieutenant.

"Leo, since you're the senior ranking officer here, (he was a lance sergeant by this time) why don't you go over, offer our respectful apologies for not greeting him sooner and make some excuse."

Leo stepped over, launched into his excuses, and when the Lieutenant looked up our way, we stood at attention to greet him. His wife and two daughters we acknowledged with a bow that was returned. As for the others on the premises, there were people of all kinds and ranks from every walk of military life. While sipping the cognac it occurred to Charlie that maybe we should ask the Lieutenant's daughters for the pleasure of a dance, seeing that they were diligent wallflowers. Maybe the Lieutenant would not be too shocked by the notion. Hopefully he would understand our boldness was strictly a kind act of courtesy because no one else was taking his daughters out on the dance floor. Personally, this did not surprise me one iota. The girls had quite obviously forgotten to stand in line when beauty was being distributed and by the time it crossed their minds to do do, the supply had run out.

"Go over and try it, Scout!"

"Me? Why me? Why not you? I don't have enough courage in me."

"Steve you try," Charlie egged him on.

"No way! I'm not going. You ask them if you want to dance so badly."

"How about you Joe?" asked Leo.

"Perish the thought! Like hell I'll do it first, but I do have a suggestion. Walter, you're sitting with your back to them, so they can't see what you're doing. Why don't you take out a slip of paper, jot down our names and we'll make a draw. Whoever's name gets pulled has to start."

His suggestion was met with unanimous approval – my name was drawn.

"Okay Scout, go for it!" ordered Leo.

"Wait a minute. Let me sip this shot of brandy and think about the best way to go about it."

"Only in as polite a manner as possible. For example, stand at attention in front of the Lieutenant and ask him if we can take his hussies for a toss on the floor because we happened to notice that they were doing nothing but sitting on their asses," said Leo, by way of some sound advice.

"Or," said Walter, "go over to one of the girls, give her a good slap on the back and say 'Hey Judy, wanna go for a spin?' "

"Quit jerking me around and let me think."

"What's there to think about? Go and ask one of them for a dance."

"Okay, okay, I'm going. But let me say this much, if you guys act up and don't dance decently with those girls, then I'm gone. You Charlie, the way you squirm around when you're dancing just won't do with these particular young ladies. The last time I saw you, you were holding that woman's waist like you would hold a lamp post at three in the morning. A cigarette paper wouldn't have fit between you two, you were holding her so close. So pretend you're standing at attention in front of her father when you dance with this one, and be sure to leave at least a half-step gap between you. This applies to all of you," I said, and leaped up suddenly, leaving them no time to lecture me with a similar sermon.

Hardly had I begun to say what I had to say as I stepped over to their table when one of the maidens revealed that she didn't know how to dance. I turned and gave the other a questioning look. She got up without saying a word. At the same time I cast a glance at their daddy, and saw that with a nod of his head, he was giving his girls permission to accept the invitation. When my dear good friends saw I had cleared the way for them, all five jumped up at once and made a beeline for the other girl. Walter got the prize, since he was the closest and got there first.

All this fervent attention was much to the spinster's liking because she let out a loud laugh. That, in turn, was not to her mother's liking, and gave the girl a reproachful look, but her laughing did break the ice. By around midnight she had loosened up so much that even her mother raised her champagne glass our way, while we in turn summoned up enough courage to stand around their table and wish them all a prosperous and happy New Year.

"You Leo, go over to the two lieutenants from our squadron and wish them too a happy New Year on behalf of us," said Charlie.

"Why are you always wanting to send someone else? Why should I go? What if they disapprove of the gesture and reprimand me?"

"That's no reason not to go, " said Joe. "You don't have to worry about that in the least, I know both of them. Lieutenant Roy is one of the most decent officers in the Battalion, and the other is just as good a guy."

"Well okay, I'll go but if I get into any trouble, don't any of you dare set foot in the infirmary again, you hear?"

He grabbed his glass of champagne and off he trotted. We kept a close eye to see what kind of an impression he would make. Leo made it to the table, stopped in front of Lieutenant Roy, raised his glass halfway and let his tongue go. The lieutenants responded. Lieutenant Roy stood up and clinked glasses with Leo. The other followed suit, then both offered Leo a seat at their table.

"See, didn't I tell you that he's a respectable kind of guy? I don't want to drop any names but had it been someone else, no way that Leo would have gotten an invitation to sit down. Most officers I can think of couldn't even be bothered to return the toast."

"Careful you guys, they're coming over here," warned Charlie.

We looked up and saw Leo coming back with the two lieutenants trailing right behind him.

We stood up as soon as they came over. Lieutenant Roy did not accept the seats so politely offered by Walter and Steve, saying, that their friends were expecting them back, and they merely wanted to return our compliments of the season. Still,they considered our offer a great honor and thanked us for the privilege. We introduced them to the partisan lieutenant with whom they also exchanged a few polite words before returning to their own party.

Everything had gone very nicely until Charlie, who was seated at the opposite end of the table facing the stage, grabbed the other bottle of champagne when the New Year's greetings were finished with and started to open it. He peeled off the paper, loosened the wire and attempted to pry out the cork while holding the bottle at a slight angle. Joe in the meantime was holding his glass by the bottle's mouth in case the costly nectar should suddenly gush forth. He didn't want it wasted on the tablecloth if that happened, he wanted to drink it himself.

The cork flew out, the nectar came spurting forth and a cry of pain was heard. The speeding cork had caught one of the musicians right on the ear. Since he was a trumpet player and was blowing into his instrument at the top of his lungs, I can well imagine what he must have felt when something gave him a good knock on the ear. The pain was instantaneous and at the impact he forgot all about his trumpet. He tried to flee and in his disoriented state took a wrong turn and ran straight into the bass drum; the drummer leapt up and crashed into the music stands, causing the smaller drums and cymbals to topple off and create an infernal din and the pianist leapt out of his chair. By now all the musicians were screaming at the others and scrambling about. None of the musicians knew what had happened. The pandemonium was at its height by the time the proprietor and two of the waiters wandered over to see what was going on. As of yet, none of the musicians were in the clear as to what actually happened. Charlie alone knew.

The victim entered into a heated discussion with the proprietor once this uproar had subsided. He was flinging his arms about madly and pointing at our table. Since the cork had come flying at him from the left, it was not difficult to ascertain conclusively that we were the source. We sat by our table while all this was going on with the look of innocence on our faces, like six newborn lambs.

I did brave a glance over to the adjoining table because I was curious to see what sort of a reaction the cork had elicited. The two girls were nearly bursting from laughter, the mother was sitting stone still, oblivious to the world around and as though nothing existed, and the Lieutenant was snickering away while giving us the odd glance. Inquisitive patrons rose to see why the musicians were in such a tizzy. Those who smelled a fight in the air were mistaken. The proprietor very deftly calmed the musicians down before the state of things had a chance to fester and get out of hand.

The music started up again soon after. The percussion section alone was found lacking to a degree, because the bass drum was lying trampled to death somewhere backstage. Nobody came over to bother us, to complain of any injustice. Is it any wonder when innocence was written all over our faces? Even the proprietor saw fit to leave the matter be and not press the point. Knowing it would only damage the reputation of his popular nightclub.

Everything went back to full swing, the dancing and the saluting in of the New Year, once the storm had spent itself. We, however, quickly and unfortunately, found ourselves without dance partners because the Lieutenant and his family had hit the road for home. In the absence of a ticket system professional dancing women for hire were not available, so there was nothing left to do but drink. Around three a.m. Charlie jumped on stage and began to sing. No sooner did he belt out a few notes when the entire band joined forces in an effort to drown out his voice. Charlie, however, still outbellowed them. One of the adjutants appeared at our table and told us to make that prima donna vanish from the stage or they would skin him alive

"He looks just like a monkey in tails. A hyena's voice is tickling to the ears compared to his."

The musicians too must have been fed up with Charlie's sense of artistry, because under such duress, they abruptly stopped and took a break. Charlie was not to be inconvenienced by this and the budding artist kept on displaying his long lost art. It took Leo some time to convince the artist to cut out his wailing if he didn't want to create a scandal larger than he had already done. But then, who was in any shape to be disgusted or shocked at half past three in the morning? Those who were still sticking it out were not in any position to care any less whether it was the musicians wailing away or someone else. Leo did nonetheless persuade Charlie off the stage, after which we sat in separate rickshaws and went home to Gia-Lam.

The weeks rolled by and I thought of asking for a transfer back to the squadron. I was missing the excitement, the primitive jungles, the skirmishes, the harassment of the Vietmins. I tried very hard to forget about the possibility of repatriation, de Carvalho was always hitting me with more responsibilities. I wrote off any notion of repatriation after Joe told me he had overheard a discussion between de Carvalho and the Gorilla in which de Carvalho had recommended I be promoted.

"Stop fooling around! And what did the Gorilla have to say about that?"

"He said that you just recently were promoted to a first class legionnaire, and besides, you've never taken an officer's training course. De Carvalho then suggested that you be sent to such a school."

"Okay, we'll send him, but then who's going to replace him? He does practically everything around here," came the Commander's objection.

"That's precisely why he should be made at least a Lance Sergeant. As a first class legionnaire, he doesn't have the same authority," reasoned de Carvalho.

"Okay, I'll give it some thought," the Commander switching the topic.

"Well what's the matter? Doesn't the prospect interest you? Aren't you glad about it? I'd be jumping up and down for joy if I was in your shoes, and you're standing there like you just heard some bad news."

"I just don't know how to respond or what to think. Truth of the matter is Joe, that since my transfer here I've been hoping they'd send me on repatriation."

"What for? You're fit as a fiddle!"

"Well that's not quite true, why the vacation in Dalat, or all those days spent in the hospital, or even my transfer here if there was nothing wrong with me? But instead of letting me go, the Gorilla promotes me to a first class legionnaire, and now, de Carvalho wants to make a Lance Sergeant out of me. They don't give a hoot about any discharge. There go my chances. And then, I've also considered asking for a transfer back to the squadron."

"Where?"

"Back to the squadron. Frankly, I'm bored to tears. This ain't my cup of tea. You wouldn't believe how monotonous the work is here, Joe. It's driving me nuts! Believe it or not, I miss the missions. A couple good rounds of shooting a trek through the jungle."

I got no further before Joe cut me off,

"Scout, you're out of your mind. I'm going to have a chat with Leo and tell him to have you taken to a looney bin. That's where anyone who says something like that belongs. You don't know when you're well off. You've never had it so good since you've been in the Legion, nor will you ever again. I mean look, you have three apprentices taking care of all your affairs for you, you're eating officer's grub, you can drink as much as you want and for free to boot, you don't ever have to go on missions, not like me who has to accompany the Gorilla every time he goes, the only action you have to participate in are the practice jumps, and with all this you want to go back to the squadron? You're not just stupid as an ass who ventures out on ice, you're a *blundering idiot!*"

"See isn't that the way it always is. A man is never satisfied with his lot. Here I am, content as a fish in water and thinking about how to bust my ass. By George, your right!"

One night we cut short our rummy game because next morning at the crack of dawn Charlie had to go on a mission. The *Devil's Bible Society* broke up well before midnight, each member dispersing to his respective cubbyhole. (Mine was an idiot's lair according to Joe.) The repose of the night was short-lived because I was woken by the rattle of firearms and loud shrieking.

"The first squadron has been attacked!" screamed someone.

Seeing that everyone else was busy imitating a greyhound, I followed their example. I pulled on my paratrooper shoes, grabbed my machine gun and ran after the others. I didn't want to be left out of this friendly round of shooting when so recently I had longed for exactly that.

The perimeter of the first squadron was a mere six hundred metres from our position, but still, twenty minutes passed by the time we got there, and by then, the party was over. It was reported that one squadron of Vietmins were responsible for the shooting that started from the opposite side of the embankment just as our side was changing guards. This left the area vulnerable since no one was around and by the time the Vietmins were on top of the embankment, half our squadron and the entire change of guard was lying in the grass, while a few dozen were spread out near the base of the embankment. Of the attacking forces, eight men in their great haste had rolled down the embankment and straight into the lake from where we had to fish them out. As for the rest, they were driven back within minutes by the squadron lying in the grass and shooting from the windows. So nothing was left for us, but the eight dripping wet Vietmins, whom we took to the squadron jail and left in the care of the guards.

The next morning began with a repeat performance of yesterday. Again, I woke to the sound of shrieking and men racing all over the place. Was it because the Vietmins were attacking again? I grabbed my things and ran outside to see what all the commotion was about and found that the excitement was focused on the jail. The prisoners, together with the guard, had cut loose and taken to their heels in the early morning. They apparently took a few weapons with them as a token of remembrance. How they got hold of the weapons is what I wanted to know.

A month later a letter arrived at the squadron, written by the legionnaire who had shifted his allegiance over to the enemy. In it, he flaunted his captain's rank in the Vietmin army and boasted about the high esteem he was granted. Among other things, he promised a certain lieutenant that he was going to track him down and skin him alive if and when he nabbed him. In addition, he warned everyone to live in constant terror of him because his thirst for revenge was insatiable. That the letter was indeed penned by him was verified beyond a shadow of a doubt, but judging by the scrawly handwriting, it was entirely possible that he may have written it under coercion and not of his own free will.

February 24, 1950

Sergeant Du Mortier and I were on a shopping trip, and had finished purchasing the necessary and listed items when we stopped in front of a store on Rue Paul Bert in which Du Mortier had some personal business to attend to. While he was inside I waited in the jeep, watching the traffic on the streets and the people sauntering back and forth.

Two women, a mother and daughter, came around the corner from the direction of the theatre square, advertising by their appearance that they were French, and belonged to the upper crust of society. Stylishly and elegantly dressed in the latest of fashions, they looked like they had just stepped down from the pages of a fashion magazine. The girl, looking to be around eighteen years of age, openly displayed a fiery temperament. Every movement of her hand was assertive and commanding. Her facial features were, however, soft and refined: the tiny pug nose, the mouth, arched and determined. I saw her for but a minute, but in that minute, the veil lifted. The veil revealed a world hundreds of millions longed for. The world of that privileged few in the upper class of society where there were no cares or woes, where servants often outnumbered the family members, where there could be more wasted in a day than what was granted in an entire lifetime to ten men elsewhere.

I still saw the noble and chiselled face of the girl in front of me, when from the store that Du Mortier was in, a woman stepped out. I was taken aback by what I saw. She couldn't have been very old, but life had taken a toll on her body. She was stepping as though wanting to mask her emfeeblement, but her troubles were weighing her down with such a force that she was incapable of hiding from view the many sufferings she endured. She wore an old and tatered black coat, one that had seen better days. Life had faded the colors of both the owner and the coat. A canvas bag hung from her hand. Were it capable of speaking, perhaps it would say it couldn't remember the last time it was full.

The woman stopped in the store's doorway, puzzled, not knowing what to do, she turned halfway around and came back out. A few steps later she went back inside the store, but turned around and came back out again before she had even closed the door behind her. She stood there, fretting, speculating. It was obvious that she wanted to buy something, but did not dare. In the middle of the sidewalk she stopped again, then suddenly turned around and hurried back in the store. The tiny and broken figure was swallowed like a leaf turned yellow in the dense autumn fog.

A few minutes later she came out holding a chocolate bar in her hand. Stopping in the middle of the sidewalk she put the chocolate in her bag, slowly and carefully, as if afraid that something might happen to it. She gathered up the bag and set off but stopping after a few steps and checked inside the bag to make sure that the chocolate was really there. She then limped off toward the theatre square and disappeared with her poverty, poor health and misery, much like the two previous figures had appeared from the same place in their wealth.

April 10, 1950

It was maybe the middle of April when Charlie ran in breathless and waving a piece of paper in his hand. It was after supper, and Steve and I were hanging around by the entrance to the dining hall.

"Guys, where's Joe? I want him to hear too! Look at this! I just received word that I can go back to Europe in three weeks! My five years have passed! Where's Joe? Come on you guys, we have to celebrate!"

He was excited as a beggar girl just asked by a prince for her hand in marriage.

"Guys, I'm going home!"

"Steve, run and get Joe, then come over to Scout's place. And you, go and bring ten bottles of wine. We're going to drink today!"

We rinsed out throats diligently as we buckled down to shower Charlie with a stream of good wishes. All the while we pounded him on the shoulders and back from which he almost choked because we did so just as he was about to swallow.

There is no rose without a thorn, and the joy was not without its taste of bitterness. We were happy for Charlie, happy that his five years were up, but at the same time we felt grieved, knowing that we had to stay. Our happiness for him was heartfelt and sincere. We were glad that he was one of the chosen few taken into the lap of the Goddess of Fortune, but how much more complete our happiness would have been had we all been given the opportunity to go home together, if the rest of us too could be aboard the *Pasteur*. That five year termination was still a long way down the road.

Charlie now spent almost all his free time in our company. He never ran out of making plans for his future. No longer was he counting the days but the hours.

There was one week to go before his date of departure when his squadron was sent on a foray around Hanoi. It was to be an insignificant patrol.

"Well guys," he said the night before, "I'm going to take one last look at the area around Hanoi. Say goodbye to the Vietmins with a couple of rounds then off I go! Scout, my friend, bring out another five or so bottles. I have to say goodbye to you guys too! One week from today I'll be drinking aboard the *Pasteur* and thinking of you!'

Around midnight I told Charlie not to go back so late. Sleep here. Never know when something might happen.

"Like hell I'm gonna stay here. What for? No big deal. I've made the trip a thousand times. Besides, I'm not alone. Here's my machine pistol!"

The next morning Charlie and his squadron departed from battalion headquarters, and the paved road stretched out behind them. It was not yet ten a.m. when the truck pulled out. We three stood on the sidewalk waving to Charlie, he waving back with his machine pistol.

It was not yet noon when a jeep pulled in front of the cadre. On it, Charlie, his body ripped into three pieces.

Vietmins had attacked the squadron, and while trying to crawl toward the enemy position, Charlie had crawled right over a mine. It exploded under his stomach and ripped him to shreds.

Two hours later the daily mail arrived, among the letters was one from Charlie's mother. Joe was the one to pick it out from the rest and showed it to Steve and I.

"Hey guys, let's open it," said Steve.

"No. Don't open it Steve!"

But it was too late, Steve had already opened the envelope. I had no desire to see it. Nor did Joe, so Steve read it alone.

A mother writing with passion to a son she had not seen in years, knowing that he was soon due to come home, was surely counting down the years, months, weeks. Such were the sentiments expressed in her letter. She wrote about how dearly they were looking forward to his coming back home, about eagerly anticipating all the stories he would have to tell, about the neighbors and friends of his who were making fervent inquiries as to his homecoming, while he, was lying in the morgue.

Charlie's death brought a big change to our lives. The card parties ceased, the high spirits vanished. If we did get together, we stared straight ahead in silence, and if someone did speak, the topic was Charlie and that a similar fate could await any one of us. At any time the mailman might deliver a letter from the French government to our homes, containing for words: "Mort pour la France! He died for France!" Outside of our group the data meant nothing more than a change in the number of staff. For our part, however, some time had to pass before we became accustomed to never again seeing Charlie's tall and lanky figure appear around battalion headquarters.

The everyday work which had to be done did not allow for an extended period of brooding and mourning. Life did not stop because of Charlie's death. A man's duties demanded that he be all there, and the void left behind by Charlie, albeit slowly to be sure, dissolved with the passing of time. Missions followed one after the other, the number of dead and injured continually grew, and the statistics were altered accordingly.

Walter, during combat jump, fell onto a bamboo rod.

"Well don't that beat everything," he said, the first time I went to visit him. "I almost followed in Charlie's footsteps. What I felt the second that bamboo rod buried itself into me, Scout, I can't begin to tell you. Only good thing was, you know, that I fainted on the spot and didn't come to 'till I was here in the hospital. First operation was last week, but the doctor tells me there's a few more to go. Looks like they couldn't flush the whole thing out all at once."

"I think you'll be resting for a few more weeks."

"A month at least is as sure as a day."

"Well, just get all the rest you need. You sure as hell deserve it. Do you know that Steve's in too with a serious injury? And the Aristocrat's dead. No one will ever find out who he really was."

"What happened to Steve?"

"A few days after you guys went jumping, they went out too. Not jumping, mind you, but on a short little foray with another squadron. They went off in two different direction, planning to meet up somewhere in the afternoon and come back together. They maintained radio contact and Steve was the one handling the radio over by the squadron's cadre. The foray went on all day without hitches. They were just making their way back to the rendezvous spot when the Vietmins made their hit. Don't know which way they were going, but whoever was with Steve, said that Steve built some kind of an entrenchment for himself out of bricks so he could handle the radio under less strain. He must have been near some large centre, else where would he have found bricks? Anyway, the Vietmins were equipped with mine throwers as well, and one of the mines caught Steve's cover right in the middle. Only good thing was that it didn't hit on the side where Steve was drawn. But pieces of brick were flying all over the place, and one cut into his stomach and slashed open his abdominal wall. I haven't seen him yet. I'm going over from here. And you, you just rest and get well as soon as possible! I'll come by again in a few days. Want me to bring you something?"

"If you can, something to read in Hungarian."

"Okay, I'll do my best."

I did find Steve, but I wasn't able to speak with him. When I looked at him I thought he was a dead man. But then I noticed the gently rising and falling chest. Dead he wasn't, but he sure the hell looked it. He didn't so much as open his eyes when I spoke to him or called him by name. I asked one of the nurses for a prognosis.

"He's past the critical stage, but he's still terribly weak. You legionnaires are made of steel. Anyone else would be long since buried from an injury like this."

As a member of the steel brigade, I was tickled by her words, and swelling with pride. I knew of certain individuals, likewise members of the guard, who were almost embarrassed to admit it.

Apart from the reports circulated about the Legion, I was not ashamed about my part in it. There was nothing to be ashamed about! That the Legion was a place of refuge for all sorts of criminals guilty of crimes did not mean that we, the thousands who had landed in the Legion after the Second World War had to feel ashamed. We bravely stood our post even if we could not call ourselves heroes. Heroes are those who crumble into the dust of a completely unknown land far from home, having fought for a purpose that even if indirectly, was in the service of their own country.

The gang was falling apart. After Charlie's death, Walter and Steve were next to fall by the wayside. Then there was Leo, who seemed at odds with himself and who we hardly saw anymore. So it was that Joe and I alone remained, and we buried ourselves in work. We visited Walter and Steve. Though both were improving, weeks had to pass before either was fit for service again.

"Hey Scout, why the hell are we moping around like this?" asked Joe. "Yesterday them; tomorrow us. Isn't that the way it is? I feel badly too that we're the only two left of such a tightly knit group, but we don't have to get all gloomy and down about it. Come on! Let's go into Hanoi and paint the town red."

"I'd go, Joe, but I hardly have any money. I've put a hold on my clever tricks at the bar. There's no reason for it that I can see. You and I don't drink enough for me to have to fool around with the portions. We've hardly gotten together since Charlie died, and since Walter and Steve have been out of commission, not once. Besides, I've been in no mood to pursue my clever tactics. It's no fun anymore. So anyway, the chest of drawers is empty."

"I'm not exactly loaded either, but there's enough that we can do something. Even if we don't paint the town red, let's give ourselves a jolt and get out of this depression."

"Okay, I'm game. Should we call Leo? Maybe he wants to tag along."

"You go over and ask. You're done with your work, and I've still got a few things to wrap up. I'll be finished by the time you come and go."

Inside the infirmary I saw Leo over by his desk, leaning back in his chair and staring off into space.

"Hi there Leo, what's the matter? Why don't you come over once in a while?"

"I don't know. Don't feel like it. Not in the mood, I guess. Atmosphere's not the same as when Charlie was around. And with Steve and Walter in the hospital . . . something wrong with you too? Want me to put you down for a week's rest?"

"I'm not sick, Leo. I don't need any rest. Glad that I have something to do all day. Keeps me from getting caught up with myself, know what I mean? That's what your problem is too. You sit here moping all day, staring into space. Come on, let's go to Hanoi! Joe and I want to go so we can shake loose this state of lethargy. First we'll visit Walter and Steve, then we'll think of something else to do. Nothing that costs though, 'cause I don't have any money. Ever since the gang broke up I haven't been saving. What for? You never come over, Joe's not the same man he was before either, I don't need . . . well, are you in the mood to come or not?"

"Well okay, let's go. There's a jeep here you can use. Don't have to walk. It's really not supposed to be used unless for official business, but what the hell. Maybe the sky won't come falling down on me because of it. There's always another one if they're really in a bind."

We picked up Joe, who was pacing in front of the cadre.

"What the hell took you so long? I've been waiting an hour."

"I'll teach your grandmother to suck eggs. Like hell you've been waiting that long! Hasn't even been ten minutes that Scout came over."

So there! They're starting to fight already. A good sign, this is. Keep it up and we won't even notice the *Devil's Bible Society* is reduced by half.

"Leave my grandmother out of this! You go and suck rocks!"

"Watch your language or I'll pulp you to a mill!"

"Are you ever dense, Leo! That's trash you to a pulp!" shouted Joe, while laughing away and pounding Leo on the back.

He was not the only one amused. My sides were split'ting from laughter over Leo's timely slip of the tongue. But the remark was made intentionally, because Leo was smiling to himself. It was with jokes like this that we wanted to, and did, pass off our misery and distress. We were still rollicking with laughter and slapping each other around long after we had left the railroad bridge behind. The mood did not dispel. Even inside the hospital, we were greeted by Walter and Steve in good spirits. True, they had not been party to Leo's slip of the tongue. Their good moods came as a result of a road to recovery so optimistic and advanced that they were permitted short walks several times a day. So what if one was forced to walk stooped over while the other strutted along? At least they weren't chained to their beds for twenty-four hours straight.

"Hey Walter, with walking around like that it looks like that bamboo rod is still stuck up your ass! It's been pulled out for a long time now," said Leo.

"You just talk! Wish you would have sat in it instead of me. Like to see how you walk around."

"Does it still hurt a lot?" I asked.

"And why the hell wouldn't it hurt? But it is getting better every day. Just wish I didn't have to go to the can. You want to hear me moan and gnash my teeth? That's where! A nurse always stands outside the door 'cause twice already I've dropped off the seat in a dead faint."

"Well don't he have it good. A nurse accompanying him to the can. Does she hold out the toilet paper on a silver platter?"

"Easy for you guys to talk. Still, I wouldn't wish similar pleasures on any one of you. Where are you going? To the lakeshore club?"

"No way. We don't have enough money for that," replied Leo.

"What do you mean by 'we'? I don't have any money at all, only you and Joe have money."

"We're off to visit Steve now," continued Leo, "then we'll go to this good little cafe I know. They serve a tasty and choice quality expresso, unlike even that offered by the finest pastry shops of Vienna. And they're usually renowned for their coffee. Well, see you later Walter, we'll look in on you some other time."

"Hey Steve, what are you looking for on the floor?" I asked when we walked into his room and I saw that he was walking around his bed bent over at a right angle.

"I think it best that for now you walk as little as possible," said Leo. "If stooped over like that is the best you can do. That wound can easily tear. When were the stitches removed?"

"Walk as little as possible you say? The nurses chase me out of bed early in the morning. A little bit every hour, they say. The little bit for this hour is up, so help me get back into bed. I'm afraid to lie back on my own because the wound gets really stretched out. It won't reopen, because the stitches are still in, but it does strain at the seams something awful."

We laid him down and then adjusted his pillow and blanket. I wanted to give him his baby bottle and asked him where it was.

"Wish I had enough strength to bash you across the mouth Scout. What a treat that would be!"

"If you did have the strength you think I would have asked?"

"You just wait! I'll teach you a lesson you won't soon forget as soon as

I get back."

"Just watch your tone. Careful how you address a Premier Class legionnaire. Lie at attention! Keep your tongue wagging like that and you'll be lying at attention beside Charlie and the Aristocrat."

"Did the Aristocrat really lose his life or did he just disappear?"

"I told you already that he was slain," interrupted Joe. "The others saw him killed in action. That's what they said."

"Then he's standing beside Charlie and expecting us at any time. They know that soon we'll line up beside them," muttered Leo.

"Don't start into the Lamentations of Jeremiah again! Let's go. See you later Steve. We'll be back."

"Leo, you don't really want to go for coffee in here, now do you?" I asked, horrified, when I saw the cafe he had mentioned. "This is a Chinese quarter! We'll never get out of this place alive."

"I'm not setting foot inside of here, Leo," voiced Joe in agreement. "Let's get out of this quarter as fast as we can. We're unarmed, and if it occurs to these guys to fondle us, in an hour's time not a trace will be left of us."

"What's with the panic? I've been here before all by myself. Would I keep coming back if there was any danger? What do you take me for? Let's go in!"

We felt somewhat uneasy but went in anyway. The coffeemaster came out to greet us with a bow, a smile and hands clasped together. He beckoned us over to a table built low to the ground and around which were pillows. It was not as comfortable as a couch, but in the absence of another mode of seating, we could not afford to be choosy. We took off our caps, placed them beside us and waited for the coffee. It was brought out soon after.

"Hey Leo, is this the famous coffee you were referring to? This looks like they poured a drop of water into a cupful of finely ground coffee. It smells good, but it's so thick I can hardly pour it. And is this it? This is no more than a mouthful. This cup is so tiny that I can barely grab hold of it. And is it supposed to be drunk so bitter?" I asked after tasting it. "Ask for some sugar. I can't eat it like this."

"You're right. It's so thick that you almost have to eat it." replied Joe. "And it's brutally strong. They should serve us coffee like this at the squadron for a week, and watch us all drop dead from heart attacks. I need some sugar too. I can't drink it bitter like this."

"Sugar will ruin the flavor. This is the real thing, not that slop of black water that we're used to calling coffee."

"Ruin the flavor or not, I want sugar brought out right now," said Joe.

It took Leo twenty minutes to suck away at his coffee. Joe and I swallowed it in one gulp. Then we circled down one street and up the next in search of some other form of entertainment. All at once, my heart started beating so strong and fast that I thought I was going to die on the spot.

"Leo stop! I feel sicker than a dog. Feels like my heart is going to leap out any minute!"

Leo felt my pulse and instead of stopping he made a beeline for the hospital. The doctor on duty examined me and told me to lie down on a bed and not move until morning.

"And don't drink any more of that coffee!" he said, then left with Leo who came back a few minutes later to say that he would come get me and take me back to Gia-Lam the next morning.

"Scout, the doctor suggested you take it as easy as possible while doing your work. Leave any running around that has to be done to your three kids, don't drink any alcohol, and most of all, don't worry!" said Leo the next morning as he was taking me back to the cadre. "So just take it easy and everything will be all right."

De Carvalho declared back at headquarters that for the time being Joe would assume my role as waiter and kitchen supervisor. All I had to do was tend the bar and attend to my administrative duties.

Two more shots of that coffee, I thought, and I'll have nothing to do all day but sit in a throne of sorts and issue orders.

This heavenly state of being was into its third week when I was summoned to the warehouse for some reason during the midday meal. I stepped into the room and saw Leo sitting beside the desk.

"And when did they make a sergeant out of you?" I asked with astonishment.

"Day before yesterday."

"Leo! Congratulations! This calls for a celebration. Come on over tonight and we'll drink a real big one to it. True that I haven't touched a drop since you told me not to, but this is such a rare event, we can't let the opportunity slip by. A few glasses can't do any harm."

"Joe, have you heard the news?" I asked back at the bar.

"If you tell me, then I'll know."

"Leo became a sergeant."

"You're kidding! When?"

"Day before yesterday. He's coming over tonight to celebrate the big event."

We could hardly wait for evening to come. Why, this would be our first go at a really good time since Charlie's death. Joe and I scraped together enough money for me to buy three bottles of wine from the bar, at cost, according to the books.

Joe had the cook make up a pile of sandwiches. Suitably set to go at last, we waited for Leo. We waited and waited. And hour and a half later, Leo was still nowhere to be found.

"I wonder what happened to him. He promised to be here by six and it's half past eight."

"Hell if I know! He probably forgot. I'm sure he'll show up. Something unforeseen likely came up."

"There's nothing that can keep anyone away for two and a half hours unless it's death."

With this, Joe grabbed one of the bottles and yanked the cork out. In the same instant the door opened and in came Steve Bidon.

"And how the hell did you find your way over here? We weren't expecting you. We're waiting for Leo!"

"Well I'll be. This is certainly a fine reception, wouldn't you say? I just get out of the hospital and I'm supposed to be glad that you don't throw me out of here."

"Don't talk nonsense! Nobody gets a release from the hospital this late at night."

"You could at least say 'boo' instead of staring at me like a stuck pig!"

"Well hello Steve and welcome. We're glad that you're out of the hospital, but truth of the matter is that it was Leo we were expecting and not you. That's why it surprised us a tad when you walked through the door, and not he, and you look like someone's puked you up five times over. But still, it's good that you're here. That makes four to celebrate Leo's promotion, if he ever gets here."

"I am here," said Leo, stepping out from behind the door. "I'm the one who brought Steve back from he hospital, that's why I'm late. And then I had to settle a couple of things that came up."

"Where's that bottle? Hop to it and open it!" came the order flying from the newly appointed sergeant master.

"A double celebration! Steve's recovery, and Leo's promotion!" I said raising two bottles of wine high.

We drank, toasted kicked up a row, but it was not the same as when all six of us were together. I had to stop drinking pretty fast, because by the third glass the room was spinning.

"Hey guys, I think the party's over as far as I'm concerned. These three glasses of wine really went to my head and I'm reeling like a goose knocked on the head."

"Indochina's gotten to your head, not the wine!" consoled Steve.

"No, really, it's driving me around the bend. Can you imagine busting apart like this from three glasses, three glasses like this here, see?" I asked, wanting to step over to Steve to show him. but if not for Leo and Joe who grabbed hold of me, I would have fallen flat on my face.

"What the hell! You really did get tipsy from this little bit of wine, didn't you!"

"Not only that, but my foot's gone to sleep. That's why I almost fell over."

"You'd better lie down, Scout. I'm going to run over to the infirmary and get you some medication. Joe, don't let him drink another drop!"

"Of course I won't drink any more. I feel like throwing up what I've already drunk."

"Yeah don't drink. Leave the drinking to us. Joe and I will take care of what's left."

"You'd better put a hold on your bravado, you hear? Don't forget that you've just come out of the hospital. You're still in pretty weak shape."

"Scout my boy, you just leave it to me! I know what's good for me and what isn't. Fill'er up Joe!"

"You know I think Scout is right. You were white as a sheet when you came in and now your face is red as a beet."

"I'm going to knock one back for Leo's health, then I'm out of here and off to bed."

But he emptied only half a glass before running out and waving so long. Leo in the meantime had returned with the pills. After making me promise that I would not take them before midnight, they left to retire. We had not exactly planned our celebration to end this way but then, what man devises God finishes!

It was a week after our abortive celebration that Joe took suddenly sick. He came down with of bout of the flu and was feverishly ill. Owing to his state, the entire lot of responsibility fell on my shoulders. I had to do everything and by the time lunch was over I was exhausted. This went on for three days before I sought out de Carvalho and asked for assistance, saying that I couldn't keep up alone like this any longer. Help was on its way, he promised, and by supper the help had arrived.

Why is it that a man's wishes are always fulfilled when he needs it least? Lo and behold this unfortunate creature who showed up to help was blessed with five left hands and the pace of a snail. Besides all I had to do, I had his blunderings to contend with. After supper I asked him very nicely to please go away, and not dare set foot inside here again, or I'd peel him out of his hide.

I dared not ask for any more help after this. One more stupid left handed idiot like this, and I'd pass away into the hereafter from a nervous breakdown before my time. Until Joe was recovered well enough to carry out his duties, I went on doing everything by myself.

July 1, 1950

I woke up completely unsuspecting on a stifling day in July.

It was not, however, a share of dressing down that I was involved in, but a clash with one of the first lieutenants who decided one morning that the breakfast specified and set out by myself with Lieutenant de Carvalho's approval (or should I say, he was one who ordered it) was not to his liking and he wanted to eat something else. And he insisted that this something else be immediately served to him.

One of my apprentices, who had overheard the demand from his place over by the outer door, wanted to run to the kitchen to fetch the pâté the lieutenant had ordered. But I beckoned him to stop and stay where he was. With the rightful respect owing to a man of his stature and summoning up all the politeness I could muster, I told him that what he wanted was not on the menu for today and barring Lieutenant de Carvalho's consent, he was not permitted to make another selection. And seeing that de Carvalho was in Hanoi until noon, permission could not be secured.

"I don't care where Lieutenant de Carvalho is. Bring me my pâté at once!" screamed the Lieutenant.

"I'm very sorry Lieutenant," I replied looking him straight in the eye, "but I refuse to bring it."

"We'll see about that. This matter is not over!" he screamed and swept the cups off the table.

I quickly grabbed my notebook from the bar counter and made note of the broken items.

"What are you scribbling down?" he screamed.

"The price of the broken cups, so I can add it to your bill, sir," I replied as calmly as I could.

At this, he took off in a rage and stormed over to the Commander's office. A good two and a half hours after, an office messenger came to tell me to go see de Carvalho.

"I heard what happened this morning with this lieutenant," he said, when I reported to him.

"Lieutenant . . ."

"There's no problem!" he interrupted. "I've taken care of everything. I explained to the Lieutenant that you were just doing you job and following my orders to the letter. Don't forget to record the price of the broken cups."

"I've already done that."

"Good. Then carry on where you left off."

Shortly after this annoying incident I and my three apprentices were getting the dining room ready. I was doing this and that behind the bar, jotting down the number of bottles already opened and setting out the necessary things for pre-dinner drinking. I was still troubled by ill-feelings from the mornings incident. True, that de Carvalho had endorsed my course of actions, but a first lieutenant was still a first lieutenant, and if he was feeling hurt by it, which was more than likely, since it was decided that I was in the right, there would be hell to pay. He'll take every advantage of me possible. That my word was greater than his in the dining room and bar meant little, because this was a tiny world compared to his. Best to stay on guard, take care, and make up for the misunderstanding as far as possible or I'd never hear the end of it.

Most of the officers were gathered, waiting for the Commander so the dinner could commence. A few were still lolling about the bar, drinking and talking when Joe poked his head in and asked me to come out to the kitchen. Apparently, the cook was finding the quantity of vegetable conserves insufficient and was worried there wouldn't be enough.

"That's impossible!" I gave him exactly what was ordered. I'll bet he hid a few cans again somewhere. Come over here while I take care of that cook."

"How can there not be enough," I asked the cook, "when you got exactly what was ordered?"

"I did not get everything. Four cans of peas were missing."

"Missing like hell! You hid them somewhere again, didn't you!"

I searched everywhere in vain. The cans were nowhere to be had. Either he found a new hiding place that I was unaware of, or it was like he said and I had shortchanged the order. I left it at that and made no effort to get to the bottom of things. I was nervous enough as it was from the morning's mishap and didn't want to get wound up any more than I already was. I'd account for the error somehow.

Then, from one second to the next on my way to the warehouse, I felt like my insides were coming apart. My limbs were becoming numb, my head was buzzing and I felt a ghastly emptiness inside.

"Joe!" I screamed, but by then I was flat on the ground.

"What's the matter Scout? What happened?" asked Joe when he raced over.

"Stand up and come in your room!" he said, as he tried to lift me.

"I can't stand. My arms and legs are gone," I tried to say but the words could not escape my throat. I was gasping for breath.

I saw him run away and come back with Steve. Together, they helped me into my room and into bed. Joe ran to get the doctor.

"What's wrong with you?" he asked leaning over me.

I tried to say but could not. I had no voice.

At this he slapped me twice across the face and waited for some reaction. There was none. Seeing that it hadn't done any good, he told Steve to go find Leo, have him arrange for hospitalization and take me in. All three helped me out to the jeep, and Leo drove me over to the hospital.

This was the last time I saw Steve, Joe and Gia-Lam. Leo too, once he had dropped me off at the hospital and waved good-bye. The official dispatch came after one week of treatment. It was an order to return to Sidi-Bel-Abbes.

July 17, 1949

I'm in Haiphong aboard a small passenger liner.

I'm feeling quite good physically, with no sign of the seizure I was afflicted with in Gia-Lam.

The ship's bow is pointed west, pointed toward the direction I had dreamed of for so long. I should be shouting for joy, but I can't And how long I waited for this day! Here it is! I made it, I had lived to see it! I was going back.

Yet I was feeling not happiness and joy but quasi-apathetic. The picture here was nearly the same as at the time of my arrival back in November of '48. Still, how different it was!

The same send-off bands, officers bidding farewell, throngs of people pressed together, hustle and bustle around me. Despite all this, I felt completely alienated and utterly alone.

Yes, my dreams had come true! What I had foretold for myself back in Vienna had come to pass. Meaning fate would lift me out of this mess the same way it had drawn me in.

I had not quite imagined my exit to be like this. I had figured in all those I was brought together with, the people whose company I became used to, and with whom I shared so much for so long in good times and in bad. You, Charlie, you were the first one to go. And how you too had longed for this day! How you were counting the hours and planning, and weaving dreams and your dreams, your dreams died with you while I'm standing in your place here by the ship's railing.

How happy we were for you when you showed us your repatriation papers, and how jealous we were because we could not go with you. I wonder if Joe and the others are jealous of me now. Are they maybe saying, "What a lucky beggar that Scout is! By now, he's sailing for Sidi-Bel-Abbes!" Are they still getting together to drink in my room in the evenings? If so, only four are left: Joe, Leo, Walter and Steve. I too had fallen by the wayside. Rejoice, Scout, and be happy. Be happy that you did not fall away like Charlie. You truly were taken into the lap of the Goddess of Fortune!

The band struck a chord, the officer's raised their hands to their caps in salute, the crowd waved and our ship's bow inched its way toward the open sea where the *Pasteur* was waiting. My thoughts transported me past the present, over Haiphong, and nearer to Gia-Lam. I see myself sneaking into the officer's mess hall, the bar, my room. It's well past the dinner hour and silence reigns throughout. The dining halls are empty; there's no one in my room. Who will replace me? Poor Joe will run himself ragged until they find someone to fill my position. Might they bring the Dutchman back? I wouldn't think so! The Gorilla can't stand him nor can de Carvalho! Steve perhaps? He and Joe always got along so well. He spent more time with us than in the company of his own squadron. Will they keep holding birthday celebrations? What good times we had, what good parties we used to throw. I'll never forget that birthday I spent in the Hollywood bar so long as I live. The *Pasteur* sounded its horn in greeting and woke me from my thoughts. Are we here already? Hard to believe how quickly these few hours flit by!

Our ship snuggled up to the *Pasteur*'s side and was shrivelled beside the gigantic proportions of the *Pasteur*. Changing ships for the one hundred passenger was over very quickly. Only one hundred when thousands had arrived. Since I was ordered to start back directly from the hospital, I was given a place in the ship's hospital along with maybe twenty others. The accommodations were of the highest standard compared to what I stayed in, way back when, on the way over.

We stopped in Cape St. Jacques to pick up others travelling to the West and we were cruising somewhere around Singapore and Ceylon. It was here that the radio signalled the approach of a storm.

The day had sunk into night, the sky was without stars or moonlight, but the ocean was quiet. The light of the lamps alone aboard the ship illuminated the agitated sea, a sea that was casting white spray as though furious at the intrusion, furious that its stillness was disturbed. The ripples were lashing at the side of the ship and the monotone sound gradually made me drowsy.

I felt the ship dancing on the water when I woke up in the morning. The few who were lying around looking green at the gills were the ones who had succumbed to seasickness. So as not to meet with the same fate, I gorged myself to make sure my stomach was stuffed. Around noon the radio signalled that the storm was intensifying in strength. Traffic by now was possible only on the sheltered walkway because the waves were already crashing through the second storey windows. To not bowl over or fall flat on our noses, we clung desperately to handrails and latches, anything that was tied down. At dinner I again ate my fill so the affliction would not catch up with me for a while.

Into its third day the dance was getting progressively worse. The Captain announced over the radio that by evening it would get even stronger. As it was, we could no longer gather even on the sheltered walkway, as men were laid flat out all over the place. Everyone was forced to stay in their quarters. Of those around me, only four of us were left who still stood up to the storm, or in spite of it. Two of these were nurses.

I don't know how those responsible managed to do it, but the meals went on as usual, smoothly and undisturbed. For those who could eat, that is. Getting down to meals was taking your life into your hands. It involved grabbing hold of anything and everything fastened down that happened to fall in the way. Ditto for during the meals. Still, those who were capable of it, did not miss a meal.

By the fourth day the waves were throwing this giant mass of steel around like a nutshell. Now it was my turn. My stomach gave out and I fell into line with the other pale faces. Now only three were left holding out, and they did so until the end of the storm. It was late afternoon by the time we left the storm area and before the dance was finally suspended.

We left Colombo behind and pushed out into the boundless Indian Ocean toward Aden. The scenes I might describe in writing are no different from those I witnessed and recorded on my way over. Dolphins, flying fish, distant ports, screaming merchants, stifling tropical days. One thing alone was absent, the singing of popular Hungarian songs, for lack of anyone to do so with. Those I sang with on the way over, Walter, Leo, Joe and the others, had stayed behind.

The days were dreadfully boring. There was absolutely nothing to do. Cards, chess, movies a thousand years old, I was fed up with it all. If only I could find another Hungarian to talk with 'till I was blue in the face. But not a Hungarian word did I hear.

My thoughts for the most part centred around those I left behind. Which part of the forest were they stomping through, who's doing the clever handed tactics behind the bar, what happened to my three apprentices, did the *Devil's Bible Society* go to pieces or did someone else take Charlie's place and mine?

One fleeting instant and I'm on the other side of the globe, standing on the spot from where I left two years ago. Forget about the fact that one had to row the boat many thousands of kilometres and suffer through many an official ceremony to get there. Just like the last two years had slipped away, the two months left to go until the final farewell counted as but a minute after the seemingly endless months spent in Indochina.

And as the *Pasteur* ploughed through the waves, the closer and closer it came to the first stop on its journey toward the ultimate goal, Marseille!

One morning I stepped out on the deck and saw an dense fog. Standing by the railing and listening to the murmur of the waves, I felt a strange burning on my face and arms. How could this be with this thick fog completely shielding the sun? I must be standing in the face of some new natural phenomenon. I've experienced a lot of oddities in the past few years, but never the burning of the sun when it wasn't even there!

The mystery was solved by a seaman who explained the nature of the fog we had wound our way into. We were sailing on the Red Sea, and a storm had broken out in the desert running parallel to the sea. Sand ground finer than flour was carried on the wind out to sea and carpeted the entire region. This fine dust bored its way into the skin's pores, and that's what was causing the unpleasant burning sensation. It was for this reason also that the color of the sea changed from a usually midnight blue to a steely bluish grey.

We left behind Suez and Port Said with their ridiculously animated and infernally loud merchants and watched the shores of Sicily rise in view in the far distance. A good feeling came over me seeing those shores, knowing that from here it was only another day and a half or so before I again touched foot on European soil.

We reached Marseille in the first days of August, from where a few days later I sailed over to Sidi-Bel-Abbes to appear before the Reformation Board.

I was granted a two month holiday, during which time the board would come to its decision. I could only hope! As a traveller in transit, I was given accommodations in the CP-1 building. I was on the verge of a discharge, I was free of responsibility and my time was my own. No matter where I wanted to go from here, the CP-3 building with all its sad memories always stood in the way. Many times a day I had an opportunity to reminisce and see myself with Leo and the gang behind the barred windows. How we gazed out into the yard with yearning at the white and blue capped legionnaires, coming and going freely without the supervision of armed guards.

How envious we were of them in those days!

And now it was other souls stranded by life who looked down from there. I watched the figures behind the bars and wondered if they were as jealous now as I was at the time. Another few weeks, and for me the Legion will be nothing but a memory, for you it's just the beginning. You men are so far removed from where I'm standing now that you can't begin to imagine. If you're lucky enough to get this far, that is.

The heat was sweltering. Blessed be those legionnaires of the thirties who built the Olympic size swimming pool. In it, I got through the hottest hours of the day along with a bunch of Hungarians. The large number of Hungarians in transit was surprising.

The evening hours were hastened by time spent in the Legion's theatre, cafe terraces, bars and dance halls. The latter was something I had to adjust to. Not to the dance hall itself but to the women. I had grown accustom to the Vietnamese women and the European women seemed enormous in comparison.

The big day was here!

I was summoned before the Reformation Board, where I received my discharge papers and instructions as to when I would return to Marseille, where final details would be cleared up and where I could once and for all bid farewell to the French Foreign Legion!

I was quite taken aback to see that of the many Hungarains present, only two of us were granted a discharge. The other Hungarian was Tom. Tom and I walked down the main street of Sidi-Bel-Abbes for one last time the night before our departure. We peeped into all the familiar bars and cafes to say goodbye to all the owners waiters and waitresses that we knew. We were offered a drink in farewell everywhere we went so that by the time we finished with our goodbyes we could hardly find the road leading to CP-1.

In Oran, we had to wait three days for the ship. I'm happy to report that nothing had changed: the food was horrible. Considering this fact, Tom and I took our meals in restaurants.

On the morning of our departure day we woke up to see, with much surprise, some mysterious blue light radiating over everything. Everybody was standing by the hallway railing on the second floor, looking at the sky and pointing. I went out, looked also toward the sky. The sun was dressed in blue!

It wore a shade of azure blue with two darker stripes that were likely rags of cloud.

Well! Africa was unveiling another surprising natural phenomenon by way of parting. A blue sun!

I later found out from one of the Marseille newspapers that this blue sun was somehow caused by the Mediterranean Sea.

We did not beat about the bush for long in Marseille. By the second day we were stripped of our legion uniforms and slipped into civilian clothing. It was definitely a weird feeling. Tom and I looked at each other and established that we both looked like a cow in drawers. but no big deal. I'd get used to this too, just like the women I danced with in Sidi-Bel-Abbes. But the change of clothing did not yet signify a break from the bonds of the Legion. Until an opportunity to earn income was secured for us both, we could not leave Marseille without permission. We had to wait until then.

Chapter Seventeen
Nice

On the fourth day of hanging around I suggested to Tom that we go to Nice. With its multitude of hotels, restaurants, bars, plus an airport, railway station and casinos there surely had to be some likelihood of employment for two men. We'd report to the office, outline our plan and barring any objection, give it a try.

The response? Affirmative, and we were aboard the early afternoon train steaming along toward Nice. We took along one bag for the two of us with enough things to last for the few days we expected to spend there. One way or another we had to come back because the Legion had to sanction our place of employment, should we find a job.

We arrived late in the afternoon and found a hotel, off on a quiet little side street not too far from the station, that suited our pocketbooks. It was a clean and well-maintained hotel. We were given a form to fill out and while doing so we mentioned to the hotel employee who we were, where we had come from and why we were here. Although there was no separate heading for it we noted on the form that we both spoke fluent Hungarian and Tom fluent German as well, thinking that it might help get us somewhere. We paid for a two day stay. Both sides of the street were lined with acacia trees. The room was nice and neat, furnished with a large bed, a table and chairs, a chest of drawers and a small table and two armchairs by the window. It contained only a sink and the communal bathroom and toilette were down at the end of the hall.

We were eye to eye with the windows of the building on the opposite side of the street. After inspecting our dwelling we locked the door and started out for a look around the city. We asked one of the hotel employees if he knew of any place where employment opportunities were registered.

"Don't know if such a place exists," he answered, "but I suggest you concentrate on checking out hotels. If there are openings to be had, that's the field where it's most likely."

We thanked him for his advice and made a tour of the town. We got back around midnight, tired, and without success. We stepped into the hotel lobby and saw another person along with the employee behind the counter who, when he saw us, came over to greet us with a smile and extended hand.

"Good evening gentlemen!" he said in Hungarian. "My friend here informs me that you're looking for work. He says you're legionnaires, just come from Marseilles."

We could hardly stammer out a hello in response from our astonishment.

"I can tell you're surprised by my Hungarian greeting. Please don't think of it as too strange. You must remember that Nice is an international centre. Anything can happen here, any language spoken can be found. Come with me. There's a restaurant a few steps from here where we can talk and drink. Come! You will be my guests."

We were always game for anything, never spoilsports, especially when the good time in question would not cost us a single Franc, so off we went after him.

"So, you guys looking for a job?" he asked, on familiar terms, his tone was already less formal than earlier even before the first toast. We were sitting in a bar, a bar by Nice's standards was the equivalent of a top notch restaurant in Budapest.

"Yes, we are looking for work," answered Tom. "We were just discharged from the Legion, and we're hoping to find a job in a better establishment such as a good restaurant, or bar like this place, or maybe a better hotel, any place where they understand that we don't come with much experience but that we learn quickly. With a little training, we can easily fit into any line of work."

"Legionnaire daredevils like yourselves are not suited for that kind of menial work. You're self-made men, you deserve to be your own bosses. Why settle for less? why be slave to someone else? What you need is something where you can assert yourselves and show off your strength. That's what you're suited for. I know legionnaires. They're tough. Used to hardships and they aren't put off by any obstacles. Especially when there's a lot of money to be had for little work. All it takes is some guts, some daring, but you're cut out for that. You know what? I'll come pick you up tomorrow morning around ten, and take you to a place where you'll meet someone who's also Hungarian, a man who was an aristocrat back home. Here, we all address him by his former formal title, Count. This pleases him very much, you should do the same. He doesn't want to disclose his real name. As legionnaires, I know this is something you can relate to. There are many in the Legion who go under assumed names, you know that. Such a practice is nothing new."

"Waiter, another bottle of wine! Keep on drinking and I'll be by to pick you up in the morning," he said. He paid the bill and left.

"So Scout, what do you think of that?"

"I don't know. We'll have to see. First, we'll have a word with the count. I'm a bit suspicious to tell you the truth. This character comes on too strong, too friendly for my taste. I wouldn't speak so informally to a perfect stranger in the first five minutes, unless he was thirty years younger than me. And this guy can't be more than two or three years older than us. Did you notice he didn't even introduce himself? He just starts talking like we were long lost friends. Something's not quite kosher."

We really don't know what his name is, do we? He knows our names from the hotel registry. But what the hell did I care what his name is? He could be Joe Smoe for all I care. Important thing is that he paid for two bottles of wine."

Next morning we woke up to someone pounding away at the door. The hotel employee called in to say that Monsieur Szamondy was waiting for us in the lobby.

So Szamondy was his name. He could have told us that yesterday. I was curious to know where we would end up. Just what kind of a job was it that called for daredevil legionnaires like us, a job that promised a lot of money for a little daring work?

We were then introduced to the Count who proved to be an elderly monocled gentleman holding a came with silver handles and attired in gaiters, grey trousers and a striped, dark blue jacket. The large diamond tie clip may have been a polished glass imitation, judging by its rather phoney sparkle. The introduction took place on the terrace cafe located on a large congested square. Monsieur Szamondy took off immediately after the introduction.

"So you're looking for work," asked the count repeating Szamondy's exact words of yesterday.

The Count's voice was surprisingly pleasant. It was a voice truly fitting of an elderly aristocratic gentleman.

"Emery, (Now I know Szamondy's first name!) told me that you'd like to find employment in a restaurant or hotel. You don't actually want to do such degrading work, do you? I'd like to propose something much more agreeable and profitable, something that involves next to no work at all. All you have to do is pocket the money. The French don't like to do such menial labor either. They like to leave that sort of stuff to vagabond strangers. And don't make me believe that you would include yourselves in their company. The work I am proposing does not call for any special skills. All it takes is a little intelligence, the ability to make a good first impression, a touch of cunning and some spunk. I have some contacts who are often good at handling the wheel. I also have some women acquaintances, and rich ones at that, who would gladly welcome an evening spent with a fine figure of a man who has the gift of gab. You guys can cut it. One can always find the means to make a lot of money with little work. All you have to know is how. And I do! Believe me, I do! If you're game, I can bring you close to these very profitable opportunities."

"My! Look how the time has flown by!" he said suddenly, glancing at his watch. "I have a very important meeting with a businessman. The man has his own yacht; that's where the meeting is scheduled to take place. I'm also expected at the cocktail party which follows. Be here tomorrow morning at 11:00 and we can discuss the matter at greater length."

"So, Tom, what do you think of that? do you want to make a lot of money? No work to do, just money to be made, at who knows what price."

"Why shouldn't we give it a try? We don't know exactly what's involved, not yet. It does sound illegal though, like we have to take part in some sort of a black market. We won't know the details until tomorrow."

On the way back to the hotel, we noticed a conspicuous looking woman dressed in red who we thought was following us.

"Hey Tom! See that women in red on our tail?"

"Of course I'm aware of her. She's always around either ahead, beside or behind us. I also couldn't help noticing her good figure and age. She can't be any older than us. Think she might be one of the Count's acquaintances?"

"It's certainly possible. Let's stop in front of a display and let her pass by. Then we can see if she really is following us."

With I in front of one, and Tom beside the display next to it, we stopped. We looked and looked for the woman, but she was nowhere to be seen.

"Where did the woman get to, Tom?"

"I haven't the foggiest idea," he said, searching right and left. "She was here just a minute ago. Looks like she wasn't one of the Count's acquaintances after all, or she'd have tailed us all the way to the hotel."

"Maybe she's spying on us from behind the doorway. Let's take a look around."

"Oh come on, don't be such a child. Why would she be spying on us? Let's go back to the hotel."

Back in our room we began to weigh the possibilities and debate the pros and cons of the issue at hand. What was worthwhile doing and what was not? During the breaks in conversation, I thought I heard some kind of rattle coming from the door. I motioned to Tom to keep on talking while I slowly crept over and flung it open. In front of it was the hotel employee, quite obviously peeping and listening through the keyhole. for a few moments he stared at me, then abruptly jumped and ran toward the exit going down.

I had barely closed the door when Tom cried out.

"Scout come quick. Look over there! There's the woman in red, standing in the window facing us. She's watching us through binoculars!"

"Not only that, there's two policemen standing up the street and two further down. Something's wrong here, Tom. Best to step down before we get mixed up over our heads in some nasty business. I'd stake my life on it that this Count is an international swindler, along with his friend Szamondy. I'm absolutely sure that they're swindlers, pimps, and who knows what else. For what else would we need daring and an aptitude for handling the wheel well? It's all starting to make sense. He was quite explicit in what he said, when you think about it, and the Italian border is not too far away, so it's easy to put two and two together. And those women who would gladly spend an evening and then some with fine young men like us, they are rich I have no doubt. How they come about their money is something else altogether, know what I mean? Let's get out of here Tom."

"Right but to where?"

"What do you mean where to? To the station, and back to Marseilles."

"We don't know when the train leaves."

"Then we have to find out."

I kept an eye on he window across the street throughout the argument, and saw that the woman in red was glued to her spot. The policemen who

who were walking up and down the street were keeping a steady eye on the hotel entrance.

"Let's do this, Tom. We'll walk over to the station to find out when the train leaves. We'll leave our bag behind and pack it in such a way that we'll be able to see right away whether someone was digging around in it or not. And while we're out on the street let's pretend we know nothing."

"Let's not go to the station," suggested Tom, "because then they'll suspect right away that we want to break loose. Two of the four policemen will follow us for sure. Let's phone from a booth on the street instead."

"Right. Let's do it that way."

We arranged our suitcase and went down. An unfamiliar face was looking at us from behind the counter in the lobby, the peeping tom had vanished. We talked as we walked along leisurely, stopping here and there to look at window displays. It took me no time at all to notice that two policemen were following at a respectable distance.

"Your prediction came true, Tom. Two of the four cops are on our tail."

"I've noticed too. But let's not concern ourselves over it. Let's find a telephone."

We found one on the main street. Tom stepped inside to make the call while I stayed outside to keep an eye on the policemen. When we stopped they drew behind a tree.

Tom stepped out of the booth. "The train leaves at 4:30."

"That leaves two and a half hours to kill. Let's go have lunch somewhere, then go back to our room and at four, we'll race over to the station."

"Let's not go for lunch. Let's keep walking, and I'll get away on a side street, go to the station and buy the tickets."

"That won't do any good. There are two policemen. One will go after you, the other will keep following me."

"Then let's go back to the hotel. We'll pick up some food on the way and eat in our room. We'll take care of the tickets somehow. If we have no other choice, we'll buy the tickets on the train. We'll tell the conductor that we came at the last minute and had no time to buy tickets from the cashier. Maybe we'll have to pay a bit more, but so what. And who knows, maybe even less if we prove that we're discharged legionnaires."

Whoever was interested in the contents of our bag made no secret of the fact. Not only was it obviously tampered with, but the curious individual had not even bothered to close the lid. It would have been nice to know what they were looking for.

"Make no mistake about it, Scout. We've gotten ourselves involved in some shady dealings." "Would you go over and see if that woman is still there?" I asked while fixing our clothes.

"She's not, but the policemen still are. Two on the right and two on the left, and now they're on bicycles."

"We can't leave by the front door because if they see us leaving with the bag, they'll seize us by the collar. We have to find out where the fire escape is and cut loose through there. Every hotel has to have a fire escape."

"Why are we sneaking around like this in the first place? After all, we've done nothing wrong. Even if they did nab us or rather take us into custody, we can prove who we are, where we came from and when. Our alibi is fool proof.

"You honestly think it would be to our advantage to have it recorded in the office of the fortress that we got into trouble with the law on our very first jaunt out because we got mixed up with a bunch of gangsters? I think it's best that we leave Nice without anybody noticing, especially the Police or that woman in red."

"How are we to know that they won't be waiting for us with open arms by the fire escape?"

"We have to get out of here somehow. We can't spend Christmas here."

"Well, if there's no other choice, let's make our escape!"

We went into the hall, looked for the fire escape, there was none. four doors to rooms down each side of the hall and the only way down was to the lobby.

"We'll have to try getting out through the bathroom," I said to Tom. "There's got to be a window in there, and hopefully something we can climb down on so we don't have to leap down a storey."

The occupied sign was not hanging on the door so we stepped in.

Standing in the shower, its door wide open, was a naked woman. This cleanliness enthusiast did not in the least seem bothered by our presence. If anything, it looked like she was a lover of not just hygiene but something else too! She continued soaping herself after we were inside, as if showering under the supervision of two male strangers was the most natural thing in the world. Seeing her nonchalance, we too continued on as if she wasn't there. (Well not quite. We did throw frequent glances her way.) We took a good look around the bathroom and were happy to discover that a large window, just happened to be open. Right below it was the tiled roof of some premise in the back, and running behind that was a narrow back street. To where it led and in which direction remained to be seen. We'd find out soon enough.

Trying not to appear too conspicuous while snooping around Tom, went in to use the toilette while I waited, leaning up against the bathtub. The woman finished with her shower in the interim, stepped out, and began to towel herself dry. I was waiting for her to finally speak up, expecting her to ask me to dry her back, but she said nothing. I was on the verge of taking the let's get acquainted initiative seeing that the bathing maiden was not about to say a single word, when Tom stepped out and I stepped into take his place.

Tom did not give the matter a second thought. Right after he came out he asked the woman if she left enough hot water, because we wanted to take a bath too.

"There's plenty. The hot water tank is large."

"Which is your room?" asked Tom.

"Number six, but don't trouble yourself over it. I'm busy now. A good friend of mine is here visiting and I don't think he'd welcome your intrusion."

"And just what would this 'good friend' of yours think if he saw you running around naked in front of us?" asked Tom.

"He can say anything he wants. Tonight, though, you can come over if you have some time. Would you kindly hand me my robe? It's right behind you. I'm free after 8:00. Knock four times, then I'll know it's you," she then put her robe on and left.

"Well Scout, what do you have to say to that?"

"What can I say? She's a member of the world's oldest profession and such women have no scruples."

"But now, we'd better step lively. It's already 3:30 and our train leaves in a hour. Let's get our things together and when the hall is clear we'll come in, put the occupied sign out, exit through the window and head straight for the Station."

Everything went smoothly and according to plan until we reached the station. We were crossing through the waiting room just a few minutes before four-thirty, when Tom suddenly grabbed my arm and pulled me aside.

"Look out Scout! There's the woman in red, standing by one of the exits to the right!"

"Set course for the exit on the left," I answered. "Make a run for it and we'll hop on whatever train happens to be right in front of us."

Luckily it was the train to Marseilles that was on the first track, but we only found that our once we had left Nice. No sooner did we place our bag on the luggage rack when the train pulled out of the station. Leaning out of the window, we saw the woman in red running with the police beside the train, but it was going too fast for them to leap abroad. With a sigh of relief we took our seats in the compartment and said

"Nice! May we never set eyes on it again!"

Chapter Eighteen
Mertzviller

Two days after our adventure in Nice, we were summoned to the fortress office and informed of various employment opportunities. We would be dispatched to the job of our choosing. A stove manufacturing factory looked to be the most promising of the offerings. The factory was located in the village of Mertzviller, about fifty kilometres to the north of Strasbourg. It was here that Tom and I became pipe and valve men, and where we manufactured stove pipes from morning 'till eve.

The village was tiny in comparison to the large factory, and thus most of the workers came in from outlying regions. Two hundred of the factory workers were housed in wooden barracks from an army camp. Meals were offered to those in the barracks at a reasonable price. While the food was tolerable, the accommodations themselves were appalling. Fifteen to twenty of us were crammed into one large section, a peaceful night's sleep was impossible. There was always a troublemaker or two, and fights were on the agenda everyday. It's not as though Tom and I weren't used to fighting, but fights here outnumbered even those in the Legion. It was for this reason that

311

I tried to find accommodation elsewhere. Tom refused my proposal to do the same, because rent in the village was at least five times higher than in the dorms.

The village residents were not particularly fond of those living in the barracks. Their belief that most of the men in the barracks were troublemakers did not make my search for alternate housing any easier. Only after a long and trying search did I find a room.

The people who took me in were in keeping with the 95 per cent of those living in the village – a family of farmers. In the house lived an old mother, whose husband had died during the War, and a young couple with two children. It would be an exaggeration to say that I was welcomed with open arms. I suspect that they were in need of the money, and overlooked my dubious character. A generalization they held because I had come from the barracks.

The mother of the two tots was young herself, and I suppose she could have been called attractive. Despite her work hardened features she still retained her feminine qualities. The two young ones, five and six-years-old, and I became "buddies" from the first few moments on. They were not at all disturbed by my origins. I was reluctant to play with the children at first, thinking that their mother might oppose my involvement with her children. Much to my surprise she didn't say a word when I played with the kids, but I did notice that she kept a close eye on our activities. The two kids always ran out to meet me when I came home in the evenings. They hung onto my neck and that's how I carried them home. Their father came home exhausted from working the fields all day, and was more than glad that I removed his responsibility of playing with his children from his shoulders. My stay here was pleasant, and in time the family became amiable toward me. The children more so, and I hardly could get away from them.

One morning before starting for work, the lady of the house asked me to come home for supper and eat with the family instead of taking the meal in the barracks kitchen. I detected a note of shyness in her voice, as though she were afraid I might turn down her kind invitation. On the contrary, I quickly accepted, afraid that she might think it over and withdraw the offer. The aromas circulating around the kitchen were proof enough that her cooking was one hundred times better than the food served in the barracks.

The two children sat beside me during supper. The kids were unquestionably cute, delightful, mischievous and forever playful. They tried to outdo each other in feeding me. And then, if I helped one cut his food first, the other clung to my neck, asking why he was being ignored. They took turns sitting on my lap, I feeding them or they me. The rest of the family sat by silently watching what the kids were up to, and marvelling at how understanding I was with children. I took their smiles to be a sign of approval.

The family asked me to go to church with them the next day. After Mass they invited me for both lunch and supper. After supper the husband asked me to go with him to the hotel which contained the village theatre. The film being shown was a good one and worth seeing, he said. I was not feeling too well and would much rather have laid down to rest, but I didn't want to refuse and risk offending him. The hotel was right next door, hardly twenty metres away, and thus I thought I could always leave the theatre and come home to lie down if my condition worsened.

Many people were already seated along long tables in the main hall of the hotel when we arrived. My host went directly over, greeted those already present and introduced me to them. From what I could tell, I was among a friendly circle of residents from the barracks. Wanting to treat my new found friends I ordered wine to be brought over, but my host refused to permit it.

"You're the guest," he said. "We'll pay."

I sure picked a fine time to be sick. I didn't want the glass in front of me to be empty, but considering the state of my health, I did choose soda water over wine. My host kept pouring for himself, but not the soda water. The movie started and ended without us. I was itching to go, to get home and lie down, while my host was itching to stay on. Finally, I decided I had had enough. I had to get up at 6:00 if I wanted to get to the factory on time, so I grabbed my host and took him home.

"Look here! There's something I want to talk to you about," he said, when he saw that I was heading for my room. "Let's sit down on this bench. I'll bring some brandy and we'll have a little chat." His speech was faltering, hesitant and disturbed by hiccups.

He went into the kitchen, brought out a bottle of brandy and filled a glass for each of us. He knocked back his in one gulp and I followed suit, thinking it would not go to waste and might even make me feel better. He poured again but this time, I was not so willing to gulp it down. The first shot had burned so much that I thought it was Dante's Inferno sliding down my throat. He, however, was not bothered by the strength of the liquor and tossed it back a second time. Once done, he started talking.

"Marry my 'wife'," he began. His wife, he claimed, was not really his wife, but his younger sister, and the two children had been fathered by American soldiers who had camped in the area during the war. The children were in dire need of a father, and his sister was in dire need of a husband. They had witnessed how good I was with the children, it was obvious that I loved kids, and they thought I would make a wonderful and understanding daddy. His sister would marry me with pleasure, despite the fact that I was a stranger and outsider, or that the villagers were ill-disposed toward strangers. They would accept me as one of them in no time: "You saw how well you were received in the hotel. Everyone would think very highly of you if you took a village girl to be your wife."

Dare I say that I almost fell off the bench from astonishment?

Their friendly attitude and behavior toward me had surprised me enough and had led me to draw numerous conclusions by it, but this? This was something I dared not think of even in my wildest dreams. (Chantal from Philippeville popped into mind, she likewise had wanted me to be her husband.)

When the "husband" had finished with his monologue, he leaned over the side of the bench and fell asleep. I ran to my room, packed my things and stole out into the night.

Scout, my boy, run so noone saddles you with a couple of bastards.

I truly did feel sorry for those two kids. Their whole lives their birth status would hang over their heads like a dark shadow because of irresponsibility on the part of their mother. I couldn't help it; but the love I had felt for them suddenly slackened.

I put an all out effort into vanishing from sight while the master of the house was still snoring away on the bench in a dead drunk. I had to sneak by him on my way out, and I was afraid I might wake him, but the way he was snoring, even the rattle of a wasted old farm wagon couldn't have roused him. His position on the bench was awkward and by way of parting, I adjusted him before stepping out on the street.

Back at the barracks I found Tom and shook him awake.

"Tom wake up!"

He looked at me with his sleepy eyes and asked: "What are you doing here Scout? What is it?"

"I'm going to Paris. Want to come?"

"Where are you going?"

"Paris! Didn't you hear what I said?"

"When?"

"Right now."

"Just how do you expect to get to Paris at 2:00 in the morning?" (By now he was sufficiently awake to look at his watch.)

"By train, you idiot! How else?"

"When does the train leave?"

"How the hell would I know? First we have to go to Hagenau, then to Strasbourg. We'll find out when the train leaves there. But what's with all the questions? Are you coming or not?"

"I'm coming!"

He got up, got dressed, packed his things and at 2:30 we hit the road for Paris.

"Hey Scout, what on earth got into you anyway? What prompted you to leave for Paris at this ungodly hour? Why not leave in the morning?" He asked as we strolled down the highway which led to Hagenau, in hopes that we would hitch a ride.

"Because, where I was living. . . ." and I gave him a full account of the grave danger threatening.

"And two kids to boot!" he commented, shocked and appalled. "You had to go live in the village didn't you! And now you have to run. Serves you right! Don't stop 'till you get to Indochina! I'd go so far if I was in your place. And they weren't even above saddling you with two kids. Imagine that!"

November 12, 1950

We made it to Paris. A local branch office of the Legion was located in the Chateau Vincen and as former legionnaires, we claimed the right to seek assistance from there. The commanding officer was a Sergeant Chef (company sergeant-major), and I explained in detail to him why I had to leave Mertzviller behind in a hurry.

"That's quite understandable," he said after I gave my report. "After all, why would anyone want to marry a woman who already has two kids hanging on her apron? Most likely I would have done what you did. But! It was irresponsible of you to leave your jobs. Work in Paris is very difficult to come by. I'll try to find you something, but don't hold your breaths. I won't make any promises. You look into it too; maybe you'll have more luck on your own. You'll be provided with room and board for the time being but for how long, I don't know. Keep in mind that as discharged soldiers, the Legion is free of further obligation to you."

We thanked him for his kindness and promised that we would not sit by and do nothing, and that we would accept any kind of work.

The same afternoon we were successful in getting in touch with the local Hungarian community who in turn put us in contact with an organization whose responsibility it was to offer assistance and support to people in our position. They were friendly up until we completed the identification form to placed on file, after which we were quickly given the boot.

I will not disclose names, but those entrusted with administering the affairs of this particular organization will receive their just punishment for sins committed against their compatriots on Judgement Day.

With Tom in Paris

In the entrance of the pensione

Tom and I tried everything imaginable, but there was no work to be had. One day, Tom happily informed me that he had heard of a salvation army where they helped those in need.

"Let's go over. Maybe something will turn up."

We got the address and found the place, but they too had nothing to offer but promises. We were told though to look in every day, because positions were few but applicants were plentiful. Our only chance at landing a job was to be on hand when a position came open. We came out of the office chestfallen. How could we afford to come by every day? Who would give us the fare for the metro? Even with the metro the trip took almost an hour. We wandered about aimlessly down one street and up the next, until we found ourselves on an abandoned side street. We saw only one other pedistrian. Tom and I were reviewing the possible courses of action, when Tom exclaimed,

"Guess what Scout, I just thought of another alternative."

"What's that?" I asked.

"Re-enlist in the Legion."

"What? Are you out of your mind?" I asked angrily.

Just then a man came up beside us, squeezing something wrapped in newspaper under his arm.

"Are you Hungarians too?" he asked, "Where are you from?"

"From the office of the Salvation Army. We were looking for a job."

"Well, is something available?"

"Nothing at all. All they said was to go back every day, but if we did that, who would give us money for the metro? It would take half the day to get here on foot."

"So, there's nothing. Too bad. That's where I was headed. I'd take anything, even a street sweeper's job. Problem is, that I'm not qualified for anything. I used to be a Baptist minister, and who needs such a minister around here? Especially when I barely speak French."

"We don't have any experience either. We're former legionnaires. We were just discharged, and things are not looking good. It's starting to look like we have no other choice but to go back and sign up for another five years."

"All the same, I hope things don't come to that. Something's bound to come up. You could be in a far worse predicament. Things will sort themselves out sooner or later, you'll see. There's always a way out. You have little reason to complain for the present; you have food and a roof over your heads."

As he was talking, he pulled the package out from under his arm and slowly opened it. It was a bottle of wine.

"Take a long swig from the bottle, my brothers," he said, "Maybe it will give rise to your spirits."

While Tom and I were tasting the wine, our comrade slowly, and almost absentmindedly, unfolded the newspaper. He held it up in a way that we couldn't fail to notice the heading staring out from the page in bold print.

Alcohol Kills The Body, Maims The Brain, And Reduces You To Ruin!

How fitting. A more appropriate piece of newspaper in which to wrap wine could not be found. Tom and I broke into such a fit of laughter when we read the heading that the street resounded with echoes.

"So you see," said our Baptist priest, "laughter is possible even in times of greatest sorrow."

With this he rewrapped the bottle, wished us well and went on his way.

December 20, 1950

After yet another wasted week of trying in vain, Tom gave up the battle, and signed up for another five years in the Legion. (I place the onus for Tom's re-joining the Legion on those who failed in their responsibility to aid people in need.) I was not permitted to do the same because my discharge had been due to illness. I continued, alone, wearing down the pavement on the streets of Paris.

One day the Sergeant Chef called me into his office to say it was essential that I find any kind of a job at once as an empty bed no longer remained available. Tom was in uniform now, and as a Corporal Chef, he assumed the roles of commander of the district and kitchen supervisor. By economizing on the other's portions Tom was able to provide me with at least one meal a day.

As long as Tom is around, I told myself, you're assured of one meal a day. But what will happen if he suddenly gets posted elsewhere? Then you can leap straight into the Seine, my boy, or take a fancy dive minus your parachute from atop the Eiffel Tower. Before you do either, pay another visit to the office of that Hungarian organization and beg for some work, even if you have to do it on bent knee. But first, I had to beg Tom for some money for the metro.

The reception did not start until 10:00 but I was on my way to the office by 6:00. I arrived with two hours to wait before it opened and at least three until guest were welcomed in. My comrades in misfortune lined up behind me like birds flocking around breadcrumb handouts, in the hopes that a crumb might fall their way too. It had passed ten when I was finally ushered into the office of his *most eminent*. When I closed the office door behind me, the man in charge sat me beside his desk, and without any prelude started to yell. I was dumbfounded. Why he was shouting was of no importance – I suspect he was unclear as to the reason himself; but my feeling was that by doing so, he wanted to scare away those still waiting outside. While screaming away he pulled out from his desk drawer a book of ten metro tickets and three hundred francs. (At the time 417 francs was equal to 1 dollar US.) He handed me the tickets and money with the warning: "Don't even think of spending this money on a movie!" With this he opened the door and shoved me out. He dismissed the others saying he had to leave immediately on urgent official business and would not be back until tomorrow.

"This pending matter concerns all of you. I am pleading your cases in trying to secure more money," he yelled, then stormed out. We followed suit and scattered.

The shortest route back to the Chateau was to take the number nine line, its station located on the corner of Montmartre and Poissonier Boulevards, from where I could reach my destination with only one transfer. So what was I fretting about, I would finally land a job and things would turn out. I was so deep in thought that I walked right past the station, and I failed to notice until I was beside the number three station on Rue Reaumur. I had to turn back, unless I wanted to ramble through half of the Paris underground.

As I walking back, it was as though an invisible hand took hold of me and led me into one of the many theatres. I purchased an admission ticket and went in. It was before noon, when very few people would consider taking in a movie, I could make out only a few figures sitting in the dark of the theatre that had seating available for several hundred. Whatever it was that prompted me in, that same uncanny force sat me right next to another man. The man turned out to be his *most eminent*, the one who chased everyone away on the pretense that he had to "leave immediately on urgent official business."

How fate directs the course of a man's life!

As to which of us was more embarrassed and bewildered, I leave that for you to decide.

December 28, 1950

Tom called to me to go to the office to see the Sergeant Chef.

"Do you know what he wants, by any chance?" I asked anxiously

"Don't know why he wants to see you, but he is in a good mood."

Prepared for anything good or bad, I went toward the office and saw through the open door that the Chef was urgently waving me over to his desk.

"Come quick, come in! I found you a job!"

"Really? Thank God!"

"Can't say it's anything all that wonderful, but at least it will secure your livelihood."

"What do I care what I have to do! Important thing is to put an end to this idleness."

"A pension is in need of a jack of all trades who will clean, cook, do dishes, do everything."

"Cook? I don't know how! I've never cooked in my life."

"You will now. Madame Schmidt will teach you. She's the owner of the place, and the widow of a former Captain of the Legion. Get going. Pack your things, because the jeep is waiting for you downstairs."

"Tom, I have a job!" I yelled as I ran to my room to throw my things together.

"Nice to hear that you're finally on your feet. What kind of work is it?"

"I'm going to cook in a boarding house. You absolutely must come and visit. Somehow, I'd like to pay you back for all the good you've done me. Here's the address: 22B, Rue d'Alesia, Pension d'Alesia. I must run now, the jeep is waiting. Please come over, Tom!"

I never saw him again.

January 2, 1951

After breaking off correspondence in Mertzviller, I re-established mail contact with my sister in Brussels. I was full of hope and confidence for the future. After all, that fifteen thousand kilometres, between myself and home had lessened to two or three hundred. What I had to do to earn my livelihood was irrelevant, and that my wages were lower than in Indochina was a disadvantage only in that some time was needed before I could save the money required for my forthcoming trip to Brussels.

This was a small bother indeed compared with all the worries and troubles of the past that I had lived through to get this far.

January 15, 1951

A surprise arrived in the mail! It was a letter from my younger sister, she wrote that she was coming to pay a visit. The fantasized reunion and plan born of years in waiting were about to come to fruition. I was so excited by the reality of it that I mixed mustard with the orange and fruit ice cream parfait intended for dessert. Thank goodness I noticed the error before it was served, thus saving myself from what my well have erupted into an embarrassing scandal. Still, the guests were forced to wait an hour while I prepared another dessert.

My sister, taken during her visit to Paris

January 30, 1951

I was up to my ears in dirty dishwater from the greasy dishes from lunch when the doorbell rang. Since Madame was taking her afternoon siesta, I now had to spice my prescribed physical exercise with a sprint to the gate. I wiped my hands on my blue work overalls while running because if I put my greasy hands on the gate latch and the Madame took notice, I'd be standing in the throes of another Indochinese war. And this was a far more dangerous proposition in Paris because words flew instead of bullets, against which no means of entrenchment could be secured. With hands scrubbed clean I opened the gate and found myself staring at my sister. For a few moments we looked at each other without saying a word. Then embraces and tears of joy.

The happy reunion lasted for a week. We were able to make the most of every minute, owing to the kindness of the Madame who found a replacement for the interim.

My sister is one of those people who is interested in everything, and Paris is a city where one never runs out of things to see and do. The one week she spent here was not enough to see and take in even one tenth of the sights. We trod the streets of Paris during that week without so much as stopping for a pause and it flew by fast as a minute. Parting was unlike that of 1948; we were certain that soon the time would come when all three siblings would be together again.

Epilogue

July 2, 1951

A few months after my sister's visit, I was finally in a position to make preparations for the last leg of a journey I had begun over three years ago. I bade Madame Schmidt, the boarding house, and Paris farewell. The Brussels Express left in the early morning from Gare St. Lazar, it journeyed between the city apartments before leaving behind this huge metropolis with all its beauty and monumental structures shrouded in two thousand years of history.

And as the rolling train ate up the kilometres, the monotone clatter of the wheels called to mind the train trip three years ago, which then had brought me so close and yet so far from my destination predetermined back home. I took a journey back through time. Kehl and the "Viennese Hungarians" materialized; the making of plans and their melting away with a last glimmer of hope because fate decreed otherwise. The short distance which had separated me from Brussels, it stretched into many thousands of kilometres. It handed me many trials and tribulations, to struggle with and overcome.

The film continued to rewind. Marseille appeared, then Sidi-Bel-Abbes and Philippeville. Cities, rows upon rows of villages, oceans, so many different parts of the world. The Far East with its tropical jungles, putrid swamps and the blood thristy enemy. I could almost hear the crack of the rifles, the rattle of machine guns, the hand grenades, the explosion of the mines. I saw the bloodied corpses of the dead, the outstretched hands of the injured pleading for assistance. The film was not without its brighter, lighter, and merrier moments: *The Devil's Bible Society*, the Lieutenant smothered in meat sauce, the succession of birthdays, Christmas, the strains of *God Bless the People of Hungary* during Midnight Mass and many other pleasant memories.

My comrades fell into line one-by-one, starting with the "Viennese Hungarians" and ending with Charlie waving his official discharge paper in his hand. They disappeared as quickly as they came. The years I struggled through not of my own free will, the months filled with dangers and combats, the daily struggle for life and death, but in the end, I can say I have no regrets. After three years and twelve days, and a detour of many tens of thousands of kilometres, I was reunited with my sisters in Brussels July 2, 1951.